FREEWAY FEAR

THE DRIFTER, VICTIMS AND BONIN

WRITTEN BY

SHARON MCQUILLAN

FREEWAY FEAR
THE DRIFTER, VICTIMS AND BONIN
WRITTEN BY:
SHARON MCQUILLAN

Disclaimer:

The author and publisher are not responsible for any adverse effects, consequences, or damages resulting from the use or application of the information contained in this book. The contents of this book are intended for your understanding and education. It contains graphic and disturbing material. If you are experiencing a mental health crisis, please contact a mental health professional immediately or call emergency services.

Rest assured, a comprehensive list of resources is at the back of this book should you need further support.

Acknowledgements

I would like to express my heartfelt gratitude to Kim McQuillan and my children, Harley, Zoe, Seth, Gabriel, and Vincent have always supported me despite their aversion to the topic.

To my previous fantastic clients, boss and friends, Eleanor Beidatch, Karen, and Kirsten, thank you for your constant encouragement and belief in me.

I would also like to thank the victims' families for sharing their precious photos and information.

Thank you to Anthony, you know who you are. Thank you for reaching out to me.

I especially want to thank Tina Munro for her candidness and invaluable insights. I could not have achieved this without you all.

Introduction

This harrowing account details the continuation of a series of brutal murders in Southern California, even after the incarceration of the notorious "Trash Bag Killer," Patrick Wayne Kearney. Detectives were faced with a disturbing pattern of homicides that mirrored Kearney's vile crimes, leading them to investigate whether 38 young men and boys, tragically murdered since 1972, were the prey of a new, sinister entity—the "Freeway Killer." Patrick Wayne Kearney, the "Trash Bag Killer," was 40 years old when he was sentenced to 21 life terms for three murders in Riverside County in 1977, and he confessed to 18 more in Los Angeles in 1978. Initially, Kearney was suspected of 34 murders. However, the sexual brutality of 11 murders between December 1972 and January 1976 prompted a re-evaluation. These victims, some of whom were known to be homosexual and endured horrific torture, castration, or had objects violently inserted into their bodies, were not disposed of in Kearney's signature green plastic trash bags. Kearney rarely left the bodies where he sodomised them. Instead, he would bring them home to drain their blood and dismember the bodies in industrial-strength plastic trash bags that he would then dump in the desert or along California's less travelled freeways, in the canyons behind Los Angeles or beneath trash in landfills.[1]

1 Rosewood, J. (2016). The True Story of The Freeway Killer: Historical Serial Killers and Murderers. CreateSpace Independent Publishing Platform.

This fundamental difference, along with the discovery of additional bodies with similar atrocious injuries, led investigators to consider the chilling notion that these could be the initial victims of another malevolent killer, infamously referred to as the "Freeway Killer."

This moving story centres on James Munro, one of the unfortunate souls entangled in the web of the notorious Freeway Killer. Now living as Tina Marie Munro, she is a transgender woman facing the harsh reality of life in a men's prison. With an intellectual disability, Tina Marie's life took a tragic detour upon crossing paths with William Bonin, the infamous California Freeway Killer. The question that haunts her narrative: Was she a monstrous accomplice or yet another victim of the Freeway Killer's cruelty? Bonin's malevolence knew no bounds; he preyed upon numerous young men, leaving a trail of tragedy in his wake. Tina Marie, tragically, became his unwitting accomplice. However, fate intervened when she managed to escape his clutches, fleeing for her life. The law, relentless in its pursuit, apprehended her, and she faced a grim sentence: 15 years to life.

Despite her circumstances, Tina Marie's quest for justice has been met with repeated denials of parole, a cruel twist of fate that underscores the inherent unfairness of her situation.

2 AP. (1980, 18 Apr). Police Probe Link between New Killings, Trash Bag Murderer. Reno Gazette Journal.

Now, unfairly denied parole multiple times, Tina Marie's quest for justice continues. While we cannot directly intervene in her case, raising awareness about her situation and advocating for fair treatment within the legal system can make a difference. Let us stand together to ensure that Tina Marie Munro receives the compassion and justice she deserves.

Tina was James Munro, born with an intellectual disability, and faced vulnerability and disadvantage throughout her life. Denied a typical childhood and formal education, she met rejection from the public elementary school due to their IQ of 75, falling below the required threshold of 80. At 19 years old, her mental age lagged significantly behind. Sadly, they became part of the distressing statistic: individuals with intellectual disabilities are disproportionately represented within the criminal justice system.

In New South Wales, approximately one per cent of the adult prison population possesses an IQ below 70, whereas only three per cent of the general public grapples with an intellectual disability. Tina Munro's story is a tragic example of how the criminal justice system fails to protect and support people with intellectual disabilities.

People with intellectual disabilities find themselves disproportionately represented within the criminal justice system for several interconnected reasons:

3 Munro, T. (2023). James Munro His life His words [Interview]. 4 Australian Bureau of Statistics. (2023). Prisoners in Australia. ABS. https://www.abs.gov.au/statistics/people/crime-and-justice/prisoners-australia/latest-release.

Vulnerability: Intellectual disabilities often make individuals more vulnerable to exploitation, manipulation, and coercion. Their limited understanding of legal processes and their rights can lead to unfavourable outcomes. Social Disadvantages: Many people with intellectual disabilities face socioeconomic challenges, including poverty, lack of education, and limited access to resources. These factors can increase the likelihood of involvement in criminal activities.
Communication Difficulties: Effective communication is crucial within legal contexts. Individuals with intellectual disabilities may struggle to express themselves clearly, leading to misunderstandings or inadequate legal representation.
Lack of Support Services: Insufficient community-based support services, such as mental health programs or vocational training, contribute to their vulnerability. They may engage in behaviours that lead to legal trouble without proper assistance.

Stereotypes and Bias: Stereotypes and biases persist within the criminal justice system. Law enforcement officers, judges, and jurors may hold misconceptions about intellectual disabilities, affecting decision-making and sentencing.
Inadequate Legal Representation: People with intellectual disabilities often receive subpar legal representation due to their limited financial resources or lack of understanding. This can result in harsher sentences.

Institutionalisation: Historically, individuals with intellectual disabilities were institutionalised rather than receiving proper community-based support. Institutionalisation can lead to exposure to criminal environments and behaviours. Criminal punishment often rests upon classical theory, which centres around individual choice. Jeremy Bentham and Cesare Beccaria are the foundational theorists of classical criminology. According to classicism, the root of criminal behaviour lies within the rational reasoning of the individual, framing it as a deliberate matter of choice and intent on the offender's part.
The classical school of criminology places significant emphasis on choice, responsibility, and intention. From this perspective, punishment is a crucial deterrent, proving personal accountability for one's actions and carrying a potent symbolic impact on society.

However, classical theory and its various iterations meet a critical limitation: they overlook individual differences among criminal actors. These theories assume that everyone operates as a rational actor, capable of exercising free choice. However, this assumption fails to account for specific categories of people—such as the elderly, individuals with mental illnesses, or those with intellectual disabilities—who do not possess the same capacities as others. In conclusion, the classical school of criminology underscores the principles of choice, responsibility, and intention, advocating punishment as a vital deterrent that emphasises personal accountability and is a powerful societal symbol. However, this school of thought encounters a fundamental shortcoming in its failure to recognise the diversity of criminal actors. It presumes a universal rationality, positing that all individuals can make free and informed choices. This presumption, however, does not hold for specific segments of the population, such as the ageing, those with mental illnesses, or individuals with intellectual disabilities, whose decision-making capacities may be significantly different from the norm. Criminological theories must evolve and adapt, considering the varied cognitive abilities and circumstances that influence human behaviour.

Contents

Chapter 1 James Michael Munro's Birth and Childhood

Michael Massow was born on June 17, 1961, in Fürth, West Germany. His mother, Anna Marie Massow, was a single German woman who worked as a housekeeper. Michael bore two congenital anomalies: an extra thumb on his left hand (which was surgically removed) and Polio, making his legs numb and impeding his ability to walk. Struggling to cope with her son's disability, Anna made the heart-wrenching decision to give Michael up for adoption when he was a mere five and a half months old. Tragically, they never crossed paths again. Anna's life followed its natural course, and she passed away on October 5, 1998. Marked by twists of fate, Michael's journey unfolded without the chance to reunite with the woman who brought him into this world or his biological brothers, Peter and Alford.

Michael Massow spent his early years in an orphanage until 1963. During that pivotal year, the Munros, a military couple stationed in Germany, grappled with the loss of their newborn child. Their military background shaped their character and influenced their approach to parenting. Seeking solace, they embarked on a visit to the orphanage, where fate intervened.
Their hearts were captured by a 2-year-old boy with brown hair who radiates an aura of promise. To the Munros, he

seemed like the perfect addition to their family—a son they would cherish. They saw in Munro the potential for a bright future despite his disabilities. Little did they realise that this child they affectionately chose would be a formidable challenge.

They boarded a military plane bound for the United States with everything in place. Munro became an integral part of the Munro family, his heart brimming with hope for the elusive promise of a happy ending. Leigh and Evon Munro welcomed two additional children into their family after Munro. Kathy Ann, Munro's younger sister, and Connie Munro. Kathy Ann bore a striking resemblance to Cindy Brady from the Brady Bunch.

In a transformative decision, they adopted Michael, altering his name from Michael Massow to James Michael Munro. The adoption process marked a significant chapter in their lives.

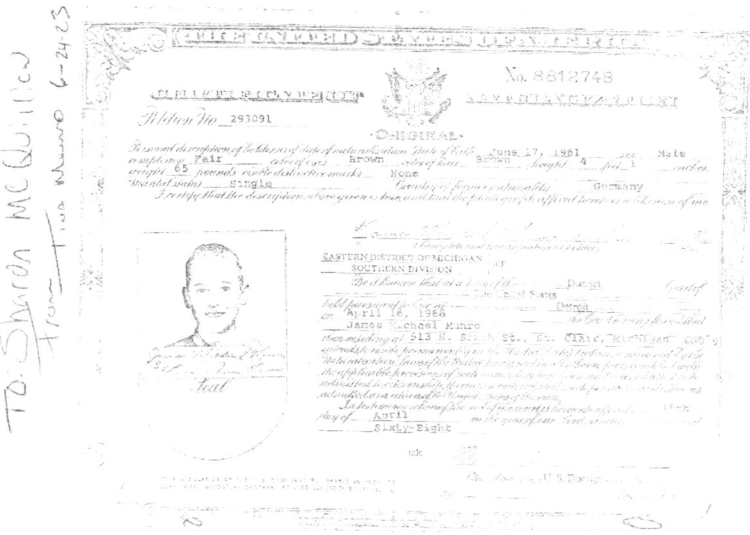
No. 8812748
Petition No. 293091
ORIGINAL
June 17, 1961
Male
Fair
Brown
Brown
4 feet 1 inches
65 pounds
None
Single
Germany
EASTERN DISTRICT OF MICHIGAN
SOUTHERN DIVISION
The United States
Detroit
April 16, 1968
James Michael Munro
April
Sixty-Eight

Munro lived with his adoptive mother and grandmother. His father served in Vietnam. Over time, the Munro family began recognising Munro's difficulties, yet understanding him was a formidable challenge. Concerned for their son's wellbeing, Munro's parents sought answers.

They took him to a United States Army hospital, where thorough examinations unfolded. Additionally, Evon, his mother, consulted a psychologist in pursuit of clarity. The medical professionals conducted a brain scan, ultimately diagnosing Munro as being borderline mentally retarded with frontal lobe damage to the brain. .[5, 6]

5 Carangelo, Lori. James Munro and the Freeway Killers. Access Press, 2018. 6 Spencer, D. A. (1970). Mental Retardation. British Journal of Psychiatry, 116(530), 127-127.

Evon's reaction was visceral, her voice echoing, "Oh My God!" Tears streamed down her face, but she stayed silent when Munro inquired, "What is wrong?" His smile masked the turmoil within.

Munro's life was burdened by Polio, rendering his legs numb and confining him to a wheelchair. Braces encased his legs, and a hearing aid bridged the gap between silence and sound. Not until he was seven did Munro defy the odds, taking his first tentative steps. His gait, reminiscent of Forrest Gump, mirrored determination and resilience. In the 1960s, metal leg braces were the only option for disabled children—a testament to both their limitations and their indomitable spirit. Despite the challenges, Munro's spirit remained unbroken, and he continued to fight for his place in the world.

Evon's wrath fell upon Munro when he dared to defy her—refusing to walk and wetting the bed. The beatings persisted until Munro's legs finally carried him upright.
Yet, life remained unkind to young Munro. At age eight, he pedalled his bike across the street, colliding with an unforgiving car. As he lay on the ground, waiting for the ambulance's arrival, his mother appeared. But instead of comforting words, she met him with more blows, lamenting the $300 the ambulance would cost her.

The accident left its mark—learning disabilities worsened. Recollection and memory became elusive, slipping through Munro's grasp like sand. His parents, once hopeful, now saw him as a burden. Ignored and rejected, Munro stood on the fringes, no longer entirely accepted as part of their family.

Munro's father, Leigh, spent much of his time away due to military service, leaving him unaware of the harsh treatment Munro endured from Evon.

While attending school in Virginia, Munro's parents, stationed at an army base, harboured hopes for his success. They envisioned him as a hall monitor, a role reflecting their aspirations. However, even this modest goal proved elusive. Munro grappled with memory lapses, struggling to find his way to classes. Concerned, the school contacted the Munros, suggesting that Munro might receive help from a specialised educational setting. In 1975, James Michael Munro and his family returned to the small town of Saint Clair in Michigan. Munro's joy knew no bounds when he finally had his room. His father, Leigh, held the rank of Master Sergeant E-8 in the United States Army, having dedicated years to military service since 1952 before retiring. Despite the challenges, the Munros remained hopeful for Munro's future, believing he could overcome his difficulties and succeed.

Leigh, Munro's adoptive father, had seen two tours of duty: one in Korea and another in Vietnam. His courage was recognised with a Medal of Valor, a Purple Heart, and a Bronze Star. In Munro's eyes, Leigh was a hero—an unwavering figure.

However, retirement altered Leigh's demeanour. Something shifted. The contrast between how he treated Munro on the military base and how he treated him after they settled into their own home became stark. Munro sensed the change at once when the Munro family relocated to 1319 St. Clair Highway in Saint Clair. Life took an unexpected turn, and the transformation was far from pleasant.

Munro attended St. Clair Elementary School, but his path was challenging. His learning disabilities, which were later diagnosed as borderline mental retardation and frontal lobe damage, posed significant hurdles. He found it challenging to retain the information taught, often experiencing memory lapses and struggling with basic tasks. Despite these challenges, Munro persisted, showing a remarkable determination to overcome his limitations.

However, sitting remained elusive—even with years of Ritalin use. His restlessness led to his removal from class, and worse yet, he was denied access to public school due to his IQ of 75, below the school's minimum requirement.

Munro's plight was heartbreaking. He endured relentless bullying and physical assaults because he could not articulate himself properly or complete schoolwork. The trauma weighed heavily on him, and even at night, he found no solace—bedwetting became a persistent companion.[7]

Finally, Munro's parents faced a pivotal decision. They recognised Munro's struggle to retain knowledge and grasp essential educational skills, so they opted for a specialised path. While Munro could read to some extent, math—addition, subtraction, and multiplication—remained elusive. To equip him for life's challenges, he needed these fundamental skills.

And so, they enrolled him in the St. Stephens Day Treatment Centre in Port Huron, Michigan. This specialised education facility catered to intellectually disabled children, supplying tailored support. A beacon of hope within a county-wide public-school program, it aimed to guide troubled youth toward brighter horizons

7 2022. NCCD [Online]. Available: https://www.nccd.edu.au/wider-support-materials/learning-differences-learning-difficulties-learning-disabilities-and-nccd [Accessed].

Chapter 2 James Munro's Teenage Years

*Image SEQ Image * ARABIC2 James Munro in the police car when first arrested (IMDb, n.d.)*

Munro's home life resembled a nightmare—a relentless cycle of fear and brutality. The constant threat of beatings etched a twitch into his head and shoulders. Far from understanding, his mother despised this involuntary

movement, punishing him with each occurrence.
Within the confines of his family, Munro felt like an outsider. Excluded from family photos and gatherings, he grappled with a growing resentment. His father, absent from baseball games and confining him to the house, perpetuated his isolation. Any attempts at friendship were sabotaged by his parents, who forbade him from conversing with anyone, especially girls. Their desire? To mould him into a loner, a captive within the walls he called home.
Munro's school life harboured a solitary beacon of light: his teacher, Jann Scheerhorn, who resembled Linda Carter from the Wonder Woman TV show. At 16, Munro found himself utterly smitten—his first crush ignited. Jann's lovely long hair and unwavering kindness left an indelible mark.
Jann went beyond her duty as a teacher, assisting Munro by taking him to her home. There, he could bathe, eat well, and prepare for his job at Wendy's. After his shift, she would drive him back to his parents' house. Munro's affection for Jann remained a secret, known only to him. This newfound emotion was unlike anything he had experienced before. In gratitude, Munro set out to repair a broken radio—a precious item given to Jann by her father. His hands worked diligently, and Jann's joy overflowed when the radio came back to life. This connection was a lifeline for Munro—a glimmer of warmth in an otherwise lonely and isolated existence.

His mother's interventions followed a pattern: Ritalin during childhood and Levpro during adolescence, all aimed at managing his anger and anxiety. But Munro's behaviour took a rebellious turn. His parents' indifference mirrored his own, leading him down a precarious path.

A stolen cigarette ignited an unexpected liking—one that spiralled into addiction. Despite Evon's efforts—forcing him to smoke an entire pack—the allure of smoking persisted. Even an attempted theft of a carton, thwarted by the store owner, failed to break the cycle. Munro remained ensnared, a captive of his vices.

Munro, hopeful that his sixteenth birthday would alter his parents' treatment, yearned for recognition as a man. However, their mistreatment persisted. Fuelled by frustration, he made a drastic decision: running away from home. He borrowed his sister's car and drove 45 miles until the gas ran dry. However, fate intervened—the police apprehended him on the highway, charging him with Grand Theft Auto. His sentence? Six months in a juvenile hall—a harsh lesson. Upon his return, life seemed to settle, albeit briefly. Munro's parents imposed a strict 9 p.m. curfew, eroding trust. His room became a prison, subjected to constant searches. One fateful night, after a family movie outing, his father, Leigh, discovered a mysterious cord dangling beneath his new car. A swift pull revealed a soldering iron. Rage consumed his father, who lashed out, striking Munro's face. Desperate,

Munro protested, blaming other neighbourhood children for garage thefts.

Nevertheless, his plea was ignored, and he was banished to his room—a captive within his own home. Munro's adoptive parents remained mysteriously silent when discussing the intricacies of the birds and the bees. They left Munro to navigate the tangled web of human reproduction like a curious explorer in an uncharted jungle. The whispers of the wind carried no secrets, and the bees buzzed their coded messages. Still, Munro needed guidance to decipher their cryptic meanings.

Even after he was caught trying on his mum's bra and playing dress-ups with his sisters, Munro remembers his younger sister showing him her breasts and letting him play with them.

Munro's father grappled with the notion that his son was embracing bisexuality. The revelation stirred a storm of emotions within him—confusion, concern, and perhaps a touch of fear. For Munro, it was a journey of self-discovery, a canvas where colours blended, creating a vibrant spectrum of identity. Munro navigated uncharted waters, seeking solace in whispered conversations with the moon and the rustling leaves. Like a compass, his heart pointed in multiple directions—drawn to both the soft curves of femininity and the rugged strength of masculinity. Leigh could not fathom the idea that Munro began to see himself as a bisexual person.

When Munro reached 16, his father stumbled upon a truth that would alter their lives forever: Munro had been exploring intimacy with other boys. This revelation hung in the air like a fragile secret, threatening to shatter the illusion of a straightforward path—the neat narrative society often prescribed.
Munro's father unleashed his fury, a storm of anger and ignorance. The blows fell like thunder, each striking pain into Munro's skin. The house, once a haven, transformed into a battleground—a place where love curdled into violence.
Thrown out, Munro stumbled into the night, his heart a fractured compass. The streets whispered their secrets—their cracked pavements bore witness to countless souls seeking refuge—Munro, with his bruises and dreams. However, Leigh, fuelled by fear, hunted him down. The streets, once a sanctuary, now betrayed him. The blows resumed—Munro's body absorbed the pain, but his spirit soared. He clung to his truth—the fragile thread that connected him to the universe.
His father, a relic of old beliefs, remained trapped in his darkness—an unwilling traveller on Munro's journey of self-discovery. The stars above, indifferent and ancient, wit-

nessed it all—the pain, the resilience, and the quiet rebellion of a boy who refused to be defined by anyone else's compass.

Munro's tumultuous journey led him to a state hospital in Michigan—once known as the Eastern Michigan Asylum for the Insane.[8] The cold walls and sterile corridors wrapped around him like a straitjacket. Munro despised the confinement, the echoes of lost sanity.
Dark humour dripped from his lips—a joke about severing his sister's head—but his parents did not laugh.
From 1976 to 1977, he existed within those institutional walls. The doctors, their eyes both curious and wary, prescribed anti-psychotic drugs to quell the storm within him. Munro's mind danced on the edge—a tightrope between violence and longing. He yearned to usurp his adoptive father to claim the throne of a fractured family.
And then, like a pendulum, Munro swung back into the world. His parents released him—a wounded bird set free. Nevertheless, freedom comes with a price. He remained an outcast in their eyes, a puzzle piece that refused to fit. The Munros, weary and defeated, surrendered. Munro roamed the town, a phantom of lost connections. Rules and boundaries eluded him.

1978 arrived, and with it, a chance for redemption. The Army National Guard beckoned—an escape route from the ghosts of family. Munro craved approval, a nod from the people who had once locked him away. His parents, eager to be rid of him, signed the papers in October 1978.

Fort Jackson South Catalina awaited—a crucible of discipline and purpose.[9] Munro shed old skin and donned a uniform. The barracks smelled of sweat and camaraderie. Drill sergeants barked orders, moulding raw recruits into soldiers. Munro, with his fractured past, stood tall. The rifle became an extension of his will—the trigger a bridge between chaos and duty.

Armed with his shots and uniform, Munro marched into Fort Bennington, Georgia, ready for boot camp. There, he learned to wield a rifle and leap from helicopters—a symphony of adrenaline and discipline. However, fate, like an erratic conductor, had other plans.

Health issues crept in. An infected leg wound, courtesy of unforgiving combat boots, led to blood poisoning. The pain seeped into his bones, a discordant note in the military symphony. Munro found himself in the hospital—a soldier sidelined by his own body.

Fort Bennington, once a beacon of purpose, became a battleground. And then, like a cruel twist, his bedwetting problem surfaced. The military, rigid in its rules, barred anyone

8 Redstone Test Stand-Huntsville, Alabama, Nasa. https://vacationsalabama.com/national-historic-landmarks/redstone-test-stand/

who wet their bed from service. South Carolina had spared him, but Fort Bennington ignited the storm.

Boot camp, relentless and unforgiving, chewed him up. They deemed Munro too slow—a misfit in their well-oiled machine. The military, with a heavy heart, granted him an honourable discharge in December 1978. Munro's relief was palpable—a ticket out of the chaos.
Nevertheless, the Munros, his adoptive family, wore disappointment-like armour. They welcomed him back, their patience tested. Munro lingered in their home until 1979 when he turned eighteen. Michigan's threshold declared him an adult—a fledgling with wings itching to soar.
Munro's eighteenth birthday, he arrived in the warm embrace of June 1979, and with it, a hunger for adventure. He could not wait to taste life beyond the familiar boundaries of St. Claire. So, he set his compass toward Port Huron, a mere five miles away—a world waiting to unfold.

The neon glow of a strip club beckoned—a siren song for a boy on the cusp of adulthood. Munro stepped inside, heart racing, eyes wide. The air smelled of anticipation and secrets. This was his inaugural visit, and he claimed a seat at a table, eyes fixed on the stage where girls danced.
Another woman occupied a nearby table—a stranger with her story etched in her eyes. Their gazes collided—a cosmic

9 Fort Jackson, SC - Coin. https://store.nwtmint.com/product_details/3655/ Fort_Jackson_SC/index.html

collision of curiosity. She saw something in Munro—a spark, perhaps. And so, she crossed the room, her heels tapping a rhythm of possibility.
"Hi," she said, her voice a velvet invitation. "I'm Lena. What's your name?"
"Munro," he replied, his heart drumming against his ribs. It's nice to meet you, Lena."
She leaned in, her perfume a whispered secret. "Munro," she murmured, "I want to take you home."
The words hung in the air—a promise, a threshold. Munro hesitated, then nodded. They left the strip club together, the night swallowing them whole. They drove through the city's veins, streetlights painting their faces in fleeting strokes. Her apartment, a sanctuary of shadows and silk, welcomed them. The door closed behind them, muffling the city's pulse. Her lips found Munro's—a map of longing. They both shed layers—their pasts, their inhibitions. Munro longed to see her voluptuous breasts to see them out of her brassiere. She finally slipped out of the last layer covering her smooth skin, and Munro raised his hands to caress as much of her breasts as he could fit in his hands.

Do you like them she asked. Hell, yeah replied Munro, so she laid back on the bed as Munro straddled her, caressing and kissing her all over. She started to moan, wanting more, so he kissed her down to her slippery cavern and slid his tongue inside her, tasting her sweetness. Munro was so hard and could not hold on for much longer, so he slid his member inside until he ejaculated. Simultaneously, he was suckling on her breasts. Munro did not want to stop. Skin met skin, and the room blurred into a symphony of touch. Munro tasted adventure on that fateful night—an elixir of lust and curiosity. The woman became his compass with her whispered promises—a guide through uncharted waters. As dawn tiptoed across the skyline, they lay tangled—a constellation of desire, etching their names into the fabric of time.

Munro's decision to bid farewell to his home felt like liberation—a taste of freedom that danced on the edge of recklessness. The Munros, his adoptive family, watched him go, unaware of the storm brewing within him.

Munro, now eighteen, was sprawled in the front yard, the sun warming his skin. His mother, concerned, approached. "Are you okay?" she asked, her voice a fragile thread connecting them.

"Just relaxing," Munro replied, eyes scanning the horizon. He waited—for her departure, for the moment when he could slip away unnoticed. A hastily penned note lay on the kitchen table: I am sorry. It is better this way.

Cash clutched in his hands; Munro packed a backpack—essentials for a journey into the unknown. California beckoned—a land of promise, where he could be free. He craved autonomy, a canvas to paint his own story.

And so, he hitched rides—trucks rumbling like thunder across state lines. Truck drivers became his mentors, teaching him the Art of navigating highways and the rhythm of gears shifting. Munro imagined his father's eyes widening, pride replacing doubt. Look, Dad, he thought, I'm not dumb. I'm surviving.

But wishes, like fragile glass, shattered. Leigh's approval remained elusive—a star just out of reach. Munro forged ahead, a wanderer with no map, no compass. He became his person, chasing sunsets and asphalt ribbons.

Yet, survival demanded sacrifice: Munro's path twisted prostitution, a desperate dance for survival. The streets whispered secrets—their cracked pavements bore witness to his choices. He yearned for acceptance, for a father's nod, but the universe remained silent.

Munro's blunder—the leap into the abyss—left scars. He learned that freedom was not just about escaping walls and finding purpose. And as he walked the edge, he wondered if redemption awaited—a chance to rewrite his story, to prove that he was more than the sum of his mistakes. Munro, a wanderer on the road to California, paused in Nashville—a pit stop in his odyssey. The motel room welcomed him—a refuge of worn sheets and fluorescent light. He sat on the bed, a hamburger in hand, hunger gnawing at his insides. But fate scratched at his door—a tiny black puppy with floppy ears. Munro's heart softened. He welcomed the pup and lifted him onto the bed. The puppy's eyes held galaxies—starving yet trusting. Munro washed him and shared his meagre meal. The puppy's gratitude warmed the room. A boy and his newfound companion slept side by side that night—the nameless yet loyal puppy nestled against Munro's chest. The world outside faded—the motel walls surrounded them.

Morning dawned, and Munro's conscience stirred. He checked every room, seeking an owner for the puppy. But fate whispered—a silent verdict. The puppy was his now—a loyal friend who loved him unconditionally.

And so, they resumed their journey. Munro walked the highway, snowflakes dancing in his wake. His gloves, fingerless and threadbare, offered little warmth. Hunger clawed at him, but the puppy's eyes kept him going. Desperation settled—a choice between survival and sacrifice. Munro was considering giving the puppy away. Then he saw a little girl playing in the front yard. Munro approached, trembling from cold and uncertainty. "Fetch your mum and dad," he asked, voice fragile as frost.

The girl darted into her house, returning with her parents—a tableau of compassion. They listened as Munro explained—

the puppy, the road, the ache in his bones. And in that snowy yard, they made a pact—a family forged from chance encounters.

Munro's loyal friend remained—a heartbeat against the cold. And as the little girl's parents welcomed them, Munro glimpsed redemption—a warmth beyond shelter, a love that defied frostbite.

The father's concern etched lines on his face while the mother listened in quiet empathy. Munro's voice trembled as he spoke, the weight of his decision heavy upon him. "Hey," he said, "I can't care for my dog Snowball anymore. Could you please take him in?" The little girl's tears flowed, joy and surprise mingling. The mother wept, too, her heart touched by this unexpected gift. They had longed for a puppy, but financial constraints had kept that dream at bay. Munro's eyes blurred—a cocktail of emotions. As he continued talking to the father, the mother's smile reached him—a lifeline in a sea of sorrow. He turned to the little girl. "Be good to Snowball for me, okay?" he whispered, tears threatening to spill.

And then, the moment arrived—the farewell to his only friend. The girl's hug held warmth, and the father's handshake conveyed gratitude. But concern lingered. "Are you okay?" the father asked. "Do you need food?"

Munro's reply was raw honesty. "I gave all my food to the little dog." The mother disappeared inside, returning with sandwiches and a steaming cup of coffee. Munro's confession spilled—he had no home or love from his parents. So, he ran.

The father's hand pressed a crumpled bill into Munro's palm—twenty dollars. And there, on the threshold of goodbye, Munro broke. Tears blurred the road ahead as he walked away. But with each step, something shifted—the weight eased. He was alone, but he had made someone happy. The farther he went, the better he felt. The road stretched, winding toward an uncertain horizon. And Munro, with Snowball's memory nestled in his heart, whispered, "Maybe I'll be okay."

Chapter 3 California/ Long Beach / Redondo / Hollywood

Munro, a wanderer with no place to call home, arrived in California in early January 1979. His pockets held only meagre coins—just enough to survive. Nights found him nestled in cardboard boxes, and hunger led him to missions, where charity meals sustained him.

In Long Beach, he contacted Tina, his sister's friend. Unbeknownst to Munro, Tina's life had taken a different path—marriage and motherhood. She picked him up from the station, her compassionate and cautious heart. Munro's intellectual disability made him vulnerable, especially in a vast and unpredictable state like California.

Tina's home became his refuge—a roof over his head, warmth against the chill. But Munro chafed against confinement. The walls whispered of freedom, and he longed to escape the well-meaning rules. One night, he slipped away—a shadow fading into the city's pulse.

Tina's worry deepened. She reported her Munro missing to the police. The streets, like a labyrinth, swallowed Munro whole. He roamed—away from safety, toward uncertainty. Killers and weirdos lurked in the shadows, but Munro had his compass—a stubborn resolve that defied caution.

And so, he wandered—a nomad with secrets, a heart seeking solace beyond walls. Tina's prayers followed him, a silent plea for his safety. But Munro had other plans—a dance with fate, a rebellion against confinement. California stretched before him—an open road, a canvas for his restless spirit.

As Munro walked, the city's mosaic absorbed him—a survivor, a dreamer, a missing piece seeking its place. The stars above, like ancient witnesses, blinked in silent approval.
"Maybe," Munro whispered, "I'll find my way."
But home awaited—a storm of emotions. Tina, his sister's friend, greeted him with sobs and screams. Munro tried to explain—an innocent outing with a guy sharing laughter over beers. But Tina's fury knew no bounds. She ordered him to his room, a prison of her making, until her husband, Jeff, returned.

Jeff arrived—a mediator in this family drama. He tried to talk to Munro, but the boy's defiance knew no bounds. Lies spilled from his lips, and mocking faces danced. Tina's anger flared—her plea for respect met with rebellion. "Discipline him," she demanded, and Jeff obliged. Munro was grounded—an adult bridled by authority.
But Munro had other plans. As they slept, he packed his bags—a fugitive in the night. Redondo beckoned—a refuge beyond their reach. Eventually, he met a gay couple who welcomed him, offering him a room in their apartment

where freedom whispered. For a while, he lived there—a survivor, a dreamer, a missing piece finding solace in the city's embrace.[5]

One February day, Munro strolled along the pier at Redondo Beach, the salty breeze kissing his face. And then, a voice—a blast from the past—echoed across the waves: "Hey Munro, I can't believe you're in California!" It was Shirley, an old friend from their days at the specialist education school. She stood there with her friend Tammy, and the universe seemed to conspire.

That night, they settled into a nearby motel—girls in separate rooms. Munro's head spun. What were the odds of reconnecting with an old friend and stumbling upon his soon-to-be girlfriend? The hours blurred—conversations, laughter, shared secrets. Munro and Tammy clicked—a symphony of hearts finding harmony. And then, in the quiet of that motel room, Munro's heart raced. He was smitten, intoxicated by the magic of the night. So, he did what any love-struck soul would do: he asked Tammy to marry him. Furthermore, she said yes to his delight—a promise etched in starlight and saltwater.

Stan Hurd, a shadow from the underbelly, soon arrived—the puppeteer pulling strings for Tammy and Shirley. Their lives entwined in a dance of survival—money and motel rooms exchanged for their bodies. Tammy, once a girl named

Rachel London, walked the streets of Hollywood—a hooker navigating neon-lit alleys.

But Munro, fuelled by love and desperation, intervened. He asked Tammy to leave this life behind and return with him to Michigan to face their parents. And she said yes—a fragile promise whispered in the night.

Together, they boarded a Greyhound bus, wheels spinning toward St. Clair. Munro's heart fluttered, swirling with a blend of relief and trepidation. His father's absence offered a brief respite, but his mother's words hung heavy. "Go," she urged, "before your father returns. He won't be pleased." Munro hugged her—a farewell etched in silence. And so, they returned to California on a pilgrimage to meet Tammy's parents. The road stretched before them—an uncertain horizon, secrets trailing in their wake.[5] Upon their return to California, Stan Hurd awaited them—a reminder of debts unpaid. His words were a warning—an ultimatum veiled in menace: Tammy was Munro's responsibility. Love her, care for her, or face the consequences.

But then, an unexpected twist—congratulations. Stan handed Munro an envelope—a promise of something more. Munro hugged him, the weight of responsibility settling on his shoulders. He vowed to cherish Tammy—a fragile oath whispered in the shadows.

And so, they settled—a cozy flat, a fresh start. Munro's days revolved around the petrol station, the engines' hum, and the gasoline scent. His fiancé Tammy became his anchor—a love story woven from chance encounters and whispered threats.

Once riding the crest of financial stability, Munro faced a fateful night—a crossroads where temptation and desperation collided. Alone in the quiet of the petrol station, he succumbed to the urge—the safe, a Pandora's box of temptation. Five hundred dollars—his fingers traced the edges, his heart racing.

But fate, like a stern accountant, had other plans. The boss checked the petrol meters and scrutinised the cash register. Numbers had to align—a delicate balance between profit and honesty. Munro's secret weighed heavy—a betrayal etched in ink.

Then, there is the request—a choice between restitution and retribution. The boss's voice held no sympathy: return the money or face the authorities. Munro hesitated, his conscience a tempest. Reluctantly, he handed over the cash—a silent farewell to security and a ticket to uncertainty.

The petrol station, once a haven, now spat him out—a job lost, a life reshuffled. Munro walked away, the taste of guilt lingering. And as the night swallowed him, he wondered if redemption awaited—a chance to balance the ledger and prove that there was room for light even in darkness.

When Munro returned home, the air thick with tension, he found Tammy at the table—rolling joints, her fingers deft and practised. His voice trembled as he demanded answers: "Where did you get the money for these drugs?" And then, the confession—a shard of truth that shattered their fragile stability. She had used their rent money.
Munro's fury erupted—a storm of disappointment and betrayal. Their voices clashed, harsh words ricocheting off walls. He stormed out—the door slamming behind him, a final punctuation mark on their brief, tumultuous relationship. Tammy, left behind, watched him vanish into the night.

Munro, seeking solace in Redondo, wandered its streets—a canvas for second chances. And then, a sign—a beacon of cleansing: "Bath House." The thought of washing away his troubles lured him—an innocent desire.

But fate, like a mischievous tide, led him astray. The door swung open—a threshold into a world he had not anticipated. Naked men swam in the pool—freedom and desire merging. Munro hesitated, then discarded his clothes, vulnerability bared.

And there, in the water's embrace, he realised his mistake. These men, circling like sharks, hungered for more than a bath. Munro felt like bait—a stranger in their territory. The water closed in, and he swam against the current, desperation and regret swirling.

Munro, heart racing, found himself surrounded Fear gnawed at him, but then, like a lifeline, another man stepped forward. His voice cut through the tension: "Leave him alone." Munro's gratitude spilled—a fragile offering in a sea of uncertainty. The man introduced himself as Art Reaz—a name etched in that pivotal moment. They talked, laughed, and found common ground—a connection forged in the crucible of that night. With his warmth and kindness, Art offered Munro a lifeline: a room in his boarding house. Eight other boarders awaited—a mix of men and women. Munro stepped into their world; their curiosity palpable. The women, eager to meet the new arrival, asked the question that hung in the air: "Are you gay like Art?"

Munro's answer was honest: "No." And in that shared grin, he glimpsed acceptance—a mosaic of souls finding their place.

One evening in March 1979, Munro was wandering the streets of Redondo, something he did often. His eyes caught a glimpse of a motorbike parked against a building, its chain dangling loosely. Temptation tugged at him—an opportunity too good to pass up.

He pulled the bike, and the lights flashed—a silent warning. But Munro's resolve solidified. This bike had already been stolen once; he would steal it again. No witnesses, no consequences. He rolled it down the road, adrenaline humming in his veins. The engine roared to life—a new ride, a taste of freedom..

He gathered his few belongings at the flat he shared with Tammy. The past was a blur—a brief, tumultuous chapter. And then, he pointed the bike toward Art's place.

June arrived, and Munro was a lone rider on his new bike. But fate had other plans. On a sun-kissed road, bikers joined him—a brotherhood of asphalt and wind. Their engines harmonised—a chorus of freedom. Munro, once adrift, is now part of something bigger—a mosaic of wheels and stories.

A lone rider on his new bike, Munro encountered a group of bikers—Men almost twice his age. They admired his bike but suggested he should consider a Harley Davidson instead. Munro responded honestly, wishing he could afford one, but money was scarce.

Clad in leather jackets adorned with Hells Angels insignia, the bikers extended an invitation. Munro hesitated only briefly and followed them—a journey into the heart of their brotherhood. Their hangout awaited—a place where legends were born.

Sonny Barger

And there, he met the boss—the man known as Sonny Ralf Barger, who went by Sonny. A living legend, Sonny's

presence was magnetic. He had consulted with the producers of the hit show *Sons of Anarchy*, and his own life echoed in the character he portrayed: Lenny "the pimp". The road had led Munro to a crossroads—a collision of fate and leather, where legends were etched in chrome and ink. [10,11]
Munro and Sonny shared more than words that day; their lives intersected like roads converging. The invitation hung in the air—a brotherhood beckoning. Munro's heart raced and agreed—a pact sealed in leather and chrome. He became a Hell Angel, the road ahead winding into a new chapter.

From June 1979 to 1980, Munro rode with them—sometimes in their company, sometimes solo, chasing the wind and the thrill. The asphalt held secrets—the roar of engines, the camaraderie of outlaws. And Sonny Badger, a legend in his own right, guided Munro through the twists and turns.
But life, like a fickle compass, shifted. In 2022, Sonny Badger succumbed to cancer—a final ride into the sunset. His legacy echoed in the wind, and now older Munro remembered those days—the brotherhood, the freedom, the roar of the open road.

Munro's 19th ---birthday arrived like a secret whispered by the wind. And then, a gift—a leather jacket—a second skin that smelled of rebellion and brotherhood. He wore it with pride; its weight reminded him that he belonged.

10 BOYLE, K. 2022. Sonny Barger Dies: Hells Angels Founder, 'Sons of Anarchy' Actor Was 83 [Online]. Online: TV Insider. Available: https://www.tvinsider.com/1050512/sonny-barger-dies-83-hells-angels-sons-of-anarchy/ [Accessed]. 11 ADRIENNE TYLER, S. B. 2023. Sons Of Anarchy: Every Real-Life Hells Angels Member in The Cast [Online].

Everywhere he went, he flaunted it—a badge of defiance. But vigilance clung to him—the Hells Angels, his guardians. Non-members circled like vultures, but Munro stayed close to the pack. They had his back—a silent promise etched in leather.

Freedom tasted sweet. Michigan beckoned—a battleground of family values and judgment. The Munros, a military clan, despised inked skin and the scent of rebellion. Munro's plan was not just about personal expression. It directly challenged his family's values, a declaration of his independence. Their disdain would fuel him—a fire to light his way. And so, he rode—a lone wolf with a pack's heart. The road stretched, and Munro grinned—a tattooed boy, a son of defiance.

Munro resided in Long Beach for several additional months, sharing a home with Art. In a generous gesture, Art gifted Munro a waterbed and a phone for his birthday and even secured him a job in Inglewood. But Art's generosity did not stop there; he also bestowed upon Munro a camera. Fuelled by curiosity and creativity, Munro turned his lens toward the world. Initially, he captured candid shots of girls in short dresses. However, his photographic pursuits took a darker turn when he delved into a practice now known as "Up Skirting"—a covert act of photographing women's panties from beneath their skirts without their knowledge or consent. This invasive behaviour is unequivocally illegal.

Undeterred, Munro continued his photographic escapades, capturing various moments. His excitement reached its peak when he managed to snap a picture of the Harlem Globe-trotters. But fate had more surprises in store for him. On the night following his 19th birthday, Munro visited Art's mother, and together, they watched *"Escape from Alcatraz"*, starring the iconic Clint Eastwood. Little did Munro know that another significant surprise awaited him back home—a revelation that would forever be etched in his dreams. Munro remembers four beautiful naked girls with big melons waiting for him, lying provocatively on Munro's bed, all wanting to please him and have a fun time. Munro was extremely nervous as he had only ever had sex with one girl at a time, "the girls told him to relax, and they would teach him everything he needed to know." Munro lay on the bed, and One girl began to undress him as another girl started licking him all over; the third girl was kissing, and the fourth girl rubbed his adulthood, giving him the best hand job he had ever felt. Munro got hard as a rock at this point. The first girl slid onto his hard erection and started riding him, bouncing up and down; the second girl was now suckling on one of the first girls' massive melons. The third girl was licking his member as it slid into the first girl's slippery opening. Munro was having an exciting time and did not want this to end; all four girls told him to relax and that this would be an all-nighter. At this point, the fourth grabbed a strap-on Dildo and started to penetrate the girl, licking his manhood. This was so fucken great.

As Munro pondered the situation, he yearned to capture it on film. However, unbeknownst to him, Art had already been recording everything. Art revealed the video recording to Munro the following day, leaving him with another surprise.

Munro does not know what happened to the tape; it most likely does not exist anymore.

Munro resided with Art until restlessness tugged at his heart. A Hollywood crush beckoned, and in January 1980, he bid farewell to Art's abode, returning to the bustling streets of Hollywood. Alas, whether fate conspired against him, the girl remained elusive, Munro never crossed paths with her again.

As Sunset Boulevard hummed with life one moonlit night, Munro found himself at Arthur Jays, a cozy café. Seated at a table, he encountered a stranger—a man who introduced himself as Cowboy. Their conversation danced between shadows, and Cowboy shared a chilling warning: a van prowled the highways, its driver a predator preying on hitchhikers. The moniker bestowed upon this menace was "The Freeway Killer." Munro, ever cautious, assured Cowboy that he never stepped into vans with unfamiliar faces, thus avoiding any grim encounters.

Cowboy and Munro meandered through the dimly lit streets, their shadows stretching across the pavement. As night settled in, Cowboy suggested finding a place to rest. With a modest stash of cash, Munro and Cowboy checked into Motel 6, where a mere $6 secured them a night's refuge.

Munro's craving for nicotine led him to the motel's restaurant. There, he concocted a clever ruse: feigning frustration, he pretended to insert 50 cents into the cigarette vending machine. The unsuspecting lady who managed the establishment sympathised with his plight and replenished the machine from the register, ensuring Munro received his coveted cigarettes.

But Munro's resourcefulness extended beyond mere smokes. He devised a more audacious scheme—dining and dashing. After ordering a meal, he would slip to the restroom, leaving the bill unpaid. His escape routes? A swift exit through a conveniently open window. To evade capture, Munro donned various disguises—a beard and a moustache—always staying one step ahead of the consequences.

While Munro strolled along the sun-kissed beaches, he stumbled upon a peculiar revelation: Hollywood—the heart of dreams and illusions—held a clandestine secret. For those seeking to peddle desire, it was the place to be. The boulevards whispered tales of forbidden transactions, where shadows danced with desire, and the city's pulse thrummed with hidden exchanges. In Hollywood's neon glow, the currency shifted from dollars to secrets.

Munro's journey led him to the vibrant streets of Santa Monica Boulevard in Hollywood. Here, the city's pulse quickened, and secrets whispered through the neon glow. Along this boulevard, young men—shrouded in shadows—peddled desire, their bodies both currency and commodity. The night held promises that daylight dared not reveal, and Munro found himself at the crossroads of allure and danger. Indeed, the streets of Hollywood whispered secrets—tales of desire, danger, and clandestine transactions. Drawn by the allure of youth, older men picked up Munro, leading him to their homes. In the shadows, transactions unfolded there. Munro navigated a world where bodies became commodities and intimacy held a price. Hollywood, with its neon glow, stood as a symbol of rock and roll, drugs, and sex—a city where dreams collided with reality, and the night held promises both thrilling and dangerous.
Indeed, within the intricate web of Hollywood's underbelly, unwritten rules governed the night. Friday and Saturday were the nights when desire flowed freely, and transactions unfolded in the neon-lit shadows. The streets pulsed with

secrets, and the currency exchanged was intimate, raw and unfiltered.

However, come Sunday, caution prevailed. The vice cops emerged from the darkness, their watchful eyes scanning the streets. To prostitute on this night was to dance with danger—a precarious waltz where the stakes were freedom itself. The risk loomed large, and those who dared faced the possibility of arrest, their illusions shattered by the harsh light of law enforcement.

In this nocturnal theatre, the players knew their roles: the seekers, the sellers, and the silent enforcers. Hollywood—the city of dreams and disillusionment—held its secrets close, revealing them only to those who dared to venture beyond the glittering façade.

Between January and May, Munro immersed himself in the pulsating heart of Hollywood—the city of dreams and illusions. Here, the rhythm of life quickened, fuelled by desire and the pursuit of fast money. Prostitution became his currency, the streets his stage, and the neon glow his spotlight. Munro's bills were paid, and life was a whirlwind of adrenaline and pleasure.

But in May of 1980, as the sun dipped below the horizon, Munro's path intersected with the LGBTQI+ community centre. Seeking refuge, he stepped inside, hoping for solace and a place to rest. The walls whispered stories of resilience and acceptance, but little did Munro know that beyond those doors, a nightmare awaited—a darkness that would forever alter the course of his life.

Chapter 4 Bonin/Munro Meeting the Devil

Munro stood outside the LGBT centre on a balmy Hollywood morning, waiting for assistance.[12] The date was May 23, 1980, a Memorial Day weekend. A blue Chevette pulled up, its engine purring to a halt, and stepped out a burly man standing at five feet nine inches and weighing around 250 pounds. His name was Bill. A fragile bridge materialised as Bill's hand extended—a tenuous connection between two souls. One sought refuge, while the other, masked in feigned solace, extended an invitation. Beneath the surface, secrets simmered, waiting to unravel in the dance of shadows and whispered promises. "I am Bill," he declared, his voice a lifeline in the night. Wearied by life's twists, Munro revealed his truth: "I need a place to stay." Bill's response echoed with false compassion: "You can stay with me for the weekend." Thus, fate wove their paths together within that fleeting exchange. This fragile connection held the promise of respite and perhaps something more.

Bill's life wove intricate threads—a home shared with brothers, a mother tending to her veteran husband at the hospital, who returned home on weekends. Munro, ever trusting, sized up Bill, his judgment whispering, "Okay, you sound trustworthy." Thus, he stepped into the car, unaware that fate's gears had shifted—a trap set, danger lurking. Blissfully ignorant, Munro rode toward an unknown horizon, destiny's hand guiding him toward an unforeseen precipice.

Munro's hunger gnawed at him as the car glided through the streets.

He confided in Bill, who responded kindly: "Okay, we will grab a sandwich near my place." Munro's grin widened; relief washed over him. Soon, they arrived at Bill's house in Downey, California. Stepping out, Munro surveyed his surroundings. The opulence struck him—this was no ordinary abode. Bill's home exuded wealth, its walls whispering secrets of prosperity. And as Munro crossed the threshold, he sensed the air thick with the scent of money, secrets, and perhaps danger.

Munro remained blissfully unaware that the house he entered was not Bill's own—it belonged to Bill's mother. The deception was seamless, and Munro's trust remained intact. Bill Bonin's mother, a woman of about 65, toiled at the Veterans Hospital, caring for her husband—a man whose needs exceeded what home could provide. Her nights were spent in Downey, tending to her responsibilities. At the same time, the house held its secrets, veiled in the tranquillity of suburban life.

Munro's encounter with Alice held a curious twist. Her gaze lingered, and she recognised him as another of Bill's gay friends. Alice, aware of Bill's orientation and his extensive

12 the Los Angeles LGBT Centre was founded in 1969 by gay and lesbian rights activists Morris Kight, Don Kilhefner, and other dedicated activists. Originally known as The Gay Community Services Centre,

male companionship, welcomed Munro into her home—a seemingly innocuous act that would ripple through fate's tapestry.

*Image SEQ Image * ARABIC4 William Bonin in court (Blanco, n.d)*

Bill and his two brothers—one older and the other younger—formed the core of the household. Robert Jr, the elder, spun tunes as a DJ at a local club, while the younger brother, Peter, managed a bustling pizza joint. Thus, Munro settled into the Bonin household, a chapter of his life unfolding from May 23 to June 11, 1980.

Munro followed Bill into the house at 10282 Angel Street in Downey, California, and encountered a layout that revealed the family's dynamics. On the right side stood two bedrooms and a den belonging to Bill's brothers—Robert Jr. and Peter. Perhaps uninterested in formalities, Munro did not bother to learn Bill's surname. At that moment, it did not

matter; the house held its secrets, and Munro's fate remained veiled.
Munro wanted a place to stay, food in his belly, and money in his pocket, and he did not care how he got it as long as he did not get arrested. Bill told Munro to go to Bill's bedroom, where Bill then firmly insisted that he needed to pay him back for giving him a place to stay and food; that was when Munro realised Bill meant sex. Bill demanded that Munro perform sexual acts with him. Munro felt he had no choice, so he let Bill do what he wanted until Bonin got his nuts off and was finished. Munro was simply happy to have food and a roof.

Munro's desperate circumstances led him to Bonin's doorstep, seeking necessities.
Nevertheless, Bill's intentions turned dark, coercing Munro into a traumatic situation. The aftermath left Munro grappling with the complexities of their newfound friendship, a bond forged in pain and betrayal. Sometimes, the true nature of a friend remains hidden until it is too late to escape the consequences.
Bonin's persuasive charm worked magic on Munro, who eagerly accepted a job offer—the prospect of driving those massive 18-wheelers excitedly filled Munro.
Munro's excitement was palpable, and the prospect of driving those massive 18-wheelers was like a dream come true.

He confided in Bonin, "Hey, I have some experience behind the wheel. Truckers taught me how to drive when I was hitchhiking my way to California." Bonin's smile widened, and he promptly called his boss. Monday morning would mark the beginning of Munro's new journey, navigating highways and mastering the art of handling those colossal rigs.

On Munro's first day at the truck company, he entered a bustling world of diesel engines, towering rigs, and the promise of open roads. The air smelled of grease and adventure, and as he walked through the yard, his eyes caught sight of a beautiful blonde woman with enormous breasts. Munro's heart raced, and blood flowed to his adulthood. Munro was bisexual and seeing her always made him horny. Still, she looked at him as if he were a child, dashing his hopes of any romantic connection. His luck, he never got a chance because she looked at him like he was a child. Munro, with one hand gripping the sturdy steering wheel and the other on the gear knob, settled into the cab of his first 18-wheeler. The engine's rumble beneath him was a symphony of power, and the promise of open roads stretched before him. As the wheels turned, he knew—he was a truck driver, and there was no better feeling.
In his mind, it was better than sex.

Munro continued his daily grind at the company, entrusted with driving long hauls. Occasionally, he and Bonin embarked on trucking adventures together. After successfully delivering their cargo, they would abandon the trusty 18-wheelers, tuck the hard-earned cash into their pockets, and return on a hitchhiking journey. The open road held freedom and uncertainty, weaving their lives together in a tapestry of asphalt and camaraderie. On that sweltering June 1, Bonin and Munro sat exhausted on the footpath, waiting for a ride back. The sun beat down mercilessly, casting long shadows across the asphalt. And then, out of nowhere, Bonin posed a chilling question to Munro: "Hey, what do you say we pick up a hitchhiker, share a night with them, and then end their life?" The words hung in the air, heavy and hateful. However, Munro, seasoned by their shared escapades, saw through the facade. He shot Bonin a look—a silent declaration that this was nothing more than a twisted prank.

Chapter 5 William George Bonin

Image 5 Bonin (Year 1963)

Image 6 Bonin at stamp club

Image 7 Bonin in Stamp Club (Year: 1963)

William George Bonin, born on January 8, 1947, in Willimantic, Connecticut, was often described as having a husky appearance. His dark, shoulder-length hair and moustache gave him an average look that was neither particularly handsome nor unattractive.

He was the second of three sons to Robert Leonard Bonin Sr. and Alice Dorothy Cote.[13] Their household was marked by dysfunction and hardship. Both parents had alcoholism, and his father was an ill-tempered World War II veteran. His father's brutality extended to gambling, and he often beat his wife and children. As a result, Bonin and his brothers were starved for care and had to rely on their neighbours for food and clothing. The abuse they endured from their parents led Bill Bonin and his brothers to spend much of their time with their grandfather.

Their grandfather was also a convicted paedophile who sexually assaulted his daughter, Alice, as a child. William George Bonin recalls those moments when he was left in the care of his grandfather. Those memories, etched into the fabric of his upbringing, would later intertwine with the darker chapters of his life as his grandpa would tickle him and make Bill suck on his genitals.

In 1953, when Bonin was only six, he and his elder brother Bobby were shipped off to an orphanage that was notorious for harshly punishing children. It inflicted both minor and significant physical abuse on them. The orphanage would brutalise and torment children with savage whippings, forcing them to hold painful poses and submerging them in

13 William Bonin - Wikipedia. https://en.wikipedia.org/wiki/William_Bonin

water-filled basins. Bonin confided about some of his childhood to Munro.

When Bonin was nine, In May of 1955, he and his brother were released from the Franco-American [14] orphanage, And Bonin began to sexually assault his brother and other young boys in the neighbourhood. This behaviour continued and escalated while Bill Bonin grew up until he was incarcerated.

*Image SEQ Image * ARABIC8 The orphanage where Bonin spent time (Orphelinat Franco-American, n.d)*

In 1957, when Bill was ten, he was caught stealing number plates and was sent to Juvenile Hall as punishment, where he was used as a sexual play toy by older children. While

14 The Franco-American Orphanage in Lowell, Massachusetts, carries a haunting history. Its three-story structure looms large, casting shadows over the lives of those who sought refuge within its walls.

there, an older boy tied Bonin up and molested him; this is where Bonin learnt to hogtie his victims and was subjected to other punishments such as submersion in ice water and being threatened at knife point. Not long after the abuse, Bonin began to ask to be restrained while engaging in sexual activity.

In 1962, Bonin and the family moved to California and lived in Torrance. Having experienced sexual abuse and a somewhat chaotic family life, Bonin constantly grappled with his social and sexual identity. He was keeping his homosexual feelings a secret.
Bonin, at 18, pleaded guilty to a first offence of Petty theft and was given a 30-day suspended sentence and a $56 fine. He did not learn from being caught; he kept committing petty crimes.

On July 4, 1965, William Bonin and his brother's friend were in a precarious situation. Their desperate act of petty theft and burglary involved pilfering a weight machine and a newspaper receipt box from a local supermarket. Nevertheless, their ill-fated endeavour turned dark when apprehended while attempting to pry open the machines, hoping for a meagre haul of coins.[15]

15 William Bonin | Found a Grave. https://www.foundagrave.com/grave/william-bonin/

*Image SEQ Image * ARABIC9 Young Bonin Screenshot (Dark Reality,2022)*

Bonin left school in late 1966, and shortly after turning 19, he secured a job alongside his father at Olympic Screw and Rivet in Downey. His desire for independence led him to a monthly payment plan to purchase a horse. Meanwhile, his mother, Alice, lived in perpetual anxiety, fearing her son's propensity for trouble. Bonin now spent considerable time with younger boys, sharing a beer and indulging in X-rated movies. This precarious path would shape his future in unforeseen ways.

Alice, a devoted Catholic mother, expressed her concerns as any caring parent would. She worried about Bonin, who had likely suffered head trauma due to the beatings she endured while pregnant. Alice persuaded Bill to enlist in the military to set him on a path of redemption. Bonin had a girlfriend during this period—perhaps to appease his mother. They made plans to marry upon his return from the war. Maybe the time away would provide clarity for Bonin, who grappled with confusion over his sexual identity.

After completing basic training, William Bonin embarked on a varied military journey. For four months, he served as a cook in Alaska. The kitchen fires and the camaraderie of fellow soldiers became his daily rhythm.

His ambition to become a helicopter pilot hit a snag—he failed the required testing. The blow to his ego was palpable, but he needed an alternative path.

Bonin shifted gears, training as a door gunner on a Chinook CH-47 twin-engine heavy-lift helicopter. Simultaneously, he honed his skills as an aircraft mechanic. The whir of rotors and the smell of aviation fuel became his new reality.

While on leave in San Francisco, fate intervened. Bonin was arrested on suspicion of *grand theft person*—stealing from another person. Denying the charges, he knew that being on leave meant he would not be around for court proceedings. His commanding officer stepped in, sending a letter to the court stating that Bonin was unavailable due to war service. Once again, he slipped through the cracks, escaping the clutches of justice.

Bonin arrived in Vietnam in 1968, two months before North Vietnamese launched the Tet Offensive. It has been published that Bonin was reportedly serving with the U.S. Air

Force on board a helicopter for search and rescue operations, looking for lost pilots, but this was not true.
According to a Disability application claim found by a private investigator, Bonin's' Army serial number was 56-700-885. Bonin obtained the Rank of Private First-Class E-3 and had been stationed at Pho Loi Base camp north of Ho Chi Minh City with the 205th Assault Support Helicopter Company, the Geronimo's of the 11th Combat Aviation Battalion nicknamed "Red Dog Firefly."
Bonin spent the last six months of his service with the 205th as a door gunner on the Chinook CH-47, Logging over 700 hours taking control of a 7.62mm M60 Machine Gun.
Bonin was awarded a commendation for risking his life to pull an injured pilot into the back of the helicopter, and he received a Marksmanship Medal, the Vietnam Service Medal, and an air medal. He also earned his high school GED while in service.
According to reports, Bonin did have at least five heterosexual encounters with prostitutes after arriving in Vietnam. However, it did not stop there. Bonin forcefully sodomised two men at gunpoint on separate occasions and had several homosexual encounters. Once again, no one was aware of the danger Bonin was becoming, as the Victims were too ashamed to come forward.
Bonin sought to deflect blame, attributing his perverse actions to the trauma of his time in Vietnam. Upon returning

in 1968, he settled in Downey, where the 105 and 605 freeways intersect. The crossroads of his life—war, guilt, and a return to familiar territory—would shape his dark path. Upon his return, Bonin discovered that his fiancée Linda had given birth to their son. However, she decided to move on, feeling Bonin was no longer necessary for her life. Thus, she married another man who would assist in raising their child. This turn of events, while seemingly harsh, may have been a fortunate twist of fate. Given Bonin's deeply ingrained predatory nature, this separation perhaps shielded his son from the potential dangers of being close to a father with such a perilous and destructive way of life.

Bonin was arrested between coming home and June 1969—for his new obsession with sodomising young boys. Bonin was charged with five counts of kidnapping, one count of sodomy, and one count of oral copulation.

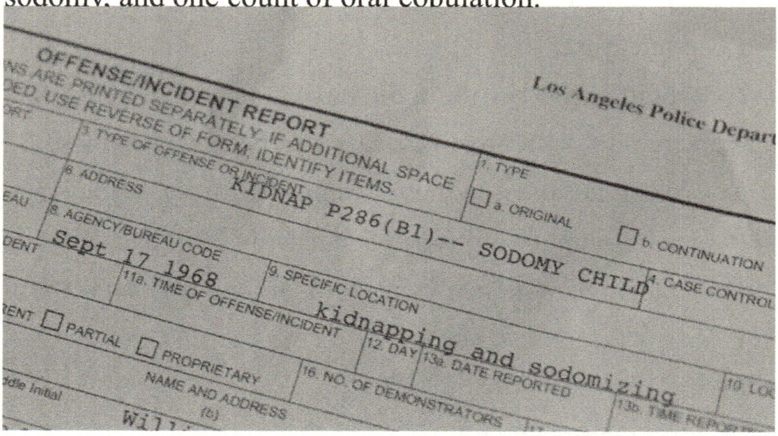

OFFENSE/INCIDENT REPORT

Los Angeles Police Depar

...NS ARE PRINTED SEPARATELY IF ADDITIONAL SPACE ...ED. USE REVERSE OF FORM, IDENTIFY ITEMS.

1. TYPE ☐ a. ORIGINAL ☐ b. CONTINUATION

3. TYPE OF OFFENSE OR INCIDENT: KIDNAP P286(B1)-- SODOMY CHILD

4. CASE CONTROL

6. ADDRESS

8. AGENCY/BUREAU CODE

9. SPECIFIC LOCATION: kidnapping and sodomizing

11a. TIME OF OFFENSE/INCIDENT: Sept 17 1968

12. DAY

13a. DATE REPORTED

13b. TIME REPORTED

☐ PARTIAL ☐ PROPRIETARY

16. NO. OF DEMONSTRATORS

NAME AND ADDRESS (b)

*Image SEQ Image * ARABIC10 Bonin offence report 1968 screenshot (Dark Reality, 2022)*

Bonin was convicted of sexually assaulting the five boys; his MO was always the same; he had to have his victims restrained somehow before raping and sodomising these young boys.

March 11, 1969, Bonin was court-ordered to undergo psychiatric examinations before he went to trial, which revealed Bonin had an IQ of 120 [16] and suffered traits of manic depression in addition to having damage to the prefrontal cortex of the brain. His body was covered in scars, which he sustained in a detention centre in the state of Connecticut Juvenile Centre.

Bonin faced formal charges on May 9, acknowledging his guilt. His sentence was handed down on June 4, 1969. Subsequently, he entered Atascadero State Hospital on June 17, 1969. Later, he was transferred to Vacaville, a state prison medical facility, on July 7, 1971. After three additional years, he earned a parole recommendation.

On June 11, 1974, he left prison, deemed safe for society by the doctors. Little did they know that Bonin harboured other, darker intentions.

In September 1975, 14-year-old David McVicker found himself hitchhiking home from a friend's house in Garden Grove, California. Fate intervened when a van pulled over, and Bonin invited McVicker inside. Little did McVicker know that this seemingly innocuous conversation would lead him down a treacherous path. The seemingly ordinary ride took a horrifying turn when Bonin immediately inquired if McVicker was gay. Alarmed, McVicker asked Bonin to stop the car, but instead, Bonin pulled out a gun and drove him to a desolate area.

There, Bonin subjected the teen to a brutal assault—forcing him to undress, beating and raping him. As he tightened a T-shirt around McVicker's neck, the boy screamed and begged for his life. Then, inexplicably, Bonin halted, offering a chilling apology. He drove McVicker home, leaving him with haunting words: "We will meet again. McVicker went home and told his parents what happened. They called the police, and Bonin was caught and charged. Bonin confessed and returned to prison on December 31, 1975.[16]

Bonin, by the late 70s, had an unsettling aura. James Hunter, a neighbour, vividly remembers an incident when Bonin tried to lure his son into his house. Meanwhile, a nearby woman heard chilling screams emanating from Bonin's residence. Despite her restless night, she dismissed it as mere domestic trouble. Little did she know that darker forces were at play. Had she suspected otherwise, she might have alerted the police—a decision that could have altered the course of events.

16 1995. Bonin v. Calderon. F. 3d. Court of Appeals, 9th Circuit.

On November 1, 1978, shortly after his release from his last crime against McVicker. Bonin moved to an apartment complex at the Kingswood Village, a block from his mother's house in Downey. His new neighbour, Scott Fraser, was around 43 well educated and a former loan officer he unwittingly helped Bonin find friends for parties, sexual partners, and murder accomplices.

Around mid-November, one night, Bonin and his friend Neil Mendez contacted Scott Fraser through the building intercom system to ask about an event at the building. Scott's place, Apartment F220, was party central for many young people, many homosexual men who gravitated to the seemingly endless festivities. Fresh out of prison with homosexual desires, Bonin gravitated to Scott, fitting in with the ever-changing scenery. It was not till later that Bonin learned his friend Neil was also gay.

Fraser's drug dealing attracted many visitors. Bonin hung out with Fraser three to four nights a week and became social friends, as Fraser said. They sometimes ate out but mostly stayed at Scott's apartment. Fraser enjoyed hosting and arranging sexual hookups for his friends. Fraser, who knew Vernon Butts from his magic show at Warren High School in Downey, introduced him to Bonin, and they hit it off.

Another Frazier showed up in April 1979. Blaine Frazier befriended Scott Fraser, and they sold at Scott's apartment on Imperial Highway. Blaine had been in jail before, and his business with Scott took a hit when they were busted for drugs. Out on bail, Blaine spent time with Bonin and found out how much Bonin liked young boys. And how he wanted to cruise around Hollywood for sex. One day, as they drove around, Bonin spotted a young boy and asked Frazier if he tried to pick him up; Frazier said, drop me off before you do anything.

Meanwhile, Bonin's attempt at picking up the boy was unsuccessful. The incident offers a first-hand account of Bonin's relentless search for young boys and a desire, even need, to recruit accomplices. Bonin hated doing things alone. Bonin was on probation, and the rules of parole, let alone the actual laws, precluded having sex with underage boys.

July 19th, 1979—the day Bonin acquired the 1972 Ford E-100 Shorty van—marked the beginning of a nightmare. The van, once innocuous, now bore the weight of malice. Its green carpeting, installed by Sunset Bank Conversions, masked secrets woven into its fabric.

Foxwood panelling and curtains cocooned the interior, shrouding it from prying eyes. No one could glimpse past the front seats through the windscreen. The van's roof vent

17 Pasqualini, K. (2023). William Bonin: Sadistic "Freeway Killer" Left Trail of Bodies. https://thecrimewire.com/true-crime/Sadistic-Freeway-Killer-Left-Trail-of-Over-22-Boys-Bodies-The-Story-of-William-Bonin

whispered secrets to the wind, while standard double doors harboured a sliding window on the right side.

Bonin's new acquisition was no ordinary van. It was a vessel of darkness, its double doors concealing more than cargo. As he climbed behind the wheel, he knowingly stepped into a macabre journey—a ride that would forever alter his life.

And so, the death van awaited its next passenger, its secrets veiled in green, its purpose insidious.

*Image SEQ Image * ARABIC11 Bonin's death van (Kurcski,2024)*

Chapter 6 Vernon Robert Butts Accomplice

*Image SEQ Image * ARABIC12 Vernon Butts Screenshot (Dark Reality, 2022)*

Vernon Robert Butts came into the world on August 29, 1957, and grew up in Norfolk. He was attending Norwalk High School.[18] His parents are Irene McVay (Butts) and Floyd Ray Butts.

Butts died on January 11, 1981, at the age of 23 and is buried at Rose Hill Memorial Park in California. [19]

Butts had a strong bond with his father, Floyd, but his father sadly died at the age of 32 when Butts was only nine.[20]

Butt's father used to teach him magic card tricks, and Butts remained fascinated with fantasy and stories based on fantasy. Butts worked at a factory and as a magician, hiring himself out to parties and claiming to be a "wizard".

18 Original data: Find a Grave. Find a Grave®. http://www.findagrave.com/cgi-bin/fg.cgi. 19 Ancestry.com. California, U.S., Death Index, 1940-1997 [database online].20 "Sellers Executed for 3 Murders." The Oklahoman (online), February 4, 1999, 1999. https://www.oklahoman.com/story/news/1999/02/04/sellers-executed-for-3-murders/62254125007/. Provo, UT, USA: Ancestry.com Operations Inc, 2000.

Butts also chose to sleep in a coffin. Butts first met Bonin at a party in 1979 and became fascinated with him. It excited Butts that Bonin was into sadistic same-gender activities. From then on, they prowled the highways in Southern California, searching for young boys and men to sodomise, rape and strangle.

Butts was a 6 ft 3 inches skinny man with long, stringy hair and a bony face. He worked at the magic store in the Knott's Berry Farm amusement park and did a simple magic act for small parties.

Another person, Ron Close, met Butts three years before through Neil Mendez at a pizza place near the Keystone Lanes bowling alley in Norwalk. They were friends who hung out, partied, and had many things in common. Ron Close joined the mystery parties that Butts set up and was aware of his occult activities. Close later said that Butts acted strangely in September of 1979, which was alarming given how odd he already was. One night at Butt's house, Butts pressed an axe blade against Close's throat and said he wanted to see his blood and hear his screams. Butts let go of the blade, and Ron Close left and never saw Butts again.

Butts was into witchcraft and black magic and joined a satanic cult with his fiancé, Cati Razook. He was bisexual and addicted to drugs and alcohol. He and Cati met at one of the mystery parties he set up.

He followed his mentors, James Meurer and Razook, in their occult/ witchcraft activities. He played Dungeons and Dragons, a fantasy role-playing game with a lot of violence and death in a magical world.
The game involved a series of supposedly authentic magical rituals. [15]
This imagined MWV (magical worldview) deviated significantly from the cultural norms of most societies, utilising the concept of manipulating the universe to achieve one's desires. The game's black magic rituals were crafted to summon demons.
The game caused many suicides and murders, primarily by young men in the 70s and 80s. Some teenagers who took their own lives by gunshot, hanging or carbon monoxide poisoning left suicide notes that showed how D&D affected their minds. Sean Sellers, another 14-year-old Satan worshipper, claimed Dungeons and Dragons made him murder. He was the youngest person on death row in Oklahoma and was put to death in 1999. Sellers admitted to killing his parents, Paul and Vonda Bellofatto, and a convenience store clerk, Robert Bower, in two separate events in 1985 and 1986. He said he was under demonic influence.

A tragic case emerged where a young individual, influenced by misconceptions surrounding a game, left a suicide note that reflected a belief in resurrection within the game's universe. This heartbreaking incident underscores the potential for dangerous misinterpretations of fantasy settings. Additionally, Butts exhibited an intense preoccupation with death and associated subcultures, often participating in rituals in places typically related to decay and the departed, such as sewers and cemeteries. These behaviours signal a concerning fascination with macabre themes and highlight the need for awareness and intervention when individuals show signs of unhealthy obsessions."

It is essential to recognise that most D&D players these days enjoy the game purely for entertainment, creativity, and social interaction. The game itself does not inherently lead to harmful behaviour.
However, like any form of media or entertainment, D&D can be misinterpreted or misused by individuals with pre-existing mental health issues or extreme beliefs. In such cases, professional help and support are vital to address the underlying problems and prevent tragic outcomes. [21]

Bonin and Butts spent time together at Fraser's apartment and became lovers and friends. Butts said Bonin was a bossy and strict type. He was a passionate lover but had

21 Henrich, S., & Worthington, R. (2023). Let Your Clients Fight Dragons: A Rapid Evidence Assessment regarding the Therapeutic Utility of 'Dungeons & Dragons'. https://doi.org/10.1080/15401383.2021.1987367

problems. Butts followed the wishes of more powerful people and had his demons, which led him to a place that he could never have imagined. He moved to a garage on Dinwiddie Street sometime in late 1979, Where the lounge room was decorated with a coffin in the corner. Another coffin for sleeping in, flashing black lights, posters, figurines, and many spider webs make a weird atmosphere. Loud music, drinking, drugs, Star Wars costumes, casual sex, and movies with violence and death were always present.

Chapter 7 Gregory Mathew Miley Accomplice

*Image SEQ Image * ARABIC13 Gregory Mathews Miley Mug Shot 1980 (Wikimedia Commons, 1980)*

Gregory Matthew Miley, born on August 5, 1961, hailed from Cincinnati, Hamilton, Ohio. He spent his formative years in the Lakewood neighbourhood of Los Angeles, conveniently close to Bonin's residence in Downey. Gregory's parents were Elmer C. Miley and Judith E. Miley (née Goldfuss). Unfortunately, their marriage ended in divorce on April 19, 1967. On the grounds of Gross Neglect of Duty, Elmer, who was 79, passed away on August 28, 2017, while Judith left this world in 2012. [22] Miley's early life was

22 Ancestry.com. U.S., Obituary Collection, 1930-Current [database on-line]. Lehi, UT, USA: Ancestry.com Operations Inc, 2006.

marked by illness, misfortune, and turmoil. As the third sibling in a quartet of children, nestled between Jeffrey, Stephen, and an unnamed fourth, Miley was met with challenges from the very beginning. His position in the family dynamic presented unique hurdles and experiences that shaped his journey. His difficult birth may have resulted in brain damage, which could explain some of his later struggles. At the tender age of two, Miley suffered a severe reaction to penicillin, leading to a high fever. These early events likely contributed to learning difficulties or even cognitive slowness.

Unfortunately, Miley's mother had a tumultuous life, marrying several abusive husbands. She was not able to provide consistent care for young Miley. His educational journey was equally rocky: he attended kindergarten twice and participated in special classes. However, by the time he reached the 11th grade, he decided to leave school altogether. [23] His life was a patchwork of short-term jobs, minor criminal activities, and drug use. Despite these challenges, he attended Bancroft Junior High School during his formative years. His life took a dark turn when he became entangled with the infamous "Freeway Killer," William Bonin, and participated in a series of horrifying crimes.In early 1980, Bonin recruited Gregory Mathew Miley, a sexual psychopath with an intellectual disability. According to his parents, met Bonin at a party when Miley was about 17, which

23 UPI. (1982, February 4). Freeway Killer accomplice gets 25 years to life sentence. Lodi News Sentinel, 29. https://news.google.com/newspapers?id=Wt4zAAAAIBAJ&pg=5776,4161244&dq/

Scott Fraser hosted; Scott was a friend of Bonin's. Miley and Bonin quickly became more than just friends. They became lovers, constantly having sex with each other. Like Vernon Butts, Miley was someone that William Bonin could easily control and manipulate. He may have been one of the easiest to influence, with a reported I.Q. of 56, way below average.

Bonin even attempted to have Miley declared incompetent to testify; the underlying basis for this claim — Miley's mental deficits —was apparent from the records. Anyone who did a cursory review of Miley's testimony would be alerted that Miley's mental acuity was less than average. In addition, the record reflected Miley's inability to read since Miley, unlike the other witnesses at the trial, needed to have the oath read to him rather than reading it aloud himself. During direct examination, Miley testified that he could not read or write and had never been able to do so. During this tumultuous period, Miley was deeply entangled in drug use, a fact that deeply troubled his mother. She implored him to sever ties with Bonin, who was a bad influence and the supplier of the substances that held Miley in thrall. Bonin's manipulative provision of drugs ensnared Miley, leaving him vulnerable to Bonin's control.

Tragically, his family's intervention proved to be heart-breakingly late. Miley's pivotal moment coincided with his parents' celebration of a new beginning—selling their home and planning a move to Texas. They envisioned a fresh start for their family, including taking Miley away from Bonin's destructive orbit. Suppose fate had only been kinder, allowing this move to occur even a day earlier. In that case, the course of Miley's life might have been drastically different.

Chapter 8 William Raymond Pugh Accomplice

William Raymond Pugh, commonly known as Billy, remains a shadowy figure due to his status as a juvenile during the time of the murders. However, some newspaper reports shed light on his troubled past. Pugh's juvenile criminal record, which began when he was just 11 years old, included convictions for robbery, burglary, and assault. These early brushes with the law, at such an early age, likely made him susceptible to manipulation, ultimately leading him down a dark path alongside the infamous "Freeway Killer," William Bonin. [24]

Pugh was the most active accomplice who was only charged with one murder. However, he confessed to killing two victims. He received six years for voluntary manslaughter in a plea bargain. [25]

Let us delve into what little we know about Pugh's family background: His mother, Loretta Camacho, was born on April 26, 1942. Her life took her to riverside California, where she eventually passed away in 2011 at the age of 68. Pugh was born on September 25, 1962 [26]

Pugh's Father, Gerald L. Pugh, was born on January 14, 1930, and shaped his life. Unfortunately, their marriage faced challenges, and they divorced in June 1973

24 UPI. (1982, February 4). Freeway Killer accomplice gets 25 years to life sentence. Lodi News Sentinel, 29. https://news.google.com/25 Profile of Serial Killer William Bonin, The Freeway Killer. https://www.thoughtco.com/serial-killer-william-bonin-973136 newspapers?id=Wt4zAAAAIBAJ&pg=5776,4161244&dq/ 26 Nevada State Health Division, Office of Vital Records. Nevada Marriage Index, 1966-2005. Carson City, Nevada: Nevada State Health Division, Office of Vital Records.

Gerald himself departed this world on December 6, 2010. [27] In 1978, Billy attended San Pedro High School, a period that may have shaped his future actions and interactions. Pugh's story is one of tragedy, poor choices, and the devastating consequences of being drawn into a web of violence, a path that he likely regretted taking.

*Image SEQ Image * ARABIC14 William Pugh (IMDb, n.d.-a)*

27 Nevada State Health Division, Office of Vital Records. Nevada Marriage Index, 1966-2005. Carson City, Nevada: Nevada State Health Division, Office of Vital Records
28 "U.S., School Yearbooks, 1880-2012"; School Name: San Pedro High School; Year:

Chapter 9 Eric Martin Wijnnaendts Accomplice

*Image SEQ Image * ARABIC15 Eric Wijnaendts (US, School Year-books, 1900-2016)*

Eric Wijnaendts was born in the Netherlands on May 23, 1960, to parents Cornelius Wijnaendts and Neeltje Merbis. He has two brothers, Robert, and Peter. He attended Bolsa Grande High School, where he began to lay the foundation for his future.

1980, it was thought William Bonin may have had another accomplice. Eric Marten Wijnnaendts, who was 20 years old, Eric crossed paths with William Bonin while they were both in Orange County jail. Not Surprisingly, Eric, a young man, became another one of Bonin's lovers during their incarceration. What's more intriguing is that their relationship did not end in prison; it continued after their release, adding a new chapter to their story.

Eric could not get into his house when he was released from incarceration. He called Bonin for help, and Bonin came over, picked him up, and took him back to where he still lived with his mother. They had time to catch up, and Bonin took Eric to a party at Scott's place. Bonin took Eric home as he was pretty intoxicated and returned to the party at Scott's to meet 17-year-old Billy Pugh. Scott often introduced Bonin to boys he fancied for romantic encounters. According to reports, Bonin was very attracted to Eric, who enjoyed spending time with him and seeking his advice. They had a curious relationship, and Bonin confessed to having some love for him, even though they barely knew each other. However, they grew distant after the first few weeks. When Eric exited prison, he said he wanted to live with Bonin but not at his mom's place. He only wanted to live with Bonin if he had his apartment and was willing to split the costs.On a Saturday in May, Bonin called Eric to ask him what he was doing. Eric was not doing much, so Bonin suggested they meet up. To avoid stirring jealousy from Eric's housemate, Bonin discreetly picked him up at the corner of Valley View and Leffingwell. . They drove around Long Beach, and Bonin brought up the Hit Squad, a subject he had mentioned to Eric before when they were in the meal line at Orange County Jail. Eric was seemingly still highly interested. Bonin told him that There' was this one guy who was thinking about turning over some contracts to him. But he will not know for a couple of weeks. "We're talking about only a bit of cash, but it's not definite yet". He was asking Eric if he was interested in being in on it. "Shit yeah. It's better money than I could get working." "Yeah, but it is not a sure thing yet. I'm lining up the people who want to join now, and I'm only choosing one. They have to be someone I can count on and won't disappoint me at the last moment." But Bonin needed proof, so he suggested that Eric and he pick someone up, someone they do not know, and kill them. "If you can handle that, you're in." In Bonin's chilling confessions, He detailed the events of that fateful night with cold precision. Eric, already inebriated before Bonin's arrival, sank deeper into his drunken state as the evening wore on. Bonin, a master of manipulation, laid out his sinister plan with a disturbing calmness. He suggested they find someone—perhaps a hustler—to satisfy his depraved desires, all while concocting a scheme to frame the act as the work of the infamous freeway killer. It was a glimpse into the mind of a man whose twisted logic operated beyond the realm of morality.

At that point, they saw Lawrence Sharpe trying to hitch a ride on Long Beach Boulevard.

A few weeks later, on May 19, Bonin wrote about another incident with Eric. Bonin was giving a lift to one of Butt's friends James Meurer and had convinced Butts to tag along in the hope of persuading him to go hunting. On the way back, they spotted Sean King. Butts was adamant he did not want to participate, but Bonin convinced Butts they were going to stop and talk. Bonin, with his trusting demeanour, managed to lure Sean into the car; this time, it was the Blue Chevette, not the Death van, Butts had managed to avoid any more murders with Bonin at this point and was grateful when Bonin took him home, but it was just so he could pick up a murder kit, as the Chevette had never been used in a murder before as Bonin never kept any torture instruments in his car. Bonin departed from Butt's place, Sean still trapped within the confines of the vehicle, and the night swallowed them as they arrived at a lonely, vacant lot—a canvas for malevolence. Here, in the shadows, Bonin's true nature emerged. Threats hung heavy in the air, and violence loomed like a spectre. Sean, a pawn in this macabre game, endured most of Bonin's rage.

But the twisted satisfaction Bonin sought remained elusive. His primal urges were unsated, and he grew impatient. Frustration gnawed at him, urging him to seek an alternative. And so, he dialled Eric—their connection forged in darkness—and they orchestrated a rendezvous at Valley View. The stage was set, the players assembled, and the night held its breath.

In the grim scene that unfolded, Bonin spun a web of deceit around Eric, weaving tales of a so-called Hit Squad. With Sean bound and concealed beneath a blanket in the front seat, Bonin issued a harrowing ultimatum: Eric must demonstrate his capacity for murder and the disposal of a body. It was a test of loyalty, a perverse rite of passage thrust upon him.

As they drove to a more isolated location, the tension was palpable. In a moment of haunting vulnerability, Sean, the frightened teenager, was forced to give Eric a blowjob—. With its shroud of secrecy, the night he was pressed in as Bonin steered them towards an uncertain fate. Bonin and Eric raped the boy before deciding on how they were going to murder him. Eric decided to use a knife; Eric started stabbing the boy on each side of his abdomen, then in the back and the neck, while Bonin egged him on. When they thought he was dead, they began to walk away. They began to hear gurgling noises and were shocked to see Sean's Body start moving in spasmodic fits. Bonin grabbed the knife and, in a frenzy, began to stab him repeatedly until he no longer moved, and the last breath had left the young boy's body.

Chapter 10 The Murder Spree

William George Bonin, also known as the Freeway Killer, was not out of the Californian state hospital for long before he resumed his sinister activities—picking up hitchhikers for sexual purposes. This time, however, the stakes were even higher.[29] On August 13, 1979, Bonin, a twice-paroled sex offender, was released from custody after spending a mere five days in Orange County for sex perversion. He confidently assured his friends that he would never be locked up again. Little did they know that Bonin had already embarked on a chilling murder spree, having taken the lives of 2 people in the preceding days.

The exact number of Bonin's victims remains shrouded in uncertainty. Officially, he was convicted of 14 murders, but suspicion lingers over 21 more. Some sources even speculate that he may have killed as many as 36 or 40 young men and boys, although conclusive evidence to support these claims is lacking.

Bonin primarily operated in Los Angeles and Orange County. Still, he also left a grim trail in other counties: Kern, Riverside, San Diego, and San Bernardino. These southern California regions witnessed the tragic discoveries of many of his victims, often found near or along freeways. Despite the horrors of the 'Freeway Killings,' there is no record of the police imposing a curfew on all kids under 18 in response. However, various towns and cities across the United States have enacted juvenile curfew laws to prevent delinquency, protect minors from predators, and maintain public order.

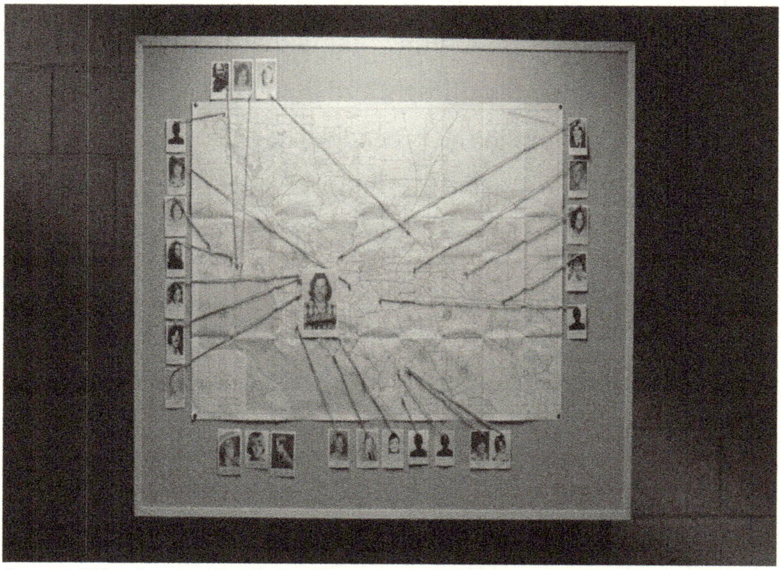

*Image SEQ Image * ARABIC16 Map of Victims and Locations. Screenshot (Dark Reality, 2022)*

29 William Bonin - Simple English Wikipedia, the free encyclopedia. https://simple.wikipedia.org/wiki/William_Bonin

Victim 1 Thomas Glen Lundgren

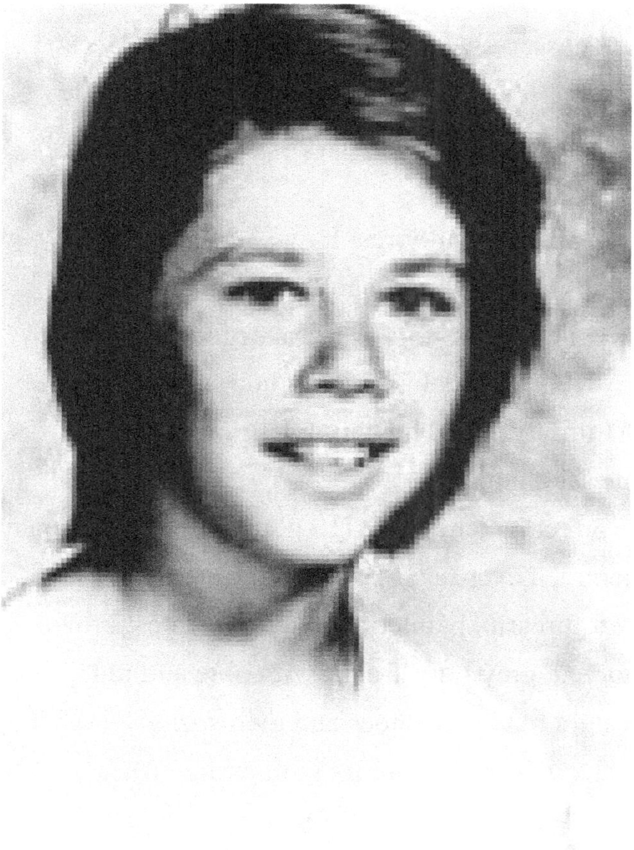

*Image SEQ Image * ARABIC17 (Thomas Glen Lundgren (1966-1979) - Find a Grave. . ., 1966)*

Thomas Glen Lundgren, born on March 24, 1966, in Northridge, Los Angeles County, California, USA, [30] was the child of Russell Lawrence Lundgren (1931-2010)

30 Ancestry.com. California Birth Index, 1905-1995 [database online]. Provo, UT, USA: Ancestry.com Operations Inc, 2005.

An Marie L White. Russell and Marie were married on September 8, 1956.[31] Thomas also had two other siblings. Sadly, Russell passed away on February 12, 2010. His son Thomas met a tragic end at the tender age of 13. His life was cut short on May 28, 1979, in Los Angeles County, California, USA.

His final resting place is at Forest Lawn Memorial Park Hollywood Hills, also in Los Angeles County.[32]

Thomas Glen Lundgren's story is heart-wrenching. On that fateful day in 1979, he left his parents' house in Reseda around 11.30 am. Little did his family know it would be their last time seeing him.

Thomas was 5 feet 2 inches tall, 110 pounds, and had brown hair and blue/green eyes. He wore a bright multi-coloured cast on his left forearm, painted with vertical lines; brown corduroy shorts; a grey Levi T-shirt with blue and red horizontal lines; light blue gym shoes and gym socks. His skateboard was a "Dog Town" Vara flux with orange wheels.

It was Memorial Day, 1979, and Thomas was abducted from Reseda. His lifeless body was discovered near a freeway in Agoura, Malibu, on the same day, roughly two hours as death. Beside his body lay his T-shirt, shoes, and socks. Not far from his body, strewn across the field, were his underwear, jeans, and genitals.

The grim details emerged during the medical examiner's autopsy: Thomas had suffered a throat slashing, emasculation,

31 Ancestry.com. U.S., Find a Grave® Index, 1600s-Current [database on-line]. Lehi, UT, USA: Ancestry.com Operations, Inc., 2012. 32 Find a Grave. Find a Grave®. http://www.findagrave.com/cgi-bin/fg.cgi.

blunt force trauma to the face with skull fractures, stab wounds, and strangulation.

Brenda Axtell, Tommy's sister, remembers the day vividly. Tommy was always hustling for money and got a job selling flowers on street corners.[33] Tommy had been approached a few days earlier by an unidentified man who offered him a job posing for photos while selling flowers on an East Los Angeles Street corner. According to his mother, he was going over to meet this stranger who was to take pictures of him on his skateboard. [34]

On May 28, 1979, His mother's behaviour took an unsettling turn around 7:00 p.m. Concerned, other family members inquired about the cause, and she revealed that Tommy had not yet returned home as the hours ticked by. Brenda, his sister, was conversing with her father while they watched television. The 11 o'clock news then delivered a chilling report: "A nude body of a young boy was found on Mulholland Drive late today. He was stabbed multiple times and sexually mutilated."

Gripped by fear, their father leapt from his chair and urgently contacted the local sheriff's department. When asked why he sought information about the murder, Mr. Lundgren's response was heart-wrenching: "I think it is my son!" Unfortunately, his intuition was tragically accurate. Tommy's lifeless body was discovered, and Brenda attested that he was nearly unrecognisable.

33 Problems Await Young Flower Hawkers." The Press Courier (Online), May 11, 1980, 10. https://news.google.com/newspapers?id=mnVKAAAAIBAJ&pg=6800,2626699&dq/. 34 Trained Dog, investigators stymied by the murder of a boy. (1979, June 4, 1979). News Chronicle.

The pain of losing a child in such a horrific manner remains etched in their memories, forever haunting the family. [35] In 1979, a friend of Tommy's recalled their last encounter on the Friday before the long Memorial Day weekend. He was in ninth grade at junior high school, and they found themselves in the cafeteria during lunchtime. There, Tommy appeared in the lunch line, sporting a cast on his arm adorned with rainbows—a creative touch from his art class earlier that day.

With his reddish/brown hair and freckled face, Tommy was passionate about skateboarding and frequented the local skate park. Like any adventurous kid, he occasionally got into trouble. He was part of a close-knit group of friends, including the ninth grader. Despite being a year younger, they had shared Boy Scout experiences and had known each other since elementary school.

The memory remains vivid: Tommy proudly showed off his rainbow-decorated cast, prompting the ninth-grader to tease, "Cool, huh?" The playful banter continued as Tommy laughed and assured them he would soon have pictures taken at the local skate park, "Skater Cross," with dreams of appearing in magazines. After lunch, their usual exchange of comments ended with a friendly punch to the arm, and Tommy ran off. That was the last time he saw Tommy alive.

35 Keel, Anna. "The Freeway Killer Lost Murder Tapes ", 1.24minIMDb Pro, 2022.

*Image SEQ Image * ARABIC18 Thomas Lundgren Screenshot (Dark Reality, 2022)*

The weekend unfolded without significant drama. The ninth grader's father, an abusive alcoholic, and his late mother, struggling with alcohol and speed abuse, each inhabited their world. His two younger brothers existed in their separate spheres.

Meanwhile, he ran a modest yard-mowing business for local realtors, employing a few neighbourhood kids. The hard-earned bucks we pocketed went toward pizzas and sodas. They were nerds, avoiding drugs.

Tuesday morning seemed unremarkable, like every other day, until lunchtime, when a female classmate rushed to him in the cafeteria. Breathless, she asked, "Hey! Did you hear the news?"

"What news?" he inquired.

"Your little friend Tommy is dead!"
Initially dismissing her words as nonsense, He began asking around at school. The messages were mixed, leaving him uncertain. However, when he returned home and opened the newspaper, a snippet confirmed the heartbreaking truth: "Body of teen found on a hiking trail in Agoura." The brief article described what the young male child had been wearing when discovered, and at that moment, his blood ran cold. [36]
Tragically, Thomas Glen Lundgren was thought to be one of the first victims of William Bonin, infamously known as The Freeway Killer. Bonin terrorised Los Angeles for over a year, committing heinous acts against teens and young men. His gruesome crimes involved rape, murder, and emasculation, with the victims' bodies dumped alongside the freeways of the San Fernando Valley and other locations.[45] The loss of Thomas at such a youthful age remains a painful chapter in the city's history.
William Bonin, infamously labelled the Freeway Killer, was acquitted in the murder case of Thomas Lundgren despite his assertions of innocence.
In a further complication, during this period of suspicion, the enigma of Thomas Lundgren's untimely departure from this world remains cloaked in the veils of the unknown. Despite exhaustive probes and legal scrutiny, the hand of justice has yet to point unwaveringly at a culprit. The hallowed

36 "Out of Horrific Tragedy the Iron Eagle Was Created." 2016, accessed September 28, 2023, https://ironeagleseries.com/fromtragedy/

halls of the judiciary, where evidence and eloquence duel, stand mute, their silence a testament to the elusive nature of truth and resolution. [37]

Concurrently. In a twist of fate, Randy Kraft, known as the Scorecard Killer, was simultaneously committing comparable atrocities, muddling the investigation as he faced allegations mirroring those against Bonin. Additionally, Rodney Alcala, a freelance photographer, emerged as a prime suspect in the deaths of both Thomas Lundgren and Russel Goudy Junior. At the time of these suspicions, Alcala had been arrested for the murder of a 12-year-old girl. Notably, his parents lived near the area where Lundgren was known to sell flowers. [38,39]

The case of Thomas Lundgren's death is still shrouded in mystery and unanswered questions. Despite investigations and inquiries, the scales of justice have yet to tip definitively. The courtroom's theatre of evidence and argument remains silent—a void where truth and closure elude us.

37 "Scorecard Killer Facing Execution." The Sydney Morning Herald (online), May 14, 1989, 10. https://news.google.com/newspapers?nid=1301&dat=19890514&id=rjJWAAAAIBAJ&pg=5146,4217770&hl=en
38 Photographer being probed in Agoura Memorial Day murder. (1979, July 26). News Chronicle 39 Jobless Photographer. (1979, July 26). The Los Angeles Times

Victim 2 Mark Duane Shelton

*Image SEQ Image * ARABIC19 (Mark Duane Shelton (1961-1979) - Find a Grave. . ., 1961)*

On a crisp December day in 1961, Mark Shelton took his first breath in the vibrant embrace of Garden Grove, nestled within the sun-kissed folds of Orange County, California.

His arrival heralded hope—a thread woven into the fabric of his family's narrative.

Mark's lineage was traced back to Donald Ray Shelton, a. His life, etched with the ink of experience, intersected with that of Ramona Ruth Walter (1933-2009). Ramona, born on May 13, 1933, had already embarked on a second journey down the aisle, her heart still echoing the memory of her first spouse.

Their union, sealed on September 12, 1959, in the arid embrace of Nevada, painted a portrait of love's resilience. But life, ever unpredictable, cast shadows across their path. Ramona followed suit, her closing chapter written on January 16, 2009, in the serene town of Burnt Ranch.

Mark's remaining siblings stood at the crossroads of legacy—Rita, Larry, Robbie, and Buck (Frank)—anchored the loss to a shared history. Together, they navigated the bittersweet currents of memory, weaving their stories into the grand design. [40,41]

Mark Duane Shelton's journey came to a premature and tragic end. At just 17 years old, his life was cut short on August 4, 1979, in San Bernardino County, California. He now rests in peace at Rose Hills Memorial Park in Whittier, Los Angeles County, California, leaving behind a legacy of youth and memories held dear by those who knew him. [42]

40 Ancestry.com. California Birth Index, 1905-1995 [database on-line]. Provo, UT, USA: Ancestry.com Operations Inc, 2005. 41 Ancestry.com. Global, find a Grave® Index for Burials at Sea and other Select Burial Locations, 1300s-Current [database on-line]. Lehi, UT, USA: Ancestry.com Operations, Inc., 2012 42 Ancestry.com. U.S., Find a Grave® Index, 1600s-Current [database on-line]. Lehi, UT, USA: Ancestry.com Operations, Inc., 2012.

The circumstances surrounding his death remain a sad chapter in history. Mark Shelton had been walking home from a movie theatre on Beach Blvd on August 4 when Bonin and Butts decided to abduct Mark. Bonin pulled his van over on Beach Boulevard and offered him a ride. Bonin did not care what his sexual orientation was. The chilling news from August 11, 79, recounts the discovery of a lifeless young man, unclothed and abandoned at Cajon Pass in San Bernardino County. The ravages of both animals and the unforgiving environment rendered his body unrecognisable—a haunting testament to the harshness of fate. Mark's parents, Donald and Ramona, grappled with the agonising uncertainty surrounding their son's fate until April 1980. Then, Mr. Shelton, driven by desperate hope, sought Mark's dental records from their trusted family dentist. Doctor Thomas Coad. [43] The grim scene at the county morgue awaited him—an unidentified body, a silent plea for answers. The police, too, appealed to the public for assistance, urging anyone with information to come forward. Yet, in the vast silence, no witness emerged—a mystery that would linger, casting shadows over Mark's memory and the hearts of those who loved him.

*Image SEQ Image * ARABIC20 Bonin's death van screenshot Wikimedia Commons, 1980)*

On that ominous Saturday, August 4, 1979, William Bonin reunited with his friend Vernon Butts. Their paths had diverged for a while—Bonin residing in Silverado Canyon with his brother, embroiled in plans to acquire the Alpine Inn restaurant and bar. But there was something else—a new van, gleaming and eager to hit the road. Bonin's desire to showcase his acquisition led them on a cinematic journey to the Highway 39 drive-in movie theatre in Westminster, a place steeped in nostalgia since its opening in 1955.

As the first feature flickered on the screen, Bonin and Butts settled into their seats, catching up on life's twists and turns

But during the intermission, their conversation took a chilling turn. The topic shifted from mundane matters to something far more sinister—a young man, desire, and the macabre dance of murder.

The conversation turned dark when Bonin, perhaps in jest, broached a sinister topic. Butts, however, found the idea enthralling. While Bonin later insisted his remarks were made in jest, Butts chillingly confessed to harbouring a longstanding fantasy about taking a life. [44] Somehow, the conversation took a more sinister turn, and they were both evaluating each other to see how far the other would go with murdering someone. No longer interested in the second movie, they unhooked the speaker from the car door and left the Drive-in. They headed towards Beach Boulevard, where Bonin had seen Hitch hikers before. On Beach Boulevard, Butts and Bonin came across young Mark Shelton; they pulled up, asked him for directions, and asked Mark if he needed a ride. Once Mark was in the van, Bonin asked him if he had ever received a blowjob from a man before; Mark replied "No" and was uneasy; it was then that Bonin offered Mark $400 to spend a few hours with him. Mark agreed after Bonin promised he would return him in the morning. They started driving towards Vegas and the Mountains of Cajun Pass. Bonin asked Mark how long he could stay out, as he had a cabin that way, but it would take a while to get there and back. Mark replied that it did not matter what

43 Victim is Identified. (1980, April 3). The San Bernadino County Sun.

time he got home, so Bonin told Mark to climb up between himself and Butts, patting the console between the two men and saying, "I want to see what you got." Mark got kneeling between the seats with his back facing the console. Bonin reached over to unzip Mark's fly, placed his hand inside Mark's pants, and began caressing his penis. Bonin seemed impressed and told Butts to check it out. Butts reached over and grabbed hold of Mark's adulthood and squeezed hard. Mark yelped in pain. That put Mark off, and he moved himself into the back of the van and zipped up his pants. Butts also jumped into the back of the van and tried to keep Mark occupied with magic tricks until they arrived at the final destination. That is when Bonin saw an old, boarded-up gas station, so he drove around, parked the van, and climbed into the back with the other two.35 Bonin told Mark the cabin would be occupied for a few more hours. Hence, they had to stay there until it was empty. They then proceeded to make out. Bonin removed Mark's clothes and managed to get him fully aroused.

Before Butts was sent to the front of the van to keep a lookout, he had given young Mark oral copulation. Once Butts was in the front, Bonin pulled down his pants and told Mark to suck his dick, and he complied, although he was nervous and shivering. Bonin then told Mark to lie on his stomach so that Bonin could penetrate him. Bonin was still calm and gentle at this point. Once Mark had obliged, Butts was now watching keenly. Bonin spat on his fingers to prepare Mark for his entry, but Mark screamed out in discomfort; Bonin was now angry. Mark had startled him, and now Bonin was no longer calm. Bonin spiralled into a rage and started punching Mark in the stomach and chest; he squeezed his testicles with enormous power and then kneed him repeatedly until he was unconscious. Now was the decisive moment: could they really kill him, or were they just talking? Unfortunately for young Mark, they were deadly serious. They flipped Mark back on his stomach, and using his long-sleeved shirt, Bonin tied the sleeves around his throat, slipped a tyre iron through the loop and started twisting. Butts was sitting on him, holding his hands behind his back while Bonin kept twisting. At this point, Mark came too and started to wriggle; Butts lost his grip, so Bonin, with one hand on the tyre iron and the other, pinned marks hands till Butts got a better grip; after 3 or 4 minutes, Mark was dead. Bonin untied the shirt from around Mark's throat, and within 10 seconds, they began to hear him gasp for air. They both panicked, and Bonin replaced the shirt and strangled him a second time. Young Mark Shelton's life was gone. Bonin and Butts got on the Interstate I-5 and drove until they found a gravel road and parked up. They carried Mark's lifeless body further down the track and dumped his body in some bushes. At this point, Butts started talking about the ice pick, they did not have one, but Bonin found

44 Butler, Vonda L Pelto PhD and Michael B. Without Redemption Creation & Deeds of Freeway Killer Bill Bonin His Five Accomplices and How One Who Escaped Justice. Flotsam Publishing 2022.pp107

some rusty wire. Therefore, Butts pushed the wire into his ear as hard and deep as he could, they got no reaction from Mark, but Bonin was not convinced Mark was dead, so on the way back to the car, Bonin saw a short, dried tree branch, Bonin went back to Marks body and rammed it up his rectum, Bonin was now sure he was dead. He claimed he could now relax.

In Bonin's written confession [16], He offered chilling thoughts on the murders and aftermath. Bonin said that after they killed Mark Shelton, they headed home.

"Butts and I were laughing. We felt that we had gotten away with it. No one knew Mark got into the van, and the guy who saw him enter the van did not know who he was. No one saw him while he was with us, and no one saw us drop him off or near the site where he was dropped off. That ended the first night of a nightmare for both Butts and me. It was the beginning of 10 months of hell for Southern California and many victims and their families and friends. No one was safe. If a youngster was out there at night or during the day and got into my van, it was all over for them." [16]

Victim 3 Markus Alexander Grabs

*Image SEQ Image * ARABIC21 Markus Grabs (IMDb, n.d.-b)*

Markus Alexander Grabs left us too soon at the tender age of 17. Born in the heart of Germany on March 4, 1962, Markus's journey led him to Los Angeles County, California, where he passed away on August 5, 1979.

In his 17 years, Markus left an indelible mark on the hearts of his family and friends. He will be remembered for his love of exploration, whether through book pages or the

*Image SEQ Image * ARABIC21 Markus Grabs (IMDb, n.d.-b) 46 William George Bonin #322. http://www.tep-online.info/laku/usa/dp/bonin322.htm 47 FilmRise True Crime. (2021, August 19). World's Most Evil Killers - Season 5, Episode 4 - William*

thrill of travel. His passion for life was contagious, inspiring others to seek adventure in their own lives.
Though Markus has departed from this world, his memory continues to shine brightly. A memorial has been placed at-Friedhof Überlingen in Baden-Württemberg, Germany, honouring his German heritage and the life he cherished.

On August 5, 1979, Bill Bonin acted alone. Between 6:00 p.m. and 10:00 p.m., he encountered 17-year-old Markus Grabs, who was hitchhiking along the Pacific Highway in Newport Beach. Markus, a German exchange student on a backpacking tour of the United States, often found himself short on funds and frequently resorted to hitchhiking to get around.
However, in *The Freeway Killer: The Shocking True Story of Serial Killer William Bonin*,[45] the following information was also stated on the Californian Department of Corrections and Rehabilitation website On August 5, 1979, the defendant and co-defendant Butts accosted Marcus Grabs, 17, in Newport Beach sometime between 6 and 10 p.m. Marcus, a German student on a backpacking tour of the United States, was sodomised, beaten and stabbed 77 times. His nude body was found the next day beside a road in Malibu, with an orange nylon cord loosely wrapped behind his head and a piece of ignition wire around one of his ankles. [45,56]
The CDCR summary states that Vernon Butts did help with

this murder. Butts also told police that he helped Bonin in eight murders and did so because he had an interest in the occult and the macabre. In the documentary *Worlds WorstSerial Killers* series 5, episode 4, it was stated that Butts was there but just watched with excitement. [47]
The Executed Inmate summary from the California Department of Corrections and Rehabilitation backs up some of this. [48] As Butts committed suicide, I guess we will never find out the truth.
Markus was sodomised, beaten, and stabbed 77 times with an orange nylon cord loosely wrapped behind his head—a piece of blue ignition wire around one of his ankles. [49, 50]
Bonin was like a rabid dog gone mad. The next day, Markus's nude body was found in Malibu Canyon, near Las Virgenes Canyon Road; except for the victim's orange back-pack, blood-splattered sunglasses, his camera, and his tennis shoes across the road, no clothing or other identifying evidence was discovered at the scene. [51,52]
Bonin says he was headed to the beach and ended up at Newport Beach when he spotted a kid hitchhiking. Bonin started to feel horny, so he decided to offer the young man

48 Réhabilitation, C. D. o. C. a. (1982). Executed Inmate Summary: Willliam George Bonin. Retrieved from https://www.cdcr.ca.gov/capital-punishment/inmates-executed-1978-to-present/william-george-bonin/ 49 William George Bonin #322. http://www.teponline.info/laku/usa/dp/bonin322.htm 50 Executed Inmate Summary - William51 People v. Bonin (1989): Supreme Court of California Decisions: California Case Law: California Law: US Law: Justia. https://law.justia.com/cases/california/supreme-court/3d/47/808.html George Bonin - Capital Punishment. https://www.cdcr.ca.gov/capital-punishment/inmates-executed-1978-to-present/william-george-bonin/ 52 William George Bonin #322. http://www.tep-online.info/laku/usa/dp/bonin322.htm

ride, he pulled over on the gravel, and Markus came straight up to the van.

Bonin asked him if he was gay, and Markus smiled and climbed into the front passenger side of the van. Bonin pulled a U-turn and headed to a more remote area for them to make out; it was pretty busy. Many cars parked along the highway overlooking the beach, so Bonin pulled up between two campers for privacy.

They both climbed into the back of the van. Each took their clothes off; they began by giving each other a blowjob; it felt good. They did that for a while, and then Bonin had an idea! Bonin wanted to try bondage; he says he had never done it before, but history says otherwise. Bonin found some electrician wire in his van, so he used that to tie up a willing Markus; Markus never objected. Looking down at the naked man lying on his stomach with his hands tied behind his back, Bonin felt good; he felt powerful. Bonin began to caress his body using his buck knife against his skin while telling Markus how easy it would be to kill him. Bonin wanted Markus to be afraid; it made him feel more powerful. Bonin said he had no intention of killing him but wanted to have fun. Bonin held the knife against Markus's throat and told him, "I should cut you." Markus started to feel scared, realising he was helpless. Markus had no idea if

Bonin was serious, but Bonin, not quite ready to give up, backed off a little and reached between his legs to check out Markus's dick; it was hard, as was Bonin's. Bonin got him up on his knees and slid inside him, rocking back and forth until his release. At that moment, Bonin grabbed his testicles real hard and squeezed.

Markus screamed, and as he launched backwards, he managed to break free, now facing Bonin with a closed fit, ready to punch him. At this point, Bonin decides he must defend himself but does not plan to kill him. Markus struck Bonin with a blow hard enough to know him backwards, and Bonin hit his head against the van. Having the knife in his hand, Bonin lunges at Markus and stabs him in the arm. Both Bonin and Markus were surprised, and Markus screamed in horror. Bonin never wanted to stab anyone. He didn't want to get blood all over his van. Something then clicked, and Bonin went on autopilot. He got a better grip on the knife and stabbed him repeatedly, not caring where the blade struck. Markus was limber even with stab wounds and was all over the place. Blood squirted everywhere. Bonin realised at that point he had gone too far; he could not let the boy live even though he had been begging to be taken to the hospital. Still, Bonin just kept stabbing until Markus stopped moving. He needed to get his head clear and dump the body. Blood was everywhere; Bonin started the van and drove towards Malibu Canyon. Bonin was worried about running out of fuel with Markus still in the back. Markus was still alive, thinking he may be going to a hospital.

Bonin reached a secluded spot and began to drag the screaming boy from the van. Bonin wrapped him in a blanket, rolled him over onto his stomach and strangled him, but he was slippery. Bonin could not get enough leverage, so he wrapped an orange cord around his neck and tried again, but that didn't work either. Bonin didn't want to use the knife; it was messy, but there was no other way. Bonin tried to put himself into a Zen state and began to stab the boy over and over again until he couldn't stab him anymore. He was now quiet but had to make sure the boy was dead, so Bonin rammed his fist up the boy's ass, he didn't move, and Markus's blood was splattered all over Bonin. Bonin dragged the lifeless body over to a bush, returned to his van and headed home. On the way home, he ran out of fuel; while waiting for a ride, a police officer drove by. Bonin waved him on so he wouldn't stop. Eventually, someone stopped and gave him a ride to a gas station. Still, luckily, he told them the blood splatters were red paint, and they seemed to believe him. Bonin found a pay phone and called Butt. He needed to get his van cleaned. The smell of all that blood was making him sick. He got to Butt's house, and they cleaned the van as best they could, but Bonin decided he had better hire a shampoo carpet cleaner as soon as he got home.[16]

On August 17, Bonin attempted to create an alibi for Grab's murder. He picked up his friend Scott Fraser and took him to the magic cork restaurant; they had a few drinks, then Bonin just blurted out I think I killed someone then went on to tell Scott the details, leaving out everything relevant to him being a murderer and acting like it was all in self-defence, he even said Butts was there which he was not. Scott was sympathetic and believed Bonin's' version of events. Bonin also told Scott about having to clean the blood from the car and also remembered that his friend Scott had a subscription to the Los Angeles Times, so they went back to the house and started going through the stacks of old copies to see if they could find anything about a possible death, Scott had almost given up looking when Bonin yells out I got it, he found the newspaper clipping. it was at that point Scotbelieved Bonin's version of events. Bonin was good at manipulating people.

*Image SEQ Image * ARABIC23 Markus Body screenshot (Dark Reality 2022)*

*Image SEQ Image * ARABIC24 Markus report screenshot (Dark Reality 2022)*

Victim 4 Donald Ray Hyden

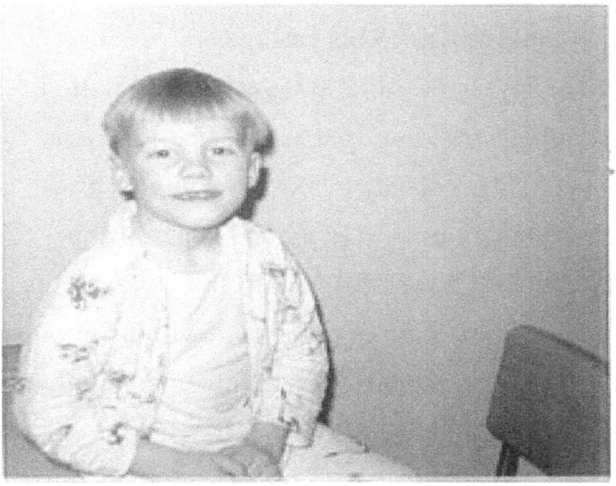

*Image SEQ Image * ARABIC25 Donald Hyden (IMDb n.d.-b)*

Donald Ray Hyden Jr.'s life was tragically cut short at the tender age of 15. Born on May 7, 1964, in Santa Monica, California, he was a young man with his entire life ahead of him. However, fate had a different plan, and on August 27, 1979, Donald's journey ended abruptly in Agoura Hills, California. He is remembered and honoured at his final resting place in the serene surroundings of Holy Cross Cemetery, Culver City, California, in a peaceful plot at Section R, Tier 15, Lot 841. His memory continues to be cherished by those who knew him and by those who honour the lives taken too soon. [53]

Donald Ray Hyden Jr.'s story is a testament to a family's resilience in navigating the complexities of life's changes. Born in Cincinnati, Ohio, in 1964, Donald Jr. was the eldest son of Donald Hyden (1936- 2020) and Mary Rutman (1940-2006). Donald Jr shared his early years with his younger brother Clayton (1966-2007) and several half-siblings from his father's previous marriages, Sheri, Dianna (1962-1996), and Robert (1958-1958) sadly passed as a baby. The family dynamics shifted when his parents divorced on May 18, 1970, leading Donald Jr, Clayton, and half-sister Diana to start anew in California with his mother. [54] In the wake of the divorce, his father welcomed another son, Mathew, with his new wife in 1974. Despite the upheaval, Donald Jr. found solace and success on the baseball diamond, showcasing his talent and passion for the game.

His untimely passing at just 15 years old left a void in the hearts of those who knew him. [55]

Donald Jr.'s journey is woven with threads of both joy and adversity. It reflects the shared human experience of countless families navigating the ebbs and flows of life. His story is a testament to the resilience of the human spirit, prevailing through the seasons of change and the shadows of loss.

In the quiet suburbs of Westchester, young Donald found solace in the comforting embrace of his grandparents' home. The crack of a baseball bat became his anthem, echoing his aspirations with each swing. Pete Rose was more than a sports hero; he embodied Donald's dreams, the guiding star in his pursuit of greatness.

As he stepped through the gates of Orville Wright Elementary School, a new chapter unfolded in California's golden light. With each lesson learned and friendship forged, Donald began to weave his legacy of courage, hope, and an unwavering spirit that danced in the face of life's intricate ballet.

Yet, amidst the triumphs on the field, a longing whispered in his heart—a yearning for the familiar warmth of his mother's presence. In 1977, drawn by this unshakeable desire, Donald returned to the bustling streets of Hollywood to a life painted with the vibrant hues of family and belonging.

[56,57]

55 Ancestry.com. Kentucky, U.S., Birth Index, 1911-1999 [database online]. Provo, UT, USA: Ancestry.com Operations Inc., 2006 56 "U.S., School Yearbooks, 1880-2012"; School Name: Orville Wright Middle School; Year: 1977 57 "People v. Bonin 1989." In. 2009. Supreme Court of California, In Bank.

On August 27 1979, at 2 am, Donald was abducted by Bonin and Butts. Donald Hyden (15) was near the LGBTQI Community Services Centre in Los Angeles. His ravaged and broken nude body was discovered near Liberty Canyon on a Ventura Highway off-ramp in a trash can on Freeway 101. Donald had been strangled by ligature and stabbed. He had also been sodomised, and attempts had been made to cut off his testicles and slash his throat. [58]

Bonin continued to monitor media reports about the crimes eagerly. Despite the police's efforts, they were no closer to apprehending him, and the public's anxiety grew as they demanded answers. The frustration among law enforcement escalated, but Bonin remained undeterred. His spree of violence persisted, and he craved another kill. With each successful crime, the sense of invincibility fueled his sinister pursuits, making each subsequent act more feasible and accessible. The darkness within him drove him forward, heedless of the consequences.

According to Bonin, the day began with a sense of anxiety and restlessness on August 26, 1979. Having already taken the lives of several young individuals in the preceding three weeks, he was acutely aware of the impending threat of arrest looming over him. The weather was sweltering, and during his work break, Bonin reached out to Butts to propose going out on a hunt. Butts, who had already assisted

*Image SEQ Image * ARABIC25 Donald Hyden (IMDb n.d.-b) 54 Ohio Department of Health; Columbus, Ohio; Ohio Divorce Index, 1962-1963, 1967-1971 and 1973-2007*

Bonin in the murder of several boys, eagerly agreed. Their shared excitement charged up Bonin, making him feel like they were a pair of big game hunters on the prowl.

Throughout Bonin's life, he preferred not being alone during such outings—a tendency that had persisted since childhood. As the afternoon unfolded, Bonin remained keyed up, contemplating fantasies and anticipating what awaited them.

"Hey Billy, you have to catch a train or something," Bonin's boss yells at him after noticing he kept checking his watch.

"Yeah, I've got a hot date later." He screamed back, laughing because his boss would never have guessed what was on his mind. Bonin had to gas up and clean the truck before leaving for the day; by the time he picked up Butts, it was mid-evening.

The streets of Long Beach yielded no results, and even Orange County proved fruitless. Frustrated, they decided to try their luck in Hollywood, a place teeming with late-night activity—hitchhikers, aspiring actors, and dreamers seeking their big break.

Around 2:00 am, as they drove west on Santa Monica Blvd, Bonin's eyes fell upon a good-looking boy crossing La Cienega Blvd. It was 15-year-old Donald Hyden, not far from his family home. Bonin's instincts kicked in. He abruptly swerved across two lanes, narrowly avoiding a police car that had witnessed his reckless manoeuvre. Despite

the risk, nothing happened. The stage was set for another horrifying chapter in Bonin's dark saga.
"Billy, you got some kind of charmed life," Butts said amid a good laugh. He was lying in the back of the Van, out of sight of the boy. Do you know where George Street is? Bonin asked, the boy using his usual ploy and employing the name George Street when familiar with the area. Donald replies, "No, I do not know that place." "Do you want to make 50 bucks?" Sure, for what? Donald said. "Give me some head," Bonin said, trying to be casual. Donald got into the Van. Already anticipating what he could do with him, fantasising about the sex and killing, Bonin was not about to let him escape after driving for hours and finally luring someone into his grasp. Sensing Donald wanted to leave after seeing Butts in the back. Bonin decided to call his bluff. "Go ahead, forget the 50 bucks, get out of the car and stop wasting my time", he said to the boy, betting he preferred not to lose the money. After Donald calmed down, Bonin said, "Look, I will have Butts Drive up and down on Sunset, so you know where we are." This remark did the trick, and the final piece of the puzzle was in place. Donald got in the back of the Van, and Butt took over driving. With a new victim firmly in his clutches, Donald and Bonin began having sex. Butt made a turn-off sunset by mistake, and Donald panicked, jumping up while tugging on his pants. Just relax. Bonin said Butt made a wrong turn, but Donald didn't listen.

"I don't care. Let me out. I want to get out here. Let me out," the boy screamed. That marked the turning point for Bonin—he was finished playing games. Consumed by rage, he seized a rope, twisting Donald's left arm behind his back and wrenching it high up between his shoulder blades, inflicting excruciating pain. With a vice-like grip, Bonin immobilised his victim, wrapping his left arm around Donald's neck. However, Donald fought back, desperate to break free. In a desperate attempt, he lunged for the side door latch, hoping to escape. Bonin's instincts kicked in—he swiftly reversed the latch. However, reality struck: the side door did not open from the inside. The grim struggle continued, and the outcome hung in the balance.

Bonin forcefully shoved the boy toward the Van's rear, pressing him against the door. In a desperate act of defiance, Donald raised his right arm, clenched his fist, and locked eyes with Bonin, ready to strike. But Bonin's warning halted him: "I would not do that if I were you." Instead of retaliating, Bonin twisted the boy's arm even higher up his back, inflicting more pain. Frustrated and enraged, the boy pounded the side of the Van repeatedly, screaming in anguish. The confined space bore witness to their grim struggle—a battle between predator and prey,

"When I get out of this, I will tell the cops. You are going to jail." "You broke my arm," Donald screams, continuing to fight. "No, I did not. Now, shut up," Bonin said as Donald tried to free his legs from his pants, but they continued to struggle. With Butts still driving, they left Sunset Blvd. and headed South to Santa Monica Blvd.

Bonin whispers into Donald's ear, "Tell you what, I'll give you another 50 bucks if you let me tie you up" "but he is not going for it. Bonin got a rope around Donald's left arm and wrapped the rest around his neck for leverage "put your right hand behind your back right fucken now" Bonin whispered menacingly. Donald stopped fighting, and Bonin tied his hands with his pants still around his ankles, preventing him from moving about with triumphant pleasure. Bonin said to Butts. See how nice he is being now? With complete control of the situation, Bonin's temper, frustration, and pent-up anxiety burst forth. In a shower of rage, he slapped the helpless 15-year-old boy hard across the face a couple of times, just like his father had done with him. "So, you are going to tell the cops on me?" Well, I may as well get my nuts off." Bonin told Donald in a threatening manner before Bonin delivered multiple punches to his chest and slapped him in the face, causing the boy to double over with pain. Hey, Butts, do you want some of this? No, Butts said from the driver's seat. Bonin drove his knee hard into the boy's side, reached between his legs, grabbed his nuts, and squeezed so hard that Donald screamed out in pain. Bonin pulled down his pants and sodomised the boy, releasing his pent-up tension in an aggressive act of sexual violence; after

58 Poole, B. (1979, August 28). Murder Scene. News Chronicle.

reaching climax, Bonin continued to beat him up as contempt and rage spilled out. Butts said, his voice low and ominous, "You've stepped into the death van. And once you're inside, there's no way out—no escape." His words hung in the air, chilling and final. Donald's heart raced, fear clawing at his chest. Bonin observed with a twisted smile. Butts seems to take pleasure in planting that seed of psychological terror in the victims' minds.
"He likes to get them scared shitless because he got a nut off on all of it." Bonin's words hung in the air, a sinister undercurrent weaving through them. Donald, however, dismissed Butt's warning as mere theatrics, assuming it was an attempt to rattle his nerves. The Van surged northbound on the Hollywood Freeway, the cityscape blurring past the windows.

Bonin's hands moved with purpose. He untied the bandana that had concealed Donald's face, and its fabric now coiled around his neck. "Don't lose this," Bonin murmured, his tone devoid of warmth. Donald's confusion deepened; he remained oblivious to the true intentions of both Bonin and Butts. The road stretched ahead, leading toward an unknown fate in the San Fernando Valley. "Here's what's going to happen. I'm just going to choke you until you're unconscious, and then we're going to drop you off. It's that, or I can squeeze your nuts and beat the shit out of you until you pass out, "Okay?" A frightened Donald whimpered. "And don't you pretend to be out because I'll know. Don't struggle, 'cause that will make it worse for you," Bonin said firmly. Bonin's actions were swift and calculated. He slid the cold, unforgiving tyre iron into the folds of the bandana, twisting it incrementally until it cinched around Donald's throat. The airway constricted, and panic flared in Donald's eyes. Bonin leaned in, his breath chilling against Donald's skin. "Sorry, kid," he murmured, devoid of remorse, "but I can't let you live to talk about this."

Donald's body convulsed, a desperate struggle for survival. But the darkness closed in, and within seconds, he slipped into unconsciousness. Bonin worked efficiently, untying him and stripping away his shoes, socks, and pants. The Van's engine roared to life as Bonin took the wheel, heading north on the Ventura Freeway, the road leading inexorably toward the ominous embrace of Malibu Canyon. The asphalt stretched ahead, a path paved with secrets and shadows. "Bonin, you know what one of my favourite fantasies has been for a long time. Yeah, I know. An Ice pick to the ear to kill someone, "he replied. "Yeah, that's one of them. But I have another one to suck on a guy after he dead" "You fucking with me? Shit. The guy wouldn't even be able to get it up." Bonin said, shocked and repulsed. "Well, that's my fantasy, "Butts said, Pleased at shocking Bonin. "Well, there's your corpse." Bonin gestured toward the Van's rear, a silent command that set events in motion. To his astonishment, Butts complied, slipping into the back and immersing himself in whatever dark purpose awaited him there. Even for someone as twisted as Bonin, Butt's behaviour stood out as peculiar, a deviation from the expected script. The truth of this macabre scene remained shrouded in uncertainty, a chilling enigma that defied easy explanation.

On Monday, August 27. 1979 Robert Cassano. A construction worker found Donald dumped on his head nude in a Dempsey dumpster. To make sure he was dead before leaving his body, Bonin had stabbed him twice in the right side of his throat, once in the middle of his back and once in the scrotum.

L.A. County Sheriff Homicide Detectives Sergeant David Kushner and his partner, Deputy Jack Fueglein, were horrified at having to view another teenage boy who had been beaten, raped and murdered by a homosexual killer. No money or I.D. was found, and Kushner observed blood running from his rectum.

Mary Hyden, the mother of Donald Hyden, was the first parent to provide testimony at the trial of William Bonin in November 1981, and having to identify before and after photos of her son.

Donald's friend, Roger Martinez, was the last person to see him alive on the Sunday evening of August 27 around Midnight in Hollywood just before his body was found.

Victim 5 David Louis Murillo

David Louis Murillo's life story is a poignant narrative of youthful promise and familial bonds shaped by the currents of migration and change. Born on May 22, 1962, in Los Angeles County, California, David's roots trace back to the vibrant landscapes of Costa Rica, from where his father, Oscar Luis Murillo (1928-2010), embarked on a journey that would lead him to the United States and to becoming a naturalised citizen on February 1, 1963. [59, 60] Oscar's path converged with that of Violet Patricia Langwell (1939-) when they united in marriage on Valentine's Day, February 14, 1959. Welcoming Marlene and David Their lives together, however, unfolded into separate paths as they divorced in September 1967. [61, 62]

David's parents, resilient in their own right, remarried and embraced new chapters.

Amidst these familial shifts, David grew up, his life tragically intersecting with the dark saga of the "Freeway Killer," William Bonin, and his accomplice Vernon Butts. On September 9, 1979, at the age of 17, Bonin cruelly took David's life in Ventura County, California.

David's memory is eternally preserved in the tranquil embrace of Rose Hills Memorial Park in Whittier, Los Angeles County. He rests in peace in Section 18, Lot 1390, Grave 31, where the whispers of his legacy and the echoes of his family's story continue to resonate.

59Ancestry.com. U.S., Find a Grave® Index, 1600s-Current [database online]. Lehi, UT, USA: Ancestry.com Operations, Inc., 2012. 60National Archives at Riverside; Riverside, California; Petitions for Naturalization, U.S. District Court for the Central District of California (Los Angeles), 1940-1991; NAI Number: 594890; Record Group Title: Records of District Courts of the United States, 1685-2009; Record Group Number: 21 61 Ancestry.com. Nevada, U.S., Marriage Index, 1956-2005 [database online]. Provo, UT, USA: Ancestry.com Operations, Inc., 2007. 62Ancestry.com. California, U.S., Divorce Index, 1966-1984 [database online]. Provo, UT, USA: Ancestry.com Operations Inc, 2007.

His life, though brief, remains a testament to the enduring spirit of those who face life's profound transformations with courage and hope. [63]

Murillo, a typical seventeen-year-old, pedalled through the streets of La Mirada. His destination was the local movie theatre, where the promise of cinematic escape awaited him. But fate had other plans.

Bill Bonin and Vernon Butts, shadows in the dim light, emerged from the darkness. Their intentions were far from innocent. Panic surged through his veins as he was thrust into the back of their van—a prison on wheels.

Bonin wielded a tyre iron, its cold metal striking David's head repeatedly. The world blurred, pain and fear merging into a chaotic symphony. Then came the unspeakable: sodomy and strangulation. The van's walls bore witness to David's desperate struggle, but it was futile. His life slipped away, leaving only a naked body discarded alongside the Ventura Highway (101), nestled in an ivy bed near the Lemon Grove overpass. No clothing, no clues—just the chilling aftermath of a predator's brutality.

Violet Murillo, her voice trembling, took the stand in the courtroom. Her eyes, filled with grief, traced the memory of her son—the last time she saw him alive. Brown Haired, slender, Seventeen and full of life, David had been heading to the movie theatre that fateful day. [64]

63 Ancestry.com. U.S., Find a Grave® Index, 1600s-Current [database online]. Lehi, UT, USA: Ancestry.com Operations, Inc., 2012. 64 UPI. (1981, November 6). Moms Identify Grisly Photos of Son in Freeway Killings. The Sacramento Bee.

Meanwhile, Bonin, the predator, operated with ruthless efficiency. His killing spree continued unabated. On the prowl once more, he set his sights on David Murillo. The unsuspecting teenager had just dismounted his bike, moving leisurely toward a bus stop on the street corner. Violet's maternal instincts flared; she warned David to be cautious and to watch out for danger.

But David, perhaps fuelled by youthful invincibility, brushed off the warning. He believed he could handle himself. Little did he know that the shadows were closing in, and Bonin's sinister figure was already lurking nearby.

According to Bonin in his chilling confession, the events unfolded as follows.

"I was travelling East and saw a kid walking his bike. I called him over and asked him where Valley View was. I used this tactic often, and then I could offer them a lift. The first thing is to get them in the van and then into the back. Then they were all mine. Before I could say anything else, he asked me if I could give him a ride, so I opened the back, and he put his bike in the back and crawled in. I asked him if he wanted to learn to earn $20 for giving him head, and he said no. he then asked if I could let him out, so I parked behind a gas station and asked why he was so scared. He said it was because kids got killed in this type of situation. I told him I was only interested in giving him fellatio, and then he told me you might have a gun in there. I told him to come over and look around, and he checked it out, and it was still against it. I said I'll give you $50. You can get in the front seat with the door open. He got back in, and I started rubbing him and said, someone may see us; let us go in the back; he refused, and I told him this was too dangerous. I'll take you where you're going. I reached over, shut the door and locked it. I now had to get him in the back. I grabbed his wrist and said, in the back, he resisted, so I put my arm around him and pulled him back. I told him to lie there on his stomach. He was terrified. I tied his hands behind his back to his neck, took his shoes and socks off, tied his feet, and then gagged him. I then told him he was being kidnapped. I called Vernon and told him I had a package. That is how I would refer to a guy who was tied up. Vern told me he had company. I told him I only needed him for about 10 minutes to get some gas. He came out, and I said, "Hey, look at this beauty." I showed him his smooth chest, which turned Vernon on.

When we returned from getting gas, Vern started fondling the kid and even gave him some head. Vern decided he was going with me. This one is too good to pass up. Vern told his friends he had to do a magic show and go to an audition. We headed off to the freeway 605 North. I told Vern to take over driving, and I got in the back with the kid and took the gag off. I slapped him once, pulled out my dick and told him to suck on it. I got his pants off and squeezed his nuts real hard. He screamed. I pulled down his pants and fucked him. I told him he was the best fuck I ever had."

"I traded places with Butts, and Butts started sucking on him; after a while, he said he couldn't get him hard. I told Butts to hit the kid a little for encouragement. Butts squeezed the kid's nuts, and he screamed. About five minutes later, but said he was half hard, I pulled over to the side of the freeway, parked and told the kid you get hard, or I fuck you up so bad you'll wish you were dead, and I squeezed his nuts. The kid was terrified. Watch this, I told Vern and started masturbating him and told him to get hard. Within a minute, he was hard. I looked at Vern and said, "See, all it takes is a little something to convince him. "Vern went back to sucking, and I continued to drive Vern got bored and told me he was through, so he took over driving, and I got in the back. I told the kid, "Sorry, kid, you're going to die." I told him how we had killed the other guys. I then took the iron bar, hit him across the chest, and squeezed his nuts. I hit him so many times in the chest and throat I am surprised he didn't cry, although I don't think he could. I told him I was going to torture him like this until he was ready to die. I told him that I'd strangle him. At that time, he asked me to stab him instead, and I told him no. I hit him some more and asked him if he was ready to die. He said yes. I put the iron bar across his neck and pushed down until I felt he was dead. I untied him and took his clothes off. I headed South, stopped along the freeway, put my flashers on, waited till there was no traffic coming, and threw him out."

On Wednesday, September 12, 1979, the grim discovery unfolded: the nude body of David lay near the 101 freeway—a life extinguished, a tragedy etched into the asphalt. Detectives, their hearts heavy, surveyed the scene. David Murillo's bruised and battered corpse bore the hallmarks of violence. The puzzle pieces clicked into place: Grabs, Hyden, and now Murillo—all likely victims of the same malevolent hand. Evidence was meticulously gathered, and the autopsy room awaited their grim task.

Dr. Kornblum, the bearer of sombre truths, revealed the aftermath. Ligature marks adorned David's neck, wrists, and ankles—a macabre signature. His skull bore an injury, and the unthinkable: his rectum distended. But it was the fractured windpipe that spoke loudest—the iron bar, pressed mercilessly against his throat, had silenced him forever. Bonin, the predator, wielded the tyre iron not merely as a tool but as an instrument of brutality. In that dark moment, the van, the highway, and the twisted mind of a killer converged, leaving behind a shattered life and a trail of horror.

Victim 6 Robert Christopher Wirostek

*Image SEQ Image * ARABIC27 (Robert Christopher "Bob" Wirostek (1960-1979)* ***-. . ., 1960)***

Robert Christopher "Bob" Wirostek entered the world on October 30, 1960, in Flint, Genesee County, Michigan, USA. His birthplace echoed with the promise of youth and dreams yet to unfold. But fate, ever capricious, had other plans.

On September 17, 1979, at the tender age of 18, Robert's journey took a tragic turn. Riverside County, California, became the backdrop for his untimely departure—a chapter cut short, leaving behind echoes of what might have been. Robert's parents, Robert Wirostek and Joan Marie Gloss, shared their love with six children: Carey, Genuine Ramona, Dominic, Renee, and Robert. Their family tapestry, woven with threads of hope and loss, bore witness to Robert's aspirations. A grocery employee by day, he harboured dreams of gracing the world as a male model. Carman High School, Michigan, witnessed his athletic prowess. The class of 1978 celebrated his achievements, but destiny had other plans. Robert's flame flickered out too soon, leaving behind memories etched in the hearts of those who knew him. 65, 66

65 Ancestry.com. Global, find a Grave® Index for Burials at Sea and other Select Burial Locations, 1300s-Current [database online]. Lehi, UT, USA: Ancestry.com Operations, Inc., 2012. 66 Youth Termed Possible 'Freeway Killer' Victim. (1980, August 27). The Los Angeles Times

*Image SEQ Image * ARABIC28 (Robert Christopher "Bob" Wirostek (1960-1979) -. . ., 1960)*

(Bob)Wirostek was kidnapped on September 17, 1979, while riding his bicycle to his job at a grocery store. Bonin and Butts pulled into the parking lot. They got him into the van, tied him up and strangled him, dumping Roberts's body along Interstate 10. Roberts's body was discovered on September 19th

The interview in question, conducted in December 1980, involved the detectives and prosecutors associated with the case. The details of this interview are chronicled in Vonda Peltos' book, providing a documented perspective on the proceedings and insights into the investigation.

Esposito: Okay, well, get to Robert Wirostek. You mentioned last night that he was hitchhiking on Pacific Coast Highway near Newport Beach.

Bonin: Correct. That would be north. As you're coming down, there is a street where you make a left turn; it goes up the hill and around that. So, it was North.

Esposito: Okay.

Bonin: That is the street we took to get to Ralph's market, to the best of my knowledge. I am trying to remember what the. I thought it was Newport….

Esposito: Newport Blvd, Interchange?

Bonin: Okay, and then that's it.

Esposito: What time of day was that?

Bonin: in the daytime, that's all I can say.

Esposito: in the afternoon?

Bonin: I don't know.

Esposito. Okay, did he say where he was going?

Bonin, yes, to work at Ralphs market.

Esposito, OK, you mentioned he was all for getting some head.

Bonin: Yes, I went. I went all the way to Ralphs Market, into a parking lot about two parking lots down from West Market, and into another big parking lot.

Esposito: Did he say how much time he had to get to work or anything like that?

Bonin: I believe he did, but I must remember how much time he had. By the time we got there, he still had half an hour.

Esposito. Okay, you said. You said last night. You tide him up. What did you tie him with?

Bonin: I'm almost sure about the string.

Esposito: how did you get him tied up?

Bonin: I tied it around one hand and wrapped it around his throat, then went round and tied it around to the other and back up the throat.

Esposito: Kind of like hog-tying?

Bonin: Yeah.

Esposito. Why Did you get him subdued? You know, to tie him up. Did you produce a knife?

Bonin: I pulled a knife.

Esposito: how long have you been with him when you pulled a knife?

Bonin: I got back there and started sucking on him, and then I said, well, I don't take the cum let me get some toilet paper, and I went up. This would have been about 15 to 30 seconds after we started, and I went up, and when I came back, I had the knife.

Esposito: Okay, so you had a knife on him.

Bonin: yes, to his throat, and he turned over, and I tied him up.

Esposito: OK, did you sodomise him?

Bonin: Yes, I believe I did.

Esposito: did you pick him up to kill him, or just for sex as it turned into killing, or what?

Bonin: Uhm, I believe. When I first picked him up, it was strictly sex. But we talked on the way up there, and the only thing we could do for $20 was let me give him head. And what I wanted to do is I wanted to fuck him, and I knew I wasn't going to be able to, so it turned around to where I was going to have to tie him up and do that.

Esposito: you have a situation where if somebody wasn't agreeable and you wound up where you had to tie them up and all that, you know, stuff to fuck them, that would prompt you to kill them.

Bonin: Yes, I would say that for a long time. As I said, I was more into the killing as I went on. If I would cum, then it would be tough for me to afterwards to kill him. I couldn't do it like, for instance. I picked up a kid living off Lakewood Blvd and Candle Stick somewhere in Los Angeles or Lakewood, and he was 16. He looked more like 12 or 13, and I got it on with him. I made him give me head. I didn't tie him up, and I butt fucked him, and I came, and then I gave him head. But I could not bring myself to kill him, and I had already come. I was by myself and ended up giving him $30, and I never heard from him again. Nothing was ever turned in. He was happy to get the $30; I am positive he didn't say anything because I played a role. I told him how sorry I was all that, and says Well, I really think I should turn myself in. We're going to find a cop. And no way did he want to find a cop because he had warrants out for him. Juvenile warrants. So, I said, okay, you got your $30, you go, and I'll go, and that was it.

In examining William Bonin's interactions with detectives, a discernible contrast emerges between his verbal and written confessions. During verbal exchanges, Bonin appears to omit the more macabre details of his crimes, seemingly attempting to minimize the perception of his sadism. However, the written confession presents a starkly different narrative that is far more explicit and vivid in depicting the events. This discrepancy highlights a calculated effort by Bonin to control the narrative and mitigate the severity of his actions in the eyes of law enforcement.

"It was a sunny day, and I felt like taking a drive. I headed for the Pacific Coast Highway, which entered the Long

Beach Traffic Circle. I wanted to do some driving and look at sailboats. I took the Coast Highway South and was at peace with myself. And then there were no hitchhikers, and the traffic was light. I found that in a short time, I was in Newport Beach, just north of Newport Beach. That is when I saw a guy hitchhiking. I picked him up and had no intentions of doing anything until he got into the van. he was around 16 to 18 and quite good-looking.

I decided to see what I could do. He said he was going to work, and I offered to drive him there. I asked him if he was into the gay scene, and he said no, and then I showed him 50 bucks to just give him head. We got in the back of the van. And I started sucking on him and rubbing his chest. Oh yeah, that was great, he said. I had him hooked. He was lying back and really enjoying it. I went in the front to get some tissue and returned with an 8-inch steak knife. I held it to his throat and said if you move, I'll stick you with the knife. He was petrified and said I would do anything you said.

So, I Tied him up and told him one false move, and I'll stick you. I could see his sweat on his tan skin, which turned me on. I pulled down my pants and butt fucked him. He started complaining, and I told him if you make any noise, your dead mother fucker I drove my dick into him and fucked him real hard. I then found a phone booth and called Vern. He kept asking me to loosen his hands because they were hurting. I told him to shut up. After I picked up Vernon in the van, we headed towards the 1-10 freeway east to the inland area.

While driving, I discovered the boy's name was Robert, but he preferred Bob. Vern gave him head and slapped him around a bit, then we swapped, and Vern drove, and I got back in there. I rolled him onto his stomach and hit some on the side. Then I asked Vern if he would like to hear him scream, and Vern said sure, why don't you do that finger trick. That was a thing we discussed the night before. It is where we break the guy's fingers. I said OKAY, grabbed Bob's little fingers, and bent it back till it snapped. He screamed in pain. After I finished, I went for his little finger on the other hand, and he begged me not to. I pushed it back for a while but didn't break it. I then grabbed his nuts and squeezed those really hard. I then took a tyre Iron, rolled him over back on his back, and hit him as hard as I could on both knees and ankles. I hit him on his shoulders and elbows, then told him we're going to let you out, but you will be unconscious. I gave him the choice of either choking him or hitting him over the head. He didn't say what he wanted initially, then said, I don't know, so I hit him.

I thought he was out, I hit him with the tyre iron again, but he moved and started yelling at me, saying, you fucking bastard. He had momentarily scared me. I said I'll choke you. Instead, just let yourself go; it won't be as bad. Don't struggle, as it will only make it worse. And do not try to pretend you're out. I can tell. I started choking him with his T-shirt and twisting it tighter with the tyre iron; after I got it tight, I saw he was fully conscious. He was trying to stay that way. I said have you tried to fight? It would use the oxygen up faster. It won't help to try and remain conscious. It's all over your one dead dude. He started to struggle. When I said that, I said struggle, baby, it will only make your death come faster 15 seconds later, he was out. I relaxed and tightened his shirt and tyre iron for five more minutes. Then we dumped him in the desert around Palm Springs and went home.

In a tragic turn of events, less than five years after the significant loss of Robert, a young man of 21 years was discovered lifeless, floating face down in a lagoon behind Cordilla Villita. This grim discovery occurred on March 28, 1984, at approximately 1:30 pm. The authorities estimated that he had been in the water for seven to ten days. He was dressed in jeans, but his upper body was bare. The man was subsequently identified as Dominic Wirostek, the brother of Robert Wirostek. A forensic autopsy concluded that drowning was the cause of death. A forensic autopsy concluded that drowning was the cause of death. Dominic stayed with his sister Ramona at Windward Village on Hilton Head Island. The Players Club employed him, and he was last seen on March 16th by his sister and a roommate when he said he was headed for Florida. Bennie Branham and Bobby Creel found the body while they were walking around the lagoon. The ongoing investigation aimed to determine whether drugs were involved or if there were any signs of foul play, such as bruises. At the time this information was made public, there was suspicion that his death might not have been accidental. However, there were also no signs of foul play either. After uncovering this information recently, I was able to find that his autopsy confirmed drowning. Still, any further details regarding the circumstances surrounding his death remain a mystery. 67

67 Man found dead in Lagoon (1984, 30 March). The Island Packet. I

Victim 7 Walter Allen Tanner

Walter Allen Tanner

On January 8, 1963, Walter Allen Tanner entered the world, cradled in the embrace of his parents, Harvey Lefran Tanner (1929 - 1994) and Anita Myra Smead (1934 - 2018). Their love, a quiet symphony, echoed through the corridors of time.

Walter was not alone in this familial tapestry. His siblings—Douglas (1957 - 2008), Clifford (1955 - 2008), and Crystal, Jocelyn and Skip—wove their threads into the fabric of shared memories.

Yet, the news reports often misstep, casting him as Wallace Tanner. But the truth remains steadfast: he is Walter Allen Tanner—a name etched in the annals of existence,

On November 17, 1979, a grim discovery was made: the body of an unidentified young man was found on a side road just a quarter mile from the San Diego Freeway. This incident occurred not far from where another victim, a 16-year-old from Milpitas, had been found the previous February, bearing similar injuries. The recent victim, initially known as John Doe, had suffered a brutal beating and strangulation. His identity remained a mystery, and his assailant was unknown. It was only later that he was identified as Walter Tanner, a 15-year-old boy who had been reported missing since November 13, 1979. The proximity of these cases and the similarity in the manner of death raised concerns about a possible connection between the incidents. 68

He was another victim of William Bonin. Bonin had been released from jail two months earlier after serving time for a previous murder.

Upon his release, he was overwhelmed by a potent compulsion to pursue his next victim. He chose to abandon Walter Tanner's remains in San Diego County, believing it would divert the police and obscure his whereabouts. His usual hunting grounds were in Los Angeles and Orange counties, where he had claimed the lives of most of his victims.

One lonely night in mid-November, he roamed the streets of Long Beach, seeking potential victims. He scoured typical youth haunts — bus stops, arcades, bars — but found the

*Image SEQ Image * ARABIC30 (Hermit, n. d.)*

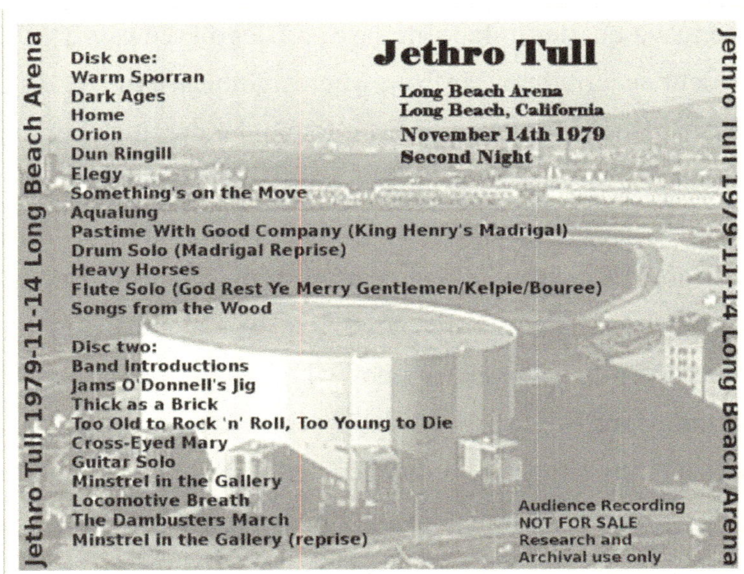

roads barren. Frustration mounted as hours ticked by fruitlessly. Resigned, he decided to retreat home.

Navigating the Pacific Coast Highway, he veered north towards Silverado Canyon, intending to traverse North Chapman. This route led directly to the canyon's seclusion, a path favoured for its darkness and solitude.

On that isolated road, he encountered Wallace Tanner, fresh from a

Jethro Tull concert and searching for a ride back to Orange—the chance sighting sealed Tanner's fate on that fateful November night.

The following narrative captures the profound tragedy of the situation: a young man, once amidst a crowd of concertgoers at a Jethro Tull performance, would soon be reduced to a mere statistic in a series of heinous acts.

Walter Tanner, a youth with his unique story, unknowingly crossed paths with Bonin. With a deceptive offer of a ride, Bonin ensnared Tanner, who was oblivious to the peril that awaited him. In a remote location, the worst fate befell Tanner at the hands of Bonin. After the atrocious act, Bonin disposed of Tanner's body in San Diego County, a calculated move to throw off the authorities. The grim satisfaction Bonin derived from his actions adds a chilling layer to the already dark tale.

Bonin stopped his vehicle and asked Tanner where he was going. "I'm heading back from the concert and trying to get home near Orange Circle. I need to reach Carson Blvd," Tanner replied. "Hop in. I'll take you there. It's on my way back home," Bonin offered. Tanner gratefully climbed into the van. "You're lucky. I live in Silverado Canyon, so it's convenient for me to drop you off. It is unsafe to hitchhike, especially late at night," Bonin cautioned.

Bonin remarked, feigning concern while engaging in casual conversation. "I'm aware, but I rarely do this," Tanner admitted. "Is that so?" Bonin replied, subtly advancing his ploy. "Do you ever get picked up by guys?" "Sure, all the time," Tanner answered. They ever approach, you know, for sex," Bonin excitedly asked. "Yeah," the innocent boy replied, sinking deeper into the net. "Have they ever offered you money? No? Well, I will do just that if you are interested," he said alluringly.

Bonin looked at him and reached over to softly run his hands up Tanner's high towards his genitals. Bonin was delighted when Tanner looked at him, smiling in disbelief at being offered 50 bucks for receiving a blowjob. Bonin, keeping his hand up against his crotch, noticed that young Tanner was responding to his touch. "You have a lot of dick for a youngster. What about it?" Bonin said with an inviting smile. "Okay," Tanner quickly responded. Bonin excitedly anticipates the emotional release from killing again. He turned right onto Carson Blvd and found a secure place to park. They entered the back of the van, and Bonin initiated the first move by pulling Tanner's pants down to his ankles and got him thoroughly excited by sucking tanners dick vigorously. Tanner responded to Bonin with moans of pleasure, appearing to be enjoying himself; after a couple of minutes, Bonin stopped and got ready for the next move. I'll get some tissues. I don't like tasting the cum. You keep jacking yourself off. Tanner was on the right side of the van, unable to see Bonin pull-out rope handcuffs and an 8-inch knife and placed them on the front seat.

Bonin snuggled up next to Tanner and prepared for the grand finale. "Would you like to earn an additional $25? Let me tie your hands behind your back. "No way, that isn't cool; you might decide to butt fuck me", Tanner protested in horror.

Bonin responded, trying to explain. "No, I just get a hard-on when I suck someone off while they're tied up," Bonin exclaimed back, trying to get him to cooperate voluntarily. "Sorry, I'm not interested in doing that," he told Bonin. Knowing it wouldn't work the easy way, Bonin reached over the seat and grabbed a knife and a slightly broken pair of handcuffs. He put the cuffs in his pocket and the knife in his right hand then spun around at full speed and pounced on the boy straddling Tanner. He placed the point of the blade knife against his throat. "Now fucking turn over or so

68 Jarlson, G. (1979, December 8). Another Male Murder Victim was identified. The Los Angeles Times.

help me. I will stick you right now" Scared and shocked by the knife, Tanner still refused to surrender without a fight. There is no way I will let you tie me up. You will butt fuck me for sure, so go ahead and stick me," Tanner bravely responded. "Look," Bonin said I am not interested in fucking you. All I wanted to do was suck you off while you were tied up. "The handcuffs aren't even working properly," Bonin said insincerely. "Forget the handcuffs," he yelled back. "Fuckin turnover," the fate of Tanner was sealed when Bonin exploded at him. The game playing is over.

Tanner refused to comply. I'm going to start pushing this blade into your throat until you turn over for penetration, or I'll shove it in.

Tanner continued refusing to comply as he still hoped to escape. Clamping the cold steel of the blade between his teeth, Bonin unleashed a ferocious punch into Tanner's stomach. The sheer force drove the breath from Tanner's lungs, folding him with pain and forcing his submission. If you waste any more of my time, I'll kill you, Bonin whispered with complete menace. He managed to manoeuvre the remaining wrist into the cuffs in clumsy haste. With deliberate care, he wrapped both hands securely, entwining them with three-inch wide surgical tape strips, ensuring they were firmly bound. At the same time, Bonin felt relieved.

Tanner's terror swirled like a vortex in the dimly lit van, threatening to engulf him. His heart hammered against his

ribcage, and each beat echoing the stark reality: he was utterly defenceless, caught in the relentless grip of an unhinged sexual predator—a walking statistic of hostility and death. So, you want to cause trouble, and you don't like getting fucked, Bonin said while stripping off the child's pants will see how you like this. "Bonin unleashed a relentless barrage of punches, each blow finding its mark on Tanner's vulnerable side and back. The room reverberated with the sickening thud of knuckles meeting flesh. But it wasn't enough—Bonin craved more than physical dominance. He lunged, fingers like vipers, and sealed Tanner's mouth shut, cutting off any desperate cries. In that chilling moment, he held absolute control, the predator's hunger gleaming in his eyes." Bonin brutally and forcefully sodomised the boy, taking out months of frustration, anger and tension on Tanner. Bonin's assault reverberated through the room—a symphony of agony and hatred. Muffled screams clawed their way out of Tanner, each one a desperate plea for escape. The air thickened with the grotesque sounds—the wet slap of skin against skin, the guttural grunts of a predator.

And then, abruptly, it was over. Bonin, driven by a primal hunger, had taken what he wanted. The sexual tension dissipated, leaving behind a void—an emptiness that gnawed at both victim and perpetrator. The release was only half complete, a fractured catharsis that lingered like a phantom ache.

"Bonin retrieved a thick chain, its links cold and unforgiving. He fashioned a loop with practised hands, the metal biting into his palm. He laid it down alongside a tyre rod, both instruments of menace. The room held its breath, the air thick with malice. Tanner, pinned and silenced, met Bonin's eyes. The unspoken threat hung heavy: not one fucking word—a pact sealed in fear and desperation." Bonin's voice sliced through the air, a blade of authority. "No," he commanded, each syllable a vice. "I won't." His eyes bore into Tanner, unyielding.

Tanner, desperate and trembling, choked out his plea. "I swear, please let me go."

With a predatory swiftness, Bonin seized him, his grip cruel and invasive. One hand tormented, seeking to degrade; the other, a vice upon Tanner's bound wrists, ensuring the chains held fast. In a sudden, wrenching motion, he forced Tanner's arms upward, contorting his body in a cruel mimicry of flight. From Tanner's lips escaped a stifled cry—a haunting note of pain that lingered in the charged air. Bonin tightened his grip on the boy's testicles fingers like a vice, and the boy's scream tore through the room—a raw, primal sound. It began with the horrifying realisation: he wasn't gagged, and his screams could summon help. Bonin, relentless, straddled Tanner, the weight of malevolence settling upon him.

"Here's what I'm going to do," Bonin whispered, a blade against Tanner's desperation. "I'll render you unconscious, dress you, and deposit you somewhere—a place where silence will be your ally."

But Tanner, eyes wide with terror, found his voice. "You don't have to do that," he pleaded. "I won't say anything."

Bonin's voice was a vicious whisper, the room's air thick with menace. "You have no choice, kid," he hissed. "That's the way it's going to be. If you don't shut up, I won't stop strangling you."

The chain, cold and unyielding, circled Tanner's neck. Bonin threaded it through the loop, the metal biting into his skin. With a cruel twist, he began to tighten, the world narrowing to a desperate struggle for air. Tanner, eyes bulging, fought against the encroaching darkness.

"If you want to struggle," Bonin murmured, satisfaction lacing his words, "will you die for it?" The predator's resignation hung heavy, a pact sealed in violence. And just as Tanner teetered on the edge of unconsciousness, his right hand broke free—a desperate defiance in the face of brutality.

Bonin moved with a chilling efficiency, seizing the chain and cinching the loop around Tanner's neck. The metal bit into flesh, and the room held its breath. With a final twist, he ensured the boy's life would drain away—a calculated act of spite.

In that moment, power surged through Bonin, intoxicating and primal. The fading pulse beneath his fingers echoed his dominance. Yet, as life ebbed, a different exhaustion settled—a weariness transcending physical exertion. The fatigue of a predator who had claimed his prey was the void left by extinguished breath.

And in that emptiness, a revelation: Bonin stood alone, untethered. He didn't need anyone else; he was strong enough to navigate the darkness solo.

Bonin steered his vehicle onto the I-5, heading south with a grim purpose. The Ortega Highway stretched before him, a ribbon of possibilities. He continued his journey southward, eyes scanning the roadsides, searching for a lonely spot shrouded in secrecy. Near San Diego, he found his grim sanctuary. Here, the coastal fog was a thief, stealing away the clarity of day, cloaking Bonin's actions in a ghostly veil. Tanner became the solitary figure abandoned in the San Diego expanse—a stark contrast to the bustling life of Long Beach. From the sun-kissed shores of Malibu to the arid stretches of Palm Springs and the rugged ascents of the Cajon Pass, Bonin had sown a trail of sorrow. Hundreds of miles lay between the resting places of the lost. This macabre breadcrumb trail left the police grappling with the enormity of Bonin's dark pilgrimage.

Victim 8 John Doe

The victim was discovered along an empty irrigation ditch or a reservoir along US Highway 99 near Taft, California and south of Bakersfield. He was savagely beaten and strangled to death. He was also found without shoes, socks, or underwear. Law enforcement believes William Bonin is responsible.

Between May 1979 and June 1980, Bonin and four accomplices were responsible for the abduction, torture, and murders of boys and young men whose bodies were dumped next to the freeways of southern California. This victim is the only unidentified victim on the list of victims. Bonin and one of his accomplices, Vernon Butts, did confess their involvement in his murder.

Also, according to Coroner Dick Gervais in the Santa Cruz Sentinel, one of the suspects admitted to killing the man as well as leading the LA County sheriff's deputies to the exact spot where the body was found. Bonin believed that the victim was around 23 and also admitted to stabbing the victim with an ice pick through the ear and nostrils before killing him. Although Bonin was charged with this victim's murder, the charge was dropped when Butts committed suicide on January 11, 1981, as his testimony was needed in court. 69

69 AP, B. (1980, 24 September). Kern County to Exhume Man Body. Santa Cruz Sentinel, 47.

This John Doe victim is buried at the West Side District Cemetery in Taft. He is one of two John Does buried in this cemetery.

Case number CT79-2742 at NamUs [70]

Kern County John Doe, located in Taft, California

Brown hair.

Clothing: Light blue OP brand pullover jacket with "California" on the back in blue. Brown corduroy pants.

Discovered: November 30, 1979

Unidentified for 44 years

Sex: Male

Age:15-27

Race: White

Height :5'1 - 5'6

Weight:140 pounds

Body condition: Skeletal

Postmortem interval: one month

Cause of death: Strangulation

The unidentified individual found in Kern County on November 30, 1979, is commonly referred to as John Doe. Despite extensive efforts, an official identification of this John Doe has yet to be made. Interestingly, the characteristics of this unidentified person bear a striking resemblance to those of Jeff Sayer.

Those characteristics that match Sayre

70 NamUs. (2024). https://www.namus.gov/UnidentifiedPersons/Case#/57039

Age: 15, Brown hair, Male, White, Height 5'6
The fact that both Killers Bonin and Kraft dumped bodies all over the place, many quite a distance from where they were picked up, does not rule out the possibility of the victim being Sayre.
While the dates do not match up, Bonin says he picked up John Doe on the 21st, but Sayre Didn't go missing until the 24th. However, as Bonin was not truthful, he may have mixed up the dates or changed them so they wouldn't connect a name to a body: nobody. No crime, right?! I realise I might be clutching at straws, but I can be hopeful until Kern County tells me John Doe has been identified or Sayre is found.
I've contacted the Kern County Sheriff's Department to share my concerns and seek further information.
I was emailed back in March 2024 that they would look for the file, as the older ones were not digitised, and get back to me. As of this book's publication date, I am still awaiting a response, even though I sent several follow-up emails.
On the same day, another victim, Frank Dennis Fox, was discovered. Unlike the John Doe in Kern County, Fox's remains were positively identified. His body was located in Orange County, not Kern. Given William Bonin's known history, it raises the question: Is it possible that Bonin was responsible for taking the lives of two individuals on that

day? Such a pattern of multiple victims in a single day was not beyond the realm of his documented crimes.

On November 21, 1979, Bonin and Butts picked up another young man; he was dumped in an irrigation ditch alongside Route 99 just south of Baker's field. Bonin had put an icepick through his nose and ear as he strangled him. Bonin had just killed Walter Tanner, a 15-year-old boy, a week after getting out of jail. He had dumped his body in San Diego County, hoping to confuse the police and hide his location. But he was not satisfied with his crime. He craved more sex and murder. He wanted to feel the thrill of hunting, raping, and killing young men and boys. He lay in bed that night, restless and eager for the next day's thrill. He wished the morning would come sooner. He had a plan to kill someone with an ice pick, a new method that Butts, his accomplice, had suggested. He agreed to do it to keep Butts as his partner in crime. He knew he needed Butt's help to lure and subdue his victims.

As dawn broke, he rose with a sense of purpose, the quiet morning air filled with anticipation. Stepping outside, he retrieved the newspaper, its crisp pages untouched by the world's awakening. Behind the wheel, he navigated the familiar streets to McDonald's, where the aroma of coffee beckoned. With a steaming cup, he settled into a secluded corner, the paper unfolding before him like a map of his desires. His eyes darted across the headlines, searching for a reflection of his deeds, a testament to the chaos he believed he had sown. He yearned for recognition, for his name to be etched in the annals of infamy, to confirm his influence over the community's heartbeat. Yet, as he combed through each line, the silence of anonymity greeted him—no whispers of fear, no echoes of his name, just the quiet hum of an ordinary day.

There was no news about Walter Tanner or any of his other victims. He felt disappointed and angry.

With the last sip of coffee leaving a bitter aftertaste, he discarded the unread stories of the day into the bin. Their significance was lost to him. He strode with a determined gait towards his van, an unassuming vehicle to the unknowing eye, yet one that harboured terrible tales within its confines. Despite its history, the van was a dependable accomplice, purring steadily on the road.

Bonin had set his sights on a familiar haunt, the residence of his acquaintance, Butts. Known for his indulgent lifestyle, Butts was the kind of person who found the mundane weekdays as fitting for revelry as any weekend. Bonin's van stopped outside the non-descript abode, its garage a silent witness to many a nocturnal escapade. With a measured knock on the door, Bonin awaited the next chapter of the day, the sun casting long shadows behind him.

When the door swung open, Bonin cut straight to the chase with a question that brooked no hesitation: "Ready for a hunt?" Butts, ever the kindred spirit in such ventures, responded with a vigorous nod, "Absolutely, let's hit the road."

Butts swiftly geared up, selecting two coils of rope, each with its sinister role and an ice pick, cold and unyielding. Together, they were a duo fuelled by a shared, dark anticipation. The air crackled with their charged energy as they leapt into the van, the engine's roar a prelude to the night's grim symphony.

The van rumbled through the suburban labyrinth, its path illuminated by the occasional streetlight that flickered with a hesitant glow. Houses stood shoulder to shoulder, their windows dark, the residents wrapped in the bliss of ignorance. Gardens lay dormant, their once vibrant hues now muted under the moon's silver wash. They roamed the streets for hours, their quest unfulfilled, the city's pulse beating in time with their growing impatience. Resolute, they steered towards the neon glow of Hollywood, a hunting ground ripe with memories of past conquests. It was here, amidst the allure of Santa Monica Blvd, that they encountered a solitary figure perched on a bus bench—a beacon in the dim light.

The youth before them was slight, no more than 5 foot 6 inches, his light brown hair cascading to his shoulders, his frame a mere 130 pounds. His claim of adulthood, marked by the number 18, seemed at odds with the innocence etched on his face—a stark contrast to the hardened streets he called home. This teenage runaway, a survivor in the urban wilderness, unwittingly drew their focus.

With a beckoning gesture, he was beckoned to the van.

"How's life treating you?" Bonin inquired, masking his intentions with feigned concern. The boy's response was tinged with caution, a single word hanging in the air: "Surviving." Bonin wasted no time, his voice cutting through the silence like a knife. "What's your game, kid? You out here hustling?" His gaze was piercing, unyielding. The boy, cornered and visibly shaken, flicked his eyes from side to side, the neon lights above casting shadows on his face. He mustered a head shake, his Adam's apple bobbing with the effort. "You… you a cop?" he stammered out, the words tumbling from his lips in a calm, breathy tone, barely audible over the distant hum of the city at night.

Bonin chuckled. "No, I'm not a cop. I'm out looking for a little action. Are you up for it?" he asked, not wanting to waste any time.

The boy hesitated for a moment, then asked the inevitable question. "How much are you offering?" Bonin named his price a meagre 20 bucks. "Does that sound alright?" he asked.

The boy shrugged and said, "Okay, I'll do it." Bonin gestured invitingly, his hand sweeping towards the open door of the nondescript van. With a subtle nod, he signalled for the young man to climb aboard. The engine hummed to life as they departed. They wove through the streets, the city's discord fading behind them, searching for a secluded enclave where their clandestine dealings could unfold away from prying eyes."

Butts, perched in the passenger seat, gazed through the window, taking in the serene beauty of the November day. The sky was a canvas of unblemished azure, stretching endlessly above. The van merged onto the Hollywood Freeway, its wheels humming a steady rhythm as they made their way north, bound for the San Fernando Valley. With each mile that slipped beneath them, the boy's heart thrummed a little louder, a symphony of nerves that reached a crescendo with the distance. Promises of a brief excursion now seemed like distant whispers as their path drew them ever further from the familiar shores of Huntington Beach."

Butts engaged the boy in light-hearted banter, weaving questions about his life and pastimes into the fabric of their conversation. With a hint of pride, the boy shared tales of a life kissed by sea breezes, where days were enhanced by the scent of fresh pastries from his family's bakery. As the journey continued, Bonin steered the van off the freeway in Studio City, navigating through the urban sprawl until they reached an isolated spot shrouded by the shadow of a long-abandoned gas station. The van's engine fell silent, and with a sense of foreboding, Bonin slipped into the back with the unsuspecting youth. He turned to Butts, offering him the lead, but Butts lost in a world of conjuring and sleight of hand, declined. His mind was a whirlwind of enchanting illusions, and he chose instead to remain seated, a solitary figure amidst the front seat's solitude."

Bonin tilted his head, initiating an intimate kiss with the boy., yet, for Bonin, the feeling was absent."; he was surprised he had no sexual arousal whatsoever. Bonin then unbuttons the boy's shirt, peels it off and runs his hands over the young boy's hairless chest. Still no arousal; he did not feel anything. Bonin offered to pay him extra money if he let himself be tied up; "To Bonin's surprise, the boy consented, albeit with a sense of urgency. 'Can we make this quick? I must return to town soon; I have made arrangements and do not want to keep them waiting.' Bonin reassured him, 'Don't worry, we'll be done here in no time.

The young boy lies down on his stomach and allows his hands and feet to be bound. Bonin rolls him over onto his back and then sits back on his haunches. The boy's anxiety is palpable as he urges, 'Let's move it along, okay? I need to be out of here soon.'

Bonin wasn't feeling any sexual excitement at all. He didn't know what was going on. Bonin looked down at the boy that was lying before him and thought back to the time when Bonin was gang raped. Suddenly, he realised it wasn't about sex anymore. It was about killing the power over life and death. Bonin was positioned over the boy's back when the boy, with a defiant tone, spoke to Bonin. I don't see how you can butt fuck me now. I still have my pants on. I don't want to fuck you anymore, Bonin whispers while leaning closer to the boy's ear. I've decided to kidnap you and hold you for ransom. In a display of intimidation, he delivered several forceful blows to the boy's chest and abdomen. The boy lying before Bonin, and Butts, recognising the odds were two against one with his bonds still in place, knew he had to cooperate to survive. Bonin took his place at the wheel and steered onto the Hollywood freeway, setting course for Interstate 5. As time passed, they found themselves amidst the Tejon Pass hills, often called the Grapevine. High in the mountains, Bonin veered off the highway and located an isolated area. Butts and Bonin wasted no time in assaulting him. Following the initial attack, Bonin wrapped his hands around the boy's neck, tightening his grip in a lethal chokehold.

In a desperate struggle, the boy fought back, causing Bonin to lose his hold. The boy freed himself, sending Bonin stumbling against the van's side. As the boy attempted to rise, Bonin shouted out, "You little shit Butts passed him the tyre iron. Bonin forced the boy down once more and began to exert intense pressure on his throat with the tyre iron." His cries of terror filled the air as Bonin applied even more force. Bonin eased his grip slightly and inquired of the boy,

"Do you want to know why you must die?" Confusion etched on his face, the boy nodded, unable to grasp the situation. Bonin leaned in closer and whispered, "Your folks hired me to track you down and end your life." The boy's gaze locked onto Bonin, his eyes expanding in disbelief at the words he heard. Bonin, unrelenting, pressed the bar down once more, extinguishing the life from the boy's body. To confirm the boy's demise, Bonin thrust the icepick into each nostril and then into his ear.

Bonin had to think about where to dump this latest victim. Bonin and Butts travelled 35 miles in the opposite direction, reaching the expansive Central Valley. From there, they veered away from Highway 5, taking a westerly route on Highway 166 toward an agricultural zone close to Taft. The boy was abandoned in a shallow irrigation depth of a lonely road between the crop fields. He was found nine days afterwards, on November 30, in Kern County. His identity remains unverified to this day.

Victim 9 James Sean Moore

*Image SEQ Image * ARABIC31 James Moore (M, A. (2024)*

In the book Without Redemption, Vonda Pelto reveals that a young man who called himself James Moore was among the victims of serial killer William Bonin. Bonin confessed to killing in writing and also gave a verbal account of the murder. He said he met him on February 1, 1980, on a ramp to the freeway, where he was trying to hitch a ride to Palm Springs. He then strangled him and disposed of his body in a trash site or a landfill. No one ever reported James Moore missing; his real identity remains unknown. According to the book, he may have used a false name or had no family or friends who cared for him. His body has never been recovered or identified, and he may still be recorded as a John Doe in the official records. 71 14

After reading the paragraph and finding the name in a list of suspected Bonin victims, I was concerned that this young man might still be missing or a John Doe. I contacted the Riverside Sheriff's Department to inquire if a young man by that name was recorded with them. I received an email back, which you can read below.

71 Eric Blair, V. J. M. (2024). [Interview].

James Moore

Contreras, Amy

Hello

I was forwarded your email regarding your interest in the James Moore investigation. I learned this tragic event did occur within our jurisdiction and was investigated by Riverside County Sheriff's Department investigators, case #E800360317. I reviewed the case in its entirety. The previous investigators assigned to the case determined William Bonin was responsible for the death of James Moore and the case was closed. It appears since Bonin was convicted of 15 murders and sentenced to death in Orange and Los Angeles county areas, Riverside County did not pursue further charges. Bonin was executed in 1996. If you are in contact with James Moore's sister and she would like to discuss further, please provide her with my below listed contact information. Thank you

Investigator Amy Contreras #2780
Riverside County Sheriff's Department
Major Crimes Bureau Cold Case Task Force
1500 Castellano Road
Riverside, California 92509
Desk 951 955-6297
Cell 951 203-1907

*Image SEQ Image * ARABIC32 Personal Email*

In the book Without Redemption, Vonda Pelto reveals that a young man who called himself James Moore was among the victims of serial killer William Bonin. Bonin confessed to killing in writing and also gave a verbal account of the murder. He said he met him on February 1, 1980, on a ramp to the freeway, where he was trying to hitch a ride to Palm Springs. He then strangled him and disposed of his body in a trash site or a landfill. No one ever reported James Moore missing; his real identity remains unknown. According to the book, he may have used a false name or had no family or friends who cared for him. His body has never been recovered or identified, and he may still be recorded as a John Doe in the official records. [71] [14]

After reading the paragraph and finding the name in a list of suspected Bonin victims, I was concerned that this young man might still be missing or a John Doe. I contacted the Riverside Sheriff's Department to inquire if a young man by that name was recorded with them. I received an email back, which you can read below.

71 Eric Blair, V. J. M. (2024). [Interview].

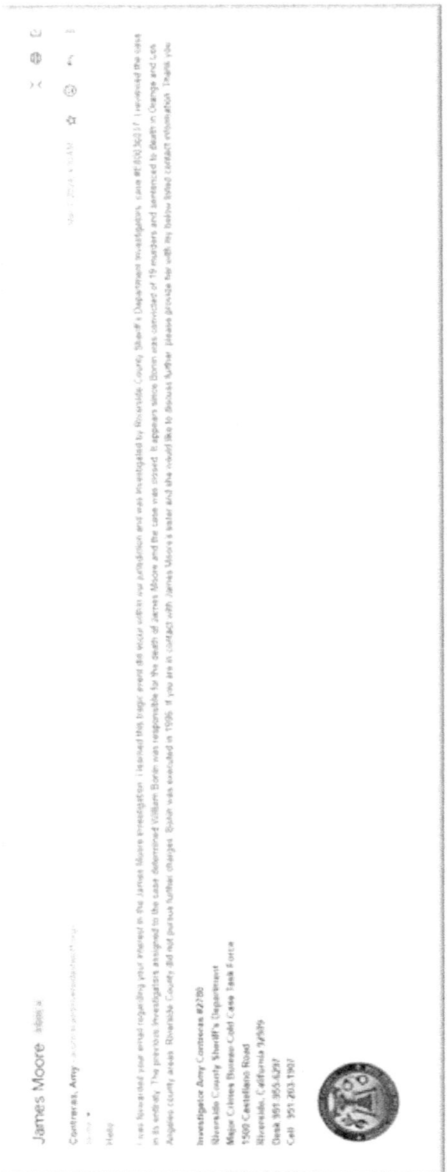

James Moore

Contreras, Amy

Hello

I was forwarded your email regarding your interest in the James Moore investigation. I learned this tragic event did occur within our jurisdiction and was investigated by Riverside County Sheriff's Department investigators, case #[illegible]. I reviewed the case in its entirety. The previous investigators assigned to the case determined William Bonin was responsible for the death of James Moore and the case was closed. It appears since Bonin was convicted of 19 murders and sentenced to death in Orange and Los Angeles county areas, Riverside County did not pursue further charges. Bonin was executed in 1996. If you are in contact with James Moore's sister and she would like to discuss further, please provide her with my below listed contact information. Thank you

Investigator Amy Contreras #2780
Riverside County Sheriff's Department
Major Crimes Bureau Cold Case Task Force
1500 Castellano Road
Riverside, California 92509
Desk 951-955-6297
Cell 951-203-1907

*Image SEQ Image * ARABIC32 Personal Email*

On March 3, 2024, I connected with the relatives of James Sean Moore via an ancestry platform. During our interaction, his sister Alicia kindly shared cherished family stories. James, born on September 13, 1960, in California, was the offspring of Elaine Nora Dias and Robert Lee Moore. He grew up with his sister, Alicia. According to family lore, their father became a distant figure after parting ways with their mother early on. The family believe that he met his untimely demise in a vehicular mishap when Alicia was approximately 12 years old. This account paints a picture of the family's history, and the gaps left by the absence of their patriarch.

As is the case for many, James Sean Moore's teenage years were turbulent. He distanced himself from his family for a period during which he struggled with substance abuse. However, James made a conscious decision to turn his life around. He returned home with a renewed determination to start anew and leave his past troubles behind. Committed to his personal growth, he resumed his education and earned his GED, a testament to his resilience and dedication. This significant achievement came less than a year before his untimely passing. Amidst this period of transformation, James also found a spark of romance, developing a fondness for a young woman with whom he was forming a closer bond.

James Sean Moore was known for his resilience, determination, and passion for fishing. He was an avid fisher who cherished the moments spent catching Bass and Catfish with his mother by the water. They would clean and prepare their catch, bonding over the shared activity.

His sister Alicia fondly recalls James's love for the music of the Eagles. The song "Hotel California" was a particular favourite of his. He played it so frequently that it became a defining soundtrack of that era for her—so much so that she now finds it overwhelming to hear.

James had diverse interests; he may not have been an athlete, but he was a dedicated stamp collector, immersing himself in the quiet pursuit of philately.

A month before his disappearance, James was present at his sister's wedding, looking dapper in a suit complemented by his favourite gold-rimmed glasses—a memory captured in a photograph that remains a treasured keepsake for his family. This image, a snapshot in time, portrays a young man full of life and potential, leaving a lasting impression on those who knew him.

In a newspaper report, friends describe Moore as an intelligent, independent youth who kept to himself. A coworker at Mimi La Marche described him as really sweet, who got along with everyone, was well adjusted, and very mature. She also said he had a girlfriend and was ready to settle down. 72

According to the Family, James Sean Moore stayed in a

72 Body may be the 11th victim in unsolved murders (1980, February 15). Santa Cruz Sentinel.

mobile home park. He told a friend he would quit his job at a nearby Carl Jr restaurant, and James was on his way there when he never arrived.

His nude body was found in a sunny mead wash near the north of Highway 60; he had been strangled and was likely the victim of a sexual assault. According to Sherrif Detective Al Hearn, he was most likely hitchhiking to visit his mother in Beaumont or towards the Los Angeles Beach area. Moore was last spotted wearing a vinyl bomber jacket with a fur collar, Denim pants, blue deck shoes, and gold-rimmed glasses. However, he had a habit of carrying those in his hand.

The distressing events surrounding James was harrowing. James was initially reported missing but was eventually found after a few days; however, despite a written confession, the absence of DNA evidence led to Bonin not being charged with his murder. The question that lingers is: Where is justice for this young man? [73]

Despite the challenges, the pursuit of justice remains unwavering, fuelled by the determination to bring closure to families like young Sean's and hold perpetrators accountable for their actions.

73 M, A. (2024). Interview [Interview].

Victim 10 Ronald Craig Gatlin

*Image SEQ Image * ARABIC33 (Ronald Craig Gatlin (1961-1980) - Find a Grave. . ., 1961)*

Cub Scouts of Pack 156 Get Awards

VAN NUYS — Cub Scout Pack 156, sponsored by the Van Nuys Optimists, held its November meeting at the Van Nuys Optimist Youth Center.

The meeting opened with the Flag ceremony led by Webelos Den 1.

New boys inducted into the pack and who received Bobcat pins were Adam DeFrance, Doug Eltringham, Mark Heffern, Dion Tretta, and Fred Tretta.

Receive Colors

Newly formed Den 2 will be led by Trudy Tretta, den coach and Katherine Schulenburg, assistant.

New Webelos receiving Webelos colors and cards were Ronald Gatlin, Richard Marker, and Fred Tretta.

Graduating from the pack was Jim Moutes. Jim won the Arrow of Light award. He also was given a trophy and certificate of graduation. Mrs. Moutes received the Arrow of Light mother's pin and her husband was presented a certificate of appreciation.

Awards were won by the following boys:

Den 4 — Richard Marker, Bear Badge.

Webelos Den 1 — Jim Moutes, three-year pin, three-year perfect attendance pin.

Webelos Den 2 — David Curtis, Geologist Badge, assistant denner; Richard Flores, Forester Badge, Geologist Badge, and Traveler Badge.

Games were led by Den 4.

Ronald Craig "Bubba" Gatlin's life journey began on August 3, 1961, in Los Angeles County, California. He was the beloved son of Lonnie Gatlin (1935-2005) and Patricia Manly (1940-2010) and a brother to Dana and Lonnie.

His life, though brief, was filled with the familial bonds that connected him deeply to his parents and siblings.

Ronald had a lot of promise; he was also a member of the Cub Scouts Pack 156 in 1971 and received his Webelos colours in November of that year.

Ronald was employed at his father's photography business on the bustling Santa Monica Boulevard.

But tragically, Ronald's life came to an untimely end on March 15, 1980, at the early age of 18, in Duarte, Los Angeles County, California. His memory and spirit are honoured and preserved at his final resting place in Forest Lawn Memorial Park, Glendale, Los Angeles County, California.

On March 14, 1980, Ronald Gatlin, an 18-year-old, was abducted by Bonin in Van Nuys around 8:30 p.m. Ronald had earlier dropped his father off at a restaurant and was on his way to a friend's house. Tragically, he was abducted after leaving his friend's house in North Hollywood. The following day, Ronald's nude body was discovered in Duart near the juncture of the 210 and 605 freeways. He had been sodomised and strangled with a ligature and lacerations to the neck and right ear made by being tortured with an ice pick. His hands and feet had been bound.

On that night in March 1980, William Bonin had set out along Van Nuys Boulevard. Steering northward from the Ventura Freeway, the boulevard was alive with activity. Near Victory Boulevard, Bonin noticed a young hitchhiker, eighteen-year-old Ronald Gatlin.

Ronald Gatlin stood by the roadside, his thumb jutting out in the universal sign for a lift. Bonin, drawn to the lone figure, eased his vehicle to a stop beside him. "Heading home?" Bonin queried. "Yeah," Gatlin confirmed, his home merely two miles away on Saticoy Street, where he resided with his family.

Gatlin's evening attire was casual yet distinctive: tan corduroys paired with a two-toned shirt, all set off by a vivid yellow ski jacket with striking orange accents.

Guided by Gatlin's decision to end his Friday night early, Bonin pressed for an explanation. Gatlin's response was reminiscent of the boredom of youth: "There's nothing else going on. "Seizing the moment, Bonin offered an alternative, "How about a spin around town? I can drop you off later." The night was young, and the road open before them. Gatlin responds with a simple "Okay."

Bonin's mind begins to wander, contemplating what lies ahead.

Having recently spent six weeks in prison, he has been plotting and waiting for the next opportunity to claim a victim.

The Conversation Takes a Disturbing Turn: Bonin's intentions become more evident as they drive around.
He asks Gatlin, "I'm horny. How about you?"
Gatlin's response is straightforward: "No, not really."
Bonin continues, "Are you into the gay scene?"
Gatlin's reply is equally direct: "No, that's not my thing."
This seemingly mundane exchange conceals the sinister reality of what was about to unfold. Bonin then asks Gatlin. Let me screw you, and I'll give you $50. No, I don't particularly appreciate getting screwed. I'll provide you with fellatio. Bonin agrees, and Gatlin gets in the back of the van. Bonin tells him to take his clothes off while he finds a place to park. Gatlin got into the back and disrobed while Bonin parked. "He was consumed by a restless yearning, an insatiable hunger for something more than an oral copulation it gnawed at him relentlessly; mere contentment was a foreign concept, forever out of reach."; Bonin wanted more. "With a swift, practised motion that betrayed his sinister intent, he unsheathed his knife, its blade glinting ominously in the flickering light and pushing the sharp edge against Gatlin's throat, telling him to lie flat on his stomach. With the knife clenched between his teeth, Bonin approached Ronald Gatlin. He was systematically tying Gatlin's limbs, securing his hands and feet.
The ominous purpose behind these actions was clear. Releasing Bonin's pent-up anger, he sodomised the young boy.

Bonin informed the boy that he had now been kidnapped, and he planned to sell him to a brothel for gay people.
Ronald Gatlin, bound and helpless, with his head, rested on the engine cover between the front seats of the van. This position allowed William Bonin to maintain constant surveillance over him. Bonin, the predator, spoke to Gatlin.
He offered a chilling deal: "I'll give you a chance to escape if I find someone I like better." Gatlin, trapped and terrified, listened intently.
Bonin instructed Gatlin on how to survive within the confines of the van.
If anyone else entered the vehicle, Gatlin was to pretend to be asleep.
It was a grim pact, a desperate attempt to survive in the presence of a remorseless killer. Bonin had fantasised about doing a double murder, and this seemed like the perfect time. Fuelled by his dark desires,
Around 1:00 a.m., Bonin was still cruising through the valley when
his eyes fell upon two young boys who appeared to be around 14 years old. Bonin pulled over, stopping the van beside them.
Bonin started the Conversation: "Hi, you two. Do you wanna earn 50 bucks?" The teenagers, likely unaware of the danger, asked, "What do we have to do?"

I want to give you a blowjob, Bonin replied, worried that Gatlin would say something from the back of the van.
Gatlin was so terrified of Bonin that he kept quiet. One of the boys agreed to Bonin's offer.
However, the other boy hesitated, having now seen the true nature of the man before them. Bonin couldn't afford to take just one of them.
He made it clear: "It's both or none."
William Bonin emphasised that many others would be willing to accept the money.
His offer hung in the air, a dark bargain with life-altering consequences. The two boys were allowed to go on their way. As Bonin continued his sinister journey, he noticed a California Highway Patrol cruiser passing. His heart raced as the patrol car slowed down, scrutinising the scene.
Miraculously, the cruiser kept going, and Bonin exhaled a sigh of relief.
The night was growing late, and Bonin knew he needed to act on Ronald Gatlin. The van held secrets, and the darkness concealed unspeakable horrors.
Still, in a highly agitated state, William Bonin drove to an isolated area. He parked the van, the engine's hum fading into the night.
Without saying a word, Bonin got into the back, where Ronald Gatlin awaited. The van's interior became a chamber of dread.

Gatlin, bound and terrified, could only imagine the horrors that awaited him. This moment began a nightmare from which there would be no escape., and without saying a word, he strangled Ronald Gatlin, ignoring his cries for mercy.

Victim 11 Frank Dennis Fox

*Image SEQ Image * ARABIC34 Dennis Fox (Dark Reality 2022)*

Frank Dennis Fox was born on June 3, 1962, in Los Angeles County, California. Unfortunately, he passed away at the youthful age of 17 on November 30, 1979, in Orange County, California, USA. He was laid to rest at El Toro Memorial Park in Lake Forest, Orange County, California, USA. Frank's family includes his mother, Geraldine, (1938-) his father, Frank, (1931- 1977) and his siblings, Julia (1958-2004) and Michael (1965- 2014). May his memory be honoured and cherished. [74] "Having the same birthday as one of my own sons, I will always remember Young Frank fondly." As his sister Julia who passed away on my birthday. While I never met them, they are always in my thoughts.

In first grade, young Frank showed a mischievous streak. He managed to sneak into the school's bell tower, where he boldly rang the bell. His escapade didn't go unnoticed, and he was promptly asked to leave. But Frank's daring spirit didn't stop there. At 15, he stowed away on a flight bound for San Francisco, seeking adventure beyond the confines of his everyday life.

Charming Conversationalist: Frank's mother fondly recalls her son as a gifted conversationalist. Armed with the cutest dimples, he could talk his way out of any situation. Whether it was a friendly chat or a tricky predicament, Frank's silver tongue and warm demeanour made him memorable to all who crossed his path.

74 Ancestry.com. California Birth Index, 1905-1995 [database online]. Provo, UT, USA: Ancestry.com Operations Inc, 2005.

The Name "Fox": To avoid confusion with his father (who also bore the name Frank), young Frank adopted the moniker "Fox." It became his distinctive identity, reflecting his independence and the bond he shared with his family. Fox's life was a blend of audacity, charm, and familial ties—a story etched in the memories of those who knew him.

Fox, a young soul with a tragic and mysterious tale, was not reported missing until he failed to attend a Thanksgiving dinner. His family, unaware of his fate, remained in the dark until the Orange County coroner's office finally identified his lifeless body. However, the grim revelation didn't occur until July 1980—months after his passing. The delay in identification added to the sorrow that enveloped Fox's loved ones.

The circumstances surrounding Fox's death were heart-wrenching. Just two years prior, tragedy had struck the family when Fox's father, a hardworking truck driver, met a gruesome end. Crushed to death by his truck against a loading dock, he left a void that would never be filled. And as if fate had a cruel sense of timing, the following year saw the passing of Fox's grandfather Millard.

In the wake of these losses, Fox's absence became a haunting echo—a young life cut short, a family forever marked by grief. 75

75Collins, Jeff. The Orange County Register.

Fox was extremely bright and with income he received from his fathers on the job death, he moved into his own apartment, his brother Michael remembers he always seemed to get good grades even though he was always on the go and never studied, he breezed through school with lousy behaviour and great grades.

Geraldine's last conversation with her son is still etched in her memory. It was a belated birthday call, but the timing didn't matter. She had recently spent time with him, handing over a few cherished items for his new apartment. In that fleeting exchange, love and connection transcended calendars and distances. 76 Fox, a self-reliant 17-year-old living in Long Beach, navigated life without a car. His preferred modes of transportation included the bus or occasional rides from his mother to attend classes at Long Beach City College on the Pacific Coast Highway campus. His independence was evident as he maintained his own apartment.

Fox was a responsible young man who always carried essential items in his wallet: his California ID, some money, and cherished pictures. However, his independence had a risky aspect—he occasionally hitchhiked around Long Beach.

Tragically, just over a week after the murder of John Doe, the notorious killer Bonin harboured a sinister desire for yet another victim. The shadows of danger loomed, and justice remained elusive for those caught in the web of violence.

76 Terrance W. McGarry. "Grieving Parents Want Killers Behind Bars." Beaver County Times (Online), September 21, 1980, 10. https://news.google.com/newspapers?id=4G0uAAAAIBAJ&pg=1345,4107664&dq.

"For the third time, Bonin ventured into the night solo, his predatory instincts leading him once more to the shadowy corridors of Long Beach. There, he roamed with a hunter's silent grace, eyes scanning for the vulnerable and the lost. There, he met Fox, a figure whose very essence seemed woven from the fabric of the streets' nocturnal "Bonin broke the silence, his voice slicing through the underbelly's murmur, 'How's it going?' Fox's reply came like a sigh lost in the wind, 'Not so good.' The following question carried the weight of an unspoken threat, 'Where are you headed?' Fox's answer was a whisper, a single word laden with resignation, 'Home.'"
Bonin probed further: "Are you into the gay scene?"
Fox's response was equally straightforward: "Yes." William Bonin asked Fox if he was interested in getting intimate. Fox replied, "Yes, for a price. I have rent to pay." William Bonin offered Fox 20 bucks and expressed his desire to fuck him.
Fox, aware of the transactional nature of the interaction, countered with a demand: 30 bucks. The deal was struck, and Bonin agreed.
Bonin and Fox found themselves in the dimly lit back of a van. The air was tense, and the engine's low hum amplified their unease.

The van's interior was cramped, and the upholstery was worn from Bonin's extracurricular activities. Fox's eyes darted around, assessing the situation.

Bonin had a release of pent-up desire in a raw, primal act. Then Bonin took out his knife…

The atmosphere shifted abruptly. Bonin's movements were deliberate, but his intentions were unclear. The glint of steel caught Fox's eye.

"Put your hands behind your back."

The command hung heavy in the air. Fox's mind raced. Was this a robbery? A betrayal? Fear clawed at his chest. "What's this?"

Fox's voice trembled. "I don't have no $30; I don't even have 5…"

Bonin's words were matter of fact, devoid of remorse. Money—such a mundane concern amidst the tension.

"So, I'm going to tie you up and put you out."

The threat hung like a guillotine blade. Fox's mind raced. What did "put you out" mean? Was it a euphemism for something darker?

Fox pleaded with him to let him go. He had no reason to do that; he could release him and walk away. Bonin glared at him and said, "Look, surrender your hands behind your back, and there will be no trouble. Either do it, or I will stop wasting my time and stab you." Fox put his hands behind his back, and Bonin bound him tightly with a thin cord.

Bonin took off his shoes and socks and secured his legs. "Since you chose not to follow my instructions initially, I'll be leaving you at a distant location from this spot." Bonin said coldly. Fox begged him, "Come on, man. I did what you wanted me to do". Bonin punched him repeatedly and then squeezed his testicles, making Fox scream. Bonin slapped him hard and said, "I told you, don't say one word unless I ask you a question. If you do, I will stop and really make you suffer. Do you understand?" Fox nodded silently, fearing for his life.

In the dead of night, the only sound was the engine's roar as Bonin's car tore down the 91 East freeway. His sharp and calculating eyes scanned the desolate landscape for the perfect hideaway. The headlights cut through the darkness, revealing a narrow frontage road that snaked away from the main thoroughfare. With a swift turn of the wheel, he veered off the freeway, gravel crunching under the tyres as he stopped.

He parked the car right on the road, the beams of the headlights illuminating a small clearing ahead. The night was still, the air thick with tension. Bonin stepped out of the driver's seat and went to the back, where Fox sat, unaware of the fate that awaited him. The door opened with a creak, and Bonin climbed in beside him.

Bonin's fists flew without a word, connecting with Fox's face with brutal force. Each strike was a thunderclap in the silence, and each groan from Fox was a chilling echo in the night. The assault was relentless, a dance of shadows and pain playing out in the confines of the car.

Bonin told Fox he was going to strangle him until he was unconscious. Fox had no chance of talking him out of it. If he tried, Bonin said he would just kill him instead. Bonin convinced him it was easier to let himself go, not that he had any choice. If he fought against him, Bonin said he might accidentally kill him.

After Bonin strangled him to death, he untied his limbs and removed the rest of his clothing. Scanning the surroundings to make sure it was safe to dump his body. However, he spotted a car approaching behind him, so he had to abort his plan. He thought he had chosen this spot carefully before he killed Fox, but now Bonin had to find another dumping ground. Bonin got back in the driver's seat and started the van. He drove until he reached a junction where he could make a U-turn. A median strip separated the lanes right after he turned and headed back toward the freeway. As Bonin glanced in the rearview mirror, he noticed a vehicle approaching rapidly; it turned out to be a patrol car. The officer reduced his speed, but unfortunately, Bonin was not pulled over; he barely escaped potential trouble. Bonin resumed his journey on the 91 West and continued until he took the exit for the 55 South; he then switched to the I-5 South, left at Ortega highway, drove until he reached the wilderness park, and located a spot to dispose of Fox's lifeless body.

Bonin did not turn off the van or the lights. Instead, he pretended to be having mechanical problems. He stayed alert for passing cars, and only when he was sure there was no sound around him did he leave the van. He dragged Fox from the back of the van and dumped him on the spot.

Fox's naked corpse was discovered in the early evening of Sunday, December 2. A criminalist collected penal swabs and a ball of fibres from Fox's penis; his body had been found at the bottom of an embankment, lying on his right side. It looked like he had been rolled down the hill, stopping at a metal post. The body had ligature marks on his wrist, ankles and neck, and he had been there for a few days before being discovered; no clothes or ID was located near the body, a sample of saliva was taken from his left nipple as well as on his penis, with abrasions to his scrotum, cause of death was strangulation.

Ten days later, Bonin decided he needed to rape and murder another young man, So Bonin drove to Long Beach.

Victim 12 John Frederick Kilpatrick

On February 24, 1964, John Fredrick Kilpatrick was born in Los Angeles County, California. He passed away at age 15 on December 12, 1979, in San Bernardino, San Bernardino County, California, USA. They rested him at Rose Hills Memorial Park in Whittier, Los Angeles County, California, USA. His parents were Priscilla Hill (1939-1992) and Charles Kilpatrick (1936-1996). He had six siblings:
Charles (1957-2001),

Cheryl (1958-2010),

Kimberley(1959-2016),

Michael (1961-2016),

Vera and unknown [77, 78]

John, a sophomore at Jordan High, was navigating the turbulent waters of adolescence amidst his parents' recent separation. His father had relocated to Cincinnati, leaving a rift in the family tapestry. During their last conversation, John's mother, Priscilla Kilpatrick, harboured deep-seated guilt. She had reprimanded him for his truancy and dalliance with marijuana. Yet, their exchange hadn't escalated into an argument; John had acquiesced with a subdued "Alright, Mum." He then slipped into his sandals, donned a pair of azure nylon shorts, and, with his skateboard underfoot, set off to meet his friends, leaving his troubles behind,

77 Ancestry.com. California Birth Index, 1905-1995 [database online]. Provo, UT, USA: Ancestry.com Operations Inc, 2005. 78 https://www.findagrave.com/memorial/199908077/john-fredrick-kilpatrick 79 McGarry, Terrance W. "Grieving Parents Want Killers Behind Bars." Beaver County Times (Online), 21 September 1980, 10.

if only for a moment. 79

On the 10th of December, a chill of foreboding settled over the Kilpatrick household as night fell, and John remained conspicuously absent. The days placed echoes of a presence that had vanished too soon. The stark reality set in: John never returned home. In February, he became an official missing person's case.

Whispers of sightings at Lakewood Centre Mall, a stone's throw from his home, had given fleeting hope, but they were misplaced echoes of a presence that had vanished too soon. The stark reality set in: John never returned home.

*Image SEQ Image * ARABIC36 (John Fredrick Kilpatrick (1964-1979) - Find A..., 1964)*

Jim Bitz, John's steadfast companion through countless games of pool, endless skateboard rides, and sun-soaked days at the beach, maintained a calm demeanour amidst John's prolonged absence. "It wasn't like him to vanish, but he had big dreams," Jim reflected. "He spoke often of making his fortune, so I figured he'd embarked on that quest." Meanwhile, Priscilla's concern deepened with each passing day. In March, her vigil by the television was interrupted by a report of an unidentified young man with blond hair. Her heart skipped a beat—could it be John? But the authorities confirmed that the John Doe on the screen bore no resemblance to her son, dashing her hopes as quickly as they had risen. 80 Mrs. Kilpatrick clung to a fragile thread of hope when the phone rang, its shrill tone slicing through the silence of her home. The voice on the other end spoke of unpaid rent—John's lingering financial obligations. Perhaps he was still out there, navigating life's twists and turns, albeit in a shadowed existence. But then, like a cruel echo, another call followed—a reminder of his impending first day at a new job. The juxtaposition of mundane responsibilities against uncertainty gnawed at her heart. Was John merely evading his duties, or had fate woven a darker tapestry? 81 The memory of the phone call was imprinted into Priscilla Kilpatrick's mind—a friend of John's, voice heavy with concern, suggesting a harrowing possibility: John might be among the victims of the notorious 'Freeway Killer.' The details of an unidentified victim shared by the authorities struck a chilling chord: a tattoo of a skull wearing a hat on the right bicep and the letter 'F' inked on the left hand. A visceral certainty washed over Priscilla; these were the indelible marks her other son had etched onto John's skin.

80UPI. "Mother Identifies Son "Freeway Killer "Victim." The Bryan Times (Online), 6 August 1980, 2. 81 UPI. (1980, 6 Aug). Mother Learns of Son's Death. The Chico Enterprise.

John's disappearance had initially sparked little concern; his penchant for impromptu escapades was well-known. Sandals were on his feet, blue nylon shorts fluttered in the breeze, and he had a habit of slipping away, his whereabouts often a mystery. Friends and family thought they glimpsed him around town, his absence a whisper rather than a scream. But as winter gave way to February's chill and a police bulletin spoke of an unidentified boy's funeral, Priscilla's heart sank. The pieces of a grim puzzle began to align, and she reached out to the authorities, a mother's intuition igniting a flicker of dread in the search for her missing son. The details matched John, including tattoos between his thumb, forefinger, and right bicep. Priscilla provided other identifiers not disclosed to the public: a chipped tooth, a nearly severed thumbnail, and a pierced ear, confirming it was indeed John. The police had publicised their intention to conduct a pauper's burial for the unidentified boy, hoping to pique the curiosity of the perpetrator, who might risk attending the funeral. 82. 83 As the sombre procession of the unidentified boy's funeral moved forward, law enforcement found themselves at a critical juncture.Vera is John's youngest sister, and she was only twelve when he disappeared; her memories are different, she remembers their mum giving John a haircut, and that day it was cut a little shorter then he liked, but John being the sweet kid he was,

82 UPI, L. B. (1980, 6 Aug). 'Freeway Killer' Victim. Desert Dispatch. 83 UPI. (1980, 6 Aug). Mother Learns Teenage Son Victim of 'Freeway Killer'—the Napa Valley Register.

never caused a scene, he never back chatted his mother, making him the favourite of them all. Vera remembered that that day, he was upset about his haircut, but instead of getting upset at his mum, he walked outside and slugged the wall. It just wasn't in his nature to argue with his mother. Vera mentions that he was a popular surfer and skateboarder, and all the girls loved him; she mentions that she was so sure that her friends only came over because they had a crush on John. John was a very handsome young man, yet he was humble and never conceited.
The fact that John's case was never officially closed broke Priscilla's heart, and Bonin was not convicted, which made the tragedy even harder to bare. Priscilla was never the same.

Their suspect, though in custody, remained shrouded in anonymity. The absence of a name gnawed at their investigation, urging them to seek confirmation. And so, with a delicate balance of duty and compassion, they went ahead. Priscilla Kilpatrick, her heart a mosaic of hope and dread, stood at the epicentre of this unfolding tragedy. Her son, John, had left an indelible mark on the world—a juvenile arrest history that now held the key to unlocking the boy's identity. John's unique patterns lay preserved within the labyrinthine archives of fingerprints, a testament to his past encounters with the law.

The authorities engaged Priscilla, their words gentle yet laden with urgency. They needed her consent and willingness to traverse the painful terrain of memory. And there, in the quiet of shared grief, they matched the prints—the living echoes of her son's touch—to those of the deceased. The lines intersected, converging in a solemn affirmation: John Kilpatrick, once vibrant and elusive, was forever etched into this tragic tale's fabric. The funeral became more than a farewell; it was a bridge between the known and the unknown. It was a final act of recognition that solidified the boy's place in history. [84, 85]

Bonin's eyes swept across the familiar streets of Long Beach, a city that held both secrets and shadows.

Beach Boulevard stretched before him, its asphalt veins weaving tales of desperation and desire. As he neared the bus depot, his senses sharpened—an instinct honed by countless encounters with vulnerability.

And there, bathed in the harsh fluorescent glow, stood a figure that would etch itself into the annals of infamy. A youthful blonde, barely out of adolescence, cradled a phone to his ear. Seventeen, perhaps—innocence and recklessness entwined. Bonin's pulse quickened; he had an eye for potential, a radar attuned to the vulnerable.

Circling the terminal like a vulture, he positioned himself strategically. The phone booth became his stage,

84 Dilbeck, S. R. (1980, 5 Aug). Rialto Body named; knew 'Freeway Killer Suspect'—the San Bernardino County Sun. (Some articles mentioned in the above-printed newspaper article regarding Kilpatrick knowing Bonin were deemed untrue, and corrections and apologies were made) 85 Correction. (1980, 12 Sept). The San Bernadino Sun.

and unsuspecting John stepped into the spotlight The conversation ended—a mundane exchange, a lifeline severed. Bonin's breath hitched; he could taste the anticipation, the hunger that gnawed at his insides.

With his tousled hair and the weight of youth on his shoulders, John stepped out of the booth. Their paths converged—the predator and the prey. Bonin's gaze bore into John's cerulean eyes, mapping vulnerability, tracing the contours of fate. The boy's oblivion was a canvas; Bonin's intentions, a brush poised to paint a darker reality.

And so, as the sun dipped below the horizon, casting elongated shadows, Bonin's shadow merged with John's. The phone booth whispered secrets, and the air crackled with menace. The freeway loomed—a ribbon of asphalt, a conduit for their collision. John, unknowingly, stepped into the abyss, and Bonin followed, insatiable hunger propelling them both toward a destiny etched in blood and bone.

John, a mere 15 years old but with the bravado of someone older, weaved through the traffic and set his course northward along Long Beach Boulevard. His youthful determination was palpable, each step a testament to the resilience of adolescence. Bonin shadowed him discreetly with a predator's patience, biding his time before moving.

Their conversation began casually enough, with John asserting an age of 18, a small defiance against the reality of his youth. Bonin, seizing the opportunity, extended an offer of

$20—a lure for the unsuspecting teen to guide him through the sprawling cityscape of Los Angeles. It was a simple proposition, yet it marked the threshold of a perilous journey, the start of an encounter that would echo through time. John's resolve remained unshaken despite the ominous shadows that clung to the death van. He stepped into its cavernous interior, a dance with destiny that defied reason. The air was thick with foreboding, yet hesitation eluded him. Perhaps it was the allure of adventure, the reckless curiosity that whispered, "What if?"

Bonin, too, hesitated—a rare flicker of conscience in the abyss of his depravity. The young blonde man seated across from him bore the hallmarks of vulnerability—the essence that fuelled Bonin's twisted desires. The van's walls seemed to close in, confining them to a macabre tableau. John's innocence was palpable, a canvas waiting for Bonin's brush strokes.

But then, in the dim light, Bonin glimpsed more than prey. John's features stirred something more profound—an echo of longing, a forbidden yearning. The contours of his face, the way his eyes held secrets—Bonin's mind wove fantasies of a different kind. A relationship not of blood and brutality but of shared nights and whispered confessions.

The van hurtled forward, its wheels spinning fate. Bonin grappled with conflicting impulses—the hunter and the haunted. John's proximity ignited a fire that transcended violence: a hunger for connection, a twisted romance born in the crucible of chaos. The blade at Bonin's side weighed heavy, its purpose blurred by desire.

And so, as the road stretched ahead, Bonin wrestled with his demons. The death van carried them both—two souls entangled in a dance of doom. Oblivious to the abyss yawning beneath him, John remained Bonin's enigma. Would he be a victim or a lover? But when Bonin's hands wandered to the forbidden zone, John protested as Bonin kept trying to insert his finger in John's rectum while receiving fellatio. In the throes of fear and defiance, John's voice echoed through the silence of the van."I don't get fucked," he exclaimed, his words a beacon of his will to survive. "I don't know what you're planning, but I want no part of it." His protest was a testament to his spirit, and that was all it took to trigger Bonin. Bonin's resolve solidified. The last vestiges of hesitation swept away like dust on a forgotten road. John's protest, though spirited, was a mere ripple in the current of Bonin's malevolence. The van's interior became a stage, so Bonin asked him about performing simultaneous fellatio, which John agreed to, and he calmed down; that's when Bonin made his signature move and told John he needed to get tissues and retrieved his knife and string. Bonin put the knife to Kilpatrick's throat and told him to roll over. The shocked and frightened John obeyed Bonin's wishes; after getting his hands tied behind his back, Bonin snarled, "You don't get fucked, huh well fuck you, buddy", and Bonin proceeded to sodomise John violently. However, this time, Bonin did not reach a climax. With the stealth of a practised predator, Bonin ignited the van's engine and set course for his mother's abode. The vehicle, a silent accomplice, provided cover as he guided John through the shadows, their movements a ghostly ballet, ensuring their presence stayed a secret to the world.

Once within the sanctuary of the house, the walls became silent witnesses to a chilling confession. John, his voice trembling with the vulnerability of youth, revealed his actual age—fifteen—a desperate plea cast into the void, a hope that honesty might grant him mercy. Yet, this truth, stark and raw, failed to sway Bonin.

Bonin squeezed the young boy's testicles to make him scream and told him he'd never make it to 16 if he didn't do what he was told precisely. John felt a glimmer of hope, but fear had filled the boy's mind, something Bonin had enjoyed instilling in his victims. Bonin went to the kitchen, got some more rope, and whipped John with it until he cried. Then he wrapped it around the boy's neck and strangled him to death. Bonin placed the dead boy in the van and drove 55 miles Northeast of Rialto next to Interstate 15 in San Bernardino County. Bonin dumped his body near Rialto airport in the Bush.

Victim 13 Charles Dempster Miranda

*Image SEQ Image * ARABIC37 Charles Miranda (Miranda, H. 2024. Interview)*

Charles entered the world on April 9, 1964, Under the bright skies of Los Angeles, California. His journey, though brief, left indelible marks on the hearts of those he touched. Tragically, His vibrant life was cut short on February 3, 1980, just as he was blossoming into his 15th year in the very city that witnessed his first breath.

Charles was bounded by the tranquil beauty of Santa Ana, Orange County, where memories of his spirit continue to resonate. 86

Charles was the beloved beacon of the Arneson-Miranda household, the cherished son of Mary Ann Arenson (1944-2022) and his devoted stepfather, Enrique Miranda (1932-2014) Though Siitia Leatutufu (1942-1968) was his biological father, he died in Vietnam. Enrique took on the fatherly role and nurtured him and the other children with unwavering love and guidance.

Charles' laughter and dreams were shared with his five siblings—Henry (1965-), Jessica (1967-2020), Angie, Cynthia, and Richard (1974-)—who carried a piece of his legacy. Furthermore, they possess a tapestry of familial love, rich with the threads of shared experiences and unspoken bonds.

86 Ancestry. com. California Birth Index, 1905-1995 [database online]. Provo, UT, USA: Ancestry.com Operations Inc, 2005.

*Image SEQ Image * ARABIC38 Charles and his family (Miranda, H. 2024. Interview)*

*Image SEQ Image * ARABIC39 Charles Miranda (Miranda, H. 2024. Interview)*

*Image SEQ Image * ARABIC40 Charles (Miranda, H. 2024. Interview)*

*Image SEQ Image * ARABIC41 Miranda family (Miranda, H. 2024. Interview)*

*Image SEQ Image * ARABIC42 Charles and his mother (Miranda, H. 2024. Interview)*

*Image SEQ Image * ARABIC43 Miranda family (Miranda, H. 2024. Interview)*

*Image SEQ Image * ARABIC44 Charles Miranda (Miranda, H. 2024. Interview)*

Even after over forty years, Charles' brother, Henry, vividly recalls the tragic events as if they occurred only yesterday. His friends remember Charles being at the Roxy in West Hollywood the night before he went missing. Despite his youth, he was remarkably skilled on the dance floor. Charles was typically a homebody, preferring to spend his time in-doors immersed in music. He had a passion for disco, often losing himself in the rhythms of The Bee Gees, Donna Summer, and other icons of the era, dancing alone in his bedroom.

Five months before Charles's untimely passing, Henry had moved to Fresno, CA, to live with his mother. At the same time, Charles remained in the Los Angeles area with their father, Enrique. The last memory Henry had of him is from Christmas Day, 1979, a poignant final encounter before his life was cut short.

Henry shared with me that in February 1980, his father made a concerning call to their mother. He reported that Charles had yet to return home the previous night. This was not an isolated incident; there had been instances where Charles stayed out after meeting with friends. We held onto hope that he would return later that same day. However, when Charles did not return on February 4, his father contacted the police. Given that Charles was underage, the case was brought to the Los Angeles County Sheriff's Department. The deputies thoroughly searched Charles's room and belongings contacted his acquaintances and inquired with family members to uncover his location.

Two weeks into the investigation, a pivotal lead appeared. Charles's father received a distressing call from the Los Angeles County medical examiner's office, suggesting they had an individual matching my brother's description. Bracing himself, his father went to make the identification. Meanwhile, unaware of the events, Henry's mother and he were en route to LA. It was there that his father, with a heavy heart, confirmed the unthinkable: the body was indeed Charles. Subsequent confirmation through dental records solidified this painful truth. [87]

87 Miranda, H. (2024). Interview [Interview].

During this intense period, the investigation intensified as additional sheriff's deputies descended upon our residence. They meticulously combed through his possessions and expanded their inquiries, speaking with an increasing number of individuals. The deputies also canvassed the neighbourhood, engaging with resident's door-to-door. Meanwhile, the media established a constant presence outside our homes, leading our parents to instruct us to avoid communicating with them. Our telephone rang incessantly, a relentless reminder of the ongoing situation. The media coverage was pervasive, with my brother's image broadcast across every television channel. The entire experience felt like a bizarre, almost dreamlike reality.

In the calm hours of February 3, 1980, as the first light crept across the sky, Miley and Bonin stood amidst the remnants of their morning sexual endeavour. It was then that a dark impulse stirred within Bill Bonin—the urge to kill beckoned once more. With a sinister resolve, they embarked in their van, the streets of Long Beach unfolding before them. Yet, the city did not yield what Bonin sought, prompting a detour into the glittering allure of Hollywood.

Like a scene from the films Hollywood was famed for, Charles Miranda, a youth 16, stepped into the daylight, his silhouette framed by the flickering marquee of a movie theatre. With a predator's instinct, Bonin drew near, his van idling like a beast in wait. A casual inquiry into Charles's plans revealed a day unspoken for—a blank canvas upon which Bonin could paint his dark designs. An offer of a ride was extended, its innocence a masquerade for the peril it possessed.

And so, with Charles unsuspecting, they ventured forth, the van's engine humming a foreboding tune. A few blocks distanced them from the world, and Bonin chose a secluded spot.

Bill overpowered Miranda, beat, and sodomised him. "Bonin urged Miley to participate aggressively." but Miley could not sustain an erection. Bonin told Miley the reason he could not get an erection was because he knew that this kid was going to die. So, instead, Miley sodomised him with a blunt object. After Miley swiped six dollars from Charles, the two men proceeded to bind his feet and hands together. Bonin acted with a cold and calculated precision. He stuffed a piece of cloth into Charles's mouth, silencing any hope of a cry for help. With a methodical grimness, he wrapped his shirt tightly around Charles's neck. Grasping a jack handle, Bill Bonin twisted the fabric with relentless force, each turn constricting like the coils of a serpent. The life within Charles was extinguished, leaving behind a haunting silence where once there was despair. The autopsy revealed that a blunt object had been inserted into Charles' anus. Bonin and Miley executed their grim task with a chilling detachment in the shadowed confines of a downtown

Los Angeles alley. They discarded Charles's lifeless form, stripped of dignity as well as attire, an act as callous as it was final. With the deed done, they departed, the van's engine a low growl in the night. Their dark odyssey continued the streets of Huntington Beach next to bear witness to their hunt for the unsuspecting.

In February 1980, Gregory Miley, then 15, stood on the cusp of a family move to Texas when an unexpected visitor arrived. Bill Bonin appeared at the Miley residence amidst a party celebrating the sale of their home. As the clock neared midnight, he rapped on the door, and Miley's younger sister greeted him. Curiosity piqued, Miley's brother joined Bonin at the doorway, peppering Bonin with questions.

The family's disapproval hung in the air, a thick cloud of concern for Miley's association with a man 15 years his senior. Despite this, Miley's brother handed him money for cigarettes, a gesture of brotherly care. Miley and Bonin then drove off to Fraser's car park, seeking a private moment away from prying eyes. There, in the confines of the van, they engaged in a fleeting encounter that lacked connection, prompting a visit to the liquor store before returning home.

Miley lingered only briefly at the house before rejoining Bonin outside. Their conversation meandered until Bonin posed a question, dark and probing: "Have you ever killed anybody?" The question hung between them, ominous and heavy. "Do you want to kill somebody?" he pressed further. Miley, taken aback by the gravity of the inquiry, could only muster an uncertain "I don't know, maybe."

Then, Miley's brother emerged, reminding him of the world beyond Bonin's influence. From the window, Miley's mother's silhouette was a silent plea, her gestures a wordless beckoning to the safety of home.

Miley urged Bonin to take the wheel, to lose themselves in the night's embrace. As the city lights blurred past, he posed a question laced with dark intent. 'What if,' he mused, 'we were cruising and spotted a hot chick thumbing a ride? Imagine we picked her up, and she resisted our advances—what then? What if we took what we wanted regardless of her will?' His words hung heavy in the air, a sinister proposition veiled as a hypothetical. Miley hesitated, the weight of the implication settling in my chest. 'Well…' he began, but the sentence withered on his lips, the gravity of the scenario rendering him speechless." Then, echoing the darkness in Bonin's tone, Miley said what Bonin seemed to want to hear. 'That would be crossing a line, but then again, she decided to get in the car with us,' Miley mused, his words reflecting the twisted logic he espoused. 'The real problem arises afterwards,' Bonin added, his voice a low growl. 'If we let her go, she'd run straight to the authorities, and we'd be behind bars before sunrise.

So, what should we do?" We would have to kill her, Miley said," so she couldn't tell the authorities. "You can handle that," Bonin asked. "Yeah, said Miley. Guess I could" "Miley boasted of feeling exhilarated that evening, though his confidence was merely a facade. Consequently, they set out for Long Beach in search of company. After a fruitless half-hour, they paused their search, stopping at a convenience store for chips and a drink. "It was around two in the morning when Bonin spoke, his voice tinged with a sinister calmness. 'Since you've never taken a life,' he said, 'I can drive you home. You can erase this night from your memory.'" Miley said, "fuck no" Now Miley was into this. He felt good. Bonin asked Miley if he had ever been to Hollywood, and when he said no, they decided to head up there. They started cruising the streets at three in the morning, observing the myriad of people milling about.

Charles Miranda was immersed in the energy of the evening with his companions at the Starwood Disco, located at the bustling intersection of Santa Monica and North Crescent Heights near La Cienega Blvd. Charles, a resident of Bell Gardens, spent his days working at a nearby doughnut shop, and he had just cashed his pay check. His family bid him farewell as he revelled in the night's festivities.

That evening, his friend Kathy spotted Charles at the club before she left at around 2:00 AM. Later, at approximately 2:30 AM, Charles unexpectedly arrived at her apartment, waking Kathy and her friends from their sleep. He urgently requested a ride home, but unfortunately, they were without a vehicle. Kathy empathetically suggested that he call his father for assistance. Disappointingly, Charles left without making the call.

After resolving to make his way back, Charles travelled to Santa Monica Blvd, just two blocks to the north, hoping to find a ride home.

Miley noticed someone afar and suggested, "How about that youngster there?" Bonin concurred promptly. He executed a quick U-turn and stealthily trailed the boy, biding his time until he was isolated. At the opportune moment, Bonin said, "Hey, where are you off to?

The boy stopped and approached the driver's window. "Home," he replied. "Want a ride?" Bonin offered. Although the kid declined firmly, Bonin persisted, using a calm and persuasive tone that had a powerful effect on people.

Then he said, "You wanna smoke a joint? The kid looked around, uninterested, so Bonin offered him 100 bucks for some head. He couldn't believe it. "You just want me to blow you for 100 bucks. Shit yeah," Bonin spun around and offered Miley a sly wink. Unaware of the impending events, Miley was left in uncertainty.

The boy prepares to clamber into the rear while Bonin takes the wheel, searching for a parking spot.

The kid comes up and sits between the seats, and starts rubbing Bonin's dick. Miley can tell Bonin is excited about the first chance Bonin got. He pulls off the street, turns off the engine, and crawls into the back of the van with the kid. Miley watched them from the front seat, and Bonin said he wanted me to stay there to be a lookout. Bonin started caressing the kid's gear, and the kid was jacking him off. Bonin asks the kid if he is gay, and he tells him he can suck his dick for 100 bucks. Then Bonin asks him if he likes to get fucked., The youth responded firm and resolute, a simple yet definitive "No." Bonin gently taps him on the head in a condescending manner. Miley said he had never done this with Bonin before, so he didn't know what would happen.

Bonin has the kid take off his clothes and tells him to lie down, then he starts jacking him off, rubbing his shaft up and down, getting him hard, but the kid wants to get the money and leave. Bonin unzipped his pants, whipped out his dick and told the punk to get busy, and "If you know what's good for you, you won't scrape your teeth on me." Bonin grabbed his head and shoved it down hard. He is gagging, but Bonin doesn't let up and keeps pushing his head down. Bonin stops and tells the kid to get on his hands and knees after Charles asks about the money again. Bonin stares at him, and he is furious. He punches him especially hard and screams at him, "Turn over and get on your knees." The kid is scared Shitless. Still, he does it.

Bonin starts penetrating him hard; Miranda is screaming because it hurts. The kid tried to turn over, so Bonin hit him again, grabbed some rope and tied his hands behind his back. It was pretty intense. The kid whined, and Bonin told him, "If you shut up and lay still, I will let you go." Bonin looked at Miley and said, "Hey man, back in Bellflower, you said you wanted to do it." Miley said, "hell yes, I want some", so he climbed into the back of the van and got on top of the kid and had a shot at fucking him. Though Miley couldn't stay erect. Bonin leaned over to Miley and said you know why the kids got to die. Bonin sucked Miley off, and then he was hard and ready to go again, so he got up and rode the kid. They were having a fun time, really partying, but the kid was attempting to turn over to get up.

Miley rolled off, and then Bonin threw the kid and started punching him, so Miley got the rope and tied his feet up. He was moving around, trying to kick us. Miley hit him as well, once on the side of his stomach, and Bonin kneed him in the balls, and he passed out. Bonin wanted Miley's shirt. He didn't know why, but he took his shirt and started strangling the kid, which kind of shocked Miley for a few seconds. Bonin twisted the shirt shit with all his strength. The kid was turning blue, and then he jerked him up and twisted harder. Bonin told Miley to hold it and to give him the iron bar. He removes the shirt, flips him over and presses the iron bar across the boy's throat. That's when Miley threw Bonin off and said hey man, let me have à go at that Miley jumped on him and pushed the tyre iron down on his throat real hard. He could hear the bones cracking, and then his neck went flat. The kid shit and puked all over the place, Man. It stunk. When Miley heard those bones cracking, he thought, yeah, okay, he's dead. After a while of driving, they came by a railway track, and there was this big dumpster with a forklift on the side. Bonin grabbed his legs, and Miley grabbed his head, and they dumped him in naked. They tossed a few clothes here and there and decided to split the money.

Victim 14 Michael Francis McDonald

Michael Francis McDonald, a bright and beloved young man, was born on March 31, 1963, in San Gabriel, Los Angeles County, California. A turbulent and harsh existence marked his journey through life. Michael, the son of Thomas Joseph Jr (1922-1983) and Meridyth Lou Armitage (1932-1977). He shared his childhood with his siblings, Shelley Ann (1953-2008) and William Bruce (1960-1992), trying to create memories that would last a lifetime. Michael, a student at Henry High School in Rialto, would have had a long academic journey filled with learning and growth if he had received the help he needed.

According to his niece, who was three at the time of his death, although she does not remember much, she did have her mother's Diaries.

Samantha does not have vivid memories of her Uncle Michael, who tragically passed away at a young age. But she knows his life was marked by sorrow and hardship, leaving a significant impact on the family. Sam's mother, Shelley, shared her childhood with an older sister and a younger brother, both of whom experienced the weight of loss alongside her. Their grandmother also passed away when she was relatively young, which added to the family's sense of grief. It appears that many individuals on that side of the family faced premature deaths, struggling with a pattern of loss that seems to have affected them for generations.

Sam recalls her mom sharing that Michael was shy, quiet, and sweet. Despite his gentle nature, he faced the challenging reality of living with schizophrenia. Individuals with schizophrenia often encounter stigma and misunderstandings. While support from family and friends is crucial, in the 1980s, there was little assistance available for those with schizophrenia and even less support for their families.

Sam still carries the memory of her grandmother, who tragically lost her life to alcohol poisoning when she was just three years old. This profound loss has shaped her understanding of life and the fragility of our existence.

Sam mentioned that after her grandmother's death, Michael came to live with them. However, it became too difficult for Shelley to care for two young children and her brother, with schizophrenia. She was worried that he might hurt them, so she had to ask him to leave at a young age.

William Bonin picked him up when he was hitchhiking, and that moment changed everything. Shelley rarely spoke about his death, perhaps because it was such a painful topic, but she poured her feelings into her diaries. Unfortunately, most of those diaries were burned by my stepdad's father, who went to great lengths to conceal what he had done to her over the years. Thankfully, I still have one diary that reveals the immense guilt she carried for having to make the difficult decision to kick him out. It's heart-wrenching to think about the burden she had to carry alone.

She felt that if she hadn't kicked him out, maybe he would have lived and not died such a gruesome death.

In addition to that, her family faced many tragedies. Michael's mother struggled with alcoholism, and from what Sam learned, was that her grandfather tried to kill her grandmother once by strangling her. He was pretty abusive, so she drank herself to death.

Sam's mother, Shelley, died due to prescription abuse, not a drug overdose, and Michael's brother William also died early. He was homeless and was beaten to death.

On January 1, 1980, at the tender age of 16, Michael's life came to an unexpected end in Chino, San Bernardino County, California. His departure from this world left a void in the hearts of those who knew him. Michael's family had him cremated. His ashes were returned to the sea, symbolising his free spirit and the eternal nature of life.

Michael's legacy is not defined by the length of his time on earth but by the depth of the impressions he left on the hearts of his family and friends. [88]

On the 3rd of January 1980, Michael McDonald was found fully clothed in San Bernardino County. Michael was brutalised and strangled. His discarded body was found

88 https://www.findagrave.com/memorial/217921005/michael-francis-mcdonald 89 William Bonin | Found a Grave. https://www.foundagrave.com/grave/william-bonin/

alongside Highway 71 in San Bernardino County two days after his murder and remained unidentified until March 24. 89 On the first day of 1980, while his mother vacationed in Hawaii, William Bonin marked the new year in a manner unlike any other. Eschewing the typical resolutions, Bonin sought thrill and danger. He journeyed 50 miles east of Los Angeles, along the 10 freeway, to Chino airport near Ontario. There, Bonin encountered a 15-year-old boy named Michael walking alone. Approaching him, Bonin inquired about the freeway's location. Unaware of the impending danger, Michael innocently pointed down the road from when Bonin had arrived.

On the dawn of the 1980 New Year, William Bonin engaged in dialogue with a youth named Michael. Michael disclosed his intention to return home, and seizing the moment, Bonin proposed to give him a lift. Once inside the car, Bonin presented a tempting proposition: a $50 bill for a simple task. "Sell pot for me," Bonin proposed. Michael, perhaps enticed by the promise of easy money, agreed. The terms were straightforward: sell five ounces of marijuana at $50 a piece,keep $10 from each sale, and then call Bonin when more marijuana was desired. Okay," Michael replied, sealing a fateful agreement. Little did he know that this seemingly harmless transaction would have tragic consequences. As they approached the shadowed facade of the apartment complex, Bonin deftly diverted from the illuminated main avenue and glided the car into a secluded parking bay. The sudden deviation prompted Michael to voice his confusion, "Bonin, what's the purpose of halting here?" His tone mingled with curiosity and a tinge of apprehension. "To which Bonin replied, "I need to hand over the marijuana discreetly. As Bonin searched for a secluded spot, he suggested Michael move to the vehicle's rear to avoid being seen. Michael obliged, clambering into the backseat of Bonin's other car, the Chevrolet. Once Bonin was confident, they were unobserved, eyeballing his prey. He joined Michael in the back, ensuring their privacy.

When Michael looked away, Bonin forcefully seized his knife, yanked him onto his stomach and straddled him. Bonin assured him that causing harm was not his intention; he was merely after money. Michael's protest pierced the tense silence, his voice escalating to a frantic pitch, "I swear, I don't have a single dime on me!" Bonin, sceptical, plunged his hands into the depths of Michael's pockets, rummaging with a sense of urgency. Yet, all he encountered was the void of emptiness, not a trace of currency. Bonin told Michael to put his hands behind his back then. Bonin tied his hands up, then turned Michael over and pulled out his penis. "Since you've got no money, you're going to have to suck my dick" Michael, with a mixture of fear and resignation, acquiesced to Bonin's demands, his actions reflecting the sombre realization of his precarious situation. Still, after a few minutes, Bonin told him to stop and rolled him over onto his stomach, then yanked Michael's pants down in typical Bonin fashion; he squeezed Michael's testicles, eliciting a scream from him as he writhed in agony. Bonin vigorously sodomised him, but only for a brief time. Bonin enjoyed the power of sexual domination, with Michael crying for mercy. Despite the unfolding drama, Bonin's interest waned rapidly, his attention fleeting as the thrill of the moment dissipated into the night air. Bonin was there for the murder and not the sexual activity. Bonin then strangled Michael, observing his life leave his young body. Then, searching for a place to dump the body, unlike his other victims, Michael was dumped fully clothed.

Victim 15 James Michael Macabe

*Image SEQ Image * ARABIC46 James Macabe (James Michael Macabe (1967-1980) - Find a Grave. . ., 1967)*

James's childhood was filled with joy that only a child can experience, and his laughter echoed through the streets of Walnut, Los Angeles County. James had two older sisters Diane (1952-, and Janette (1964-1965) passed away as a baby Unfortunately, James childhood came to an untimely end on February 3, 1980.

Although his years were short, the legacy of young James would remain among the whispering palms of Melrose Abbey Memorial Park in Anaheim, where memories linger. Tales of yesteryears are etched into the very soil that cradles history. 90

Sadly, James's father also passed away only seven years later (1931-1987)

Anna Macabe, (1932 -) just before Bonin's execution, was 63 and a switchboard operator at a Laughlin, Nevada, casino; she had lost touch with the other parents whose children died at Bonin's hands. James was abducted, taking a bus to Disneyland. Mrs Macabe said at the time of the interview in 1996 that regarding Bonin's impending execution, it was the 16th anniversary of James' death and the way she marks the date every February: by working to keep her mind off the tragedy. She stated that she did not know an execution date had been set. She had told the reporter. "You know that country song about 'No future in the past'?" said Macabe, who moved from Orange County and now lives in Bullhead City, Arizona. "There isn't." 91

90 "Find a Grave." 2023, https://www.findagrave.com/virtual-cemetery/1485060 91 Ellingwood, Ken. "The Other Victims of William Bonin." The Times (Online), 1996.

It was February 3 when Bonin and Miley began talking to James Macabe. He was waiting for a bus to Disney Land at a Huntington Beach bus stop. Bonin said they offered James a lift to Disneyland after they all smoked some marijuana. After James was high, Bonin tied him up. Then they drove to a gas station and got some gas. While Bonin had raped and beat him, Miley went to a secluded area where Bonin beat him, strangled him with his shirt, and crushed his neck with a jack handle while Miley jumped on the young boy's chest. Once he was dead, they removed the money from James' wallet. They discarded his fully clothed body next to a garbage dumpster near Walnut Drive in front of the Pomona freeway Walnut. Bonin and Miley used James Disneyland's entry fee to buy their lunch. James was discovered on February 6th. [92]

On the fateful night of February 2, as Miley's parents revelled in their family gathering, the air was pierced by an undercurrent of sinister intent. The same dark evening witnessed Charles Miranda's tragic end. Amidst the laughter and merriment, Bonin, a figure of solitude, infiltrated the festivities with a predatory gaze. He never preferred the company of his shadow, and on this night, he sought a companion in Miley. To Miley, Bonin was more than a mere acquaintance; he was a mentor, a guardian of sorts, despite the disdain Miley's mother harboured for him. In a moment marred by naivety and misplaced trust, Miley succumbed to

92 'Freeway Killer' Terrorized Southern California During Yearlong Murder Spree | Serial Killers | Investigation Discovery. https://www.investigationdiscovery.com/crimefeed/serial-killer/freeway-killer-terrorized-southern-california-during-yearlong-murder-spree

Bonin's influence, a decision sealed by destiny, leading him down a path of irrevocable consequence.

After murdering Miranda and dumping his body, Bonin announced to Miley that he was horny and needed another one; Miley claimed he was tired and just wanted to go home. But they did go out and find another young victim; luckily for some young kid, they avoided his torture as they were not interested when Bonin approached them; at that point, Miley decided to just fall asleep in the back of the van and leave Bonin to his hunting. Miley was woken up when they arrived at Huntington Beach. Bonin excitedly yelled at him to wake up; he had seen a kid excitedly heading somewhere. Miley stated that the child was too young, but Bonin wanted him. Bonin pulled up next to the kid and asked him where he was going, and he gleefully announced he was heading to Disneyland and didn't need a lift. Macabe was catching the bus and said he didn't need a ride, but maybe he would get in for a smoke, so Bonin offered him some weed. Macabe was interested. So, Miley jumped out and opened the door so Macabe could get in. Bonin gets Miley to drive so he can get in the back with Macabe. Miley began to hear all sorts of noises, sounding like sex, but the curtain was closed. He could not see anything. Then he heard Macabe crying and saying No, but Miley kept driving. Soon, they needed to stop for fuel, and Miley knew Macabe would not make it to Disneyland. However, trying to keep the kid calm, he told him they would drop him off at Disney Land.

Bonin is now driving again and suggests they will stop soon and let him out. Bonin stops at a grocery store and parks the van. They are all in the back of the van when Bonin tells-Macabe to take off all his clothes; the kid begins to scream at Bonin you said we were going to smoke weed, and then you were dropping me at Disneyland. Bonin just smiled at him and said yes, soon. I want to hold you for a little while. Bonin then starts kissing and hugging Macabe and rubbing his penis. Miley is getting bored just watching, so he reaches over and squeezes the kid's testicles hard. Macabe screams and tries to twist away. Bonin began to laugh, and then they decided to hook him up, tying him up around the neck and bending him backwards real hard. Then, he asks Macabe what he might be worth as a ransom, but the kid is crying and doesn't answer.

Bonin announces this is a kidnapping and begins to jump on his stomach; Macabe desperately wants to escape. Bonin attempts to defeat him, and then Miley and Bonin take turns beating him.

Bonin, now really excited, wants to fuck him, he penetrates him, but Macabe is screaming. At this point, Miley claims he pulled Bonin off, telling him he is too small, The kid is a virgin, you can't do it, he is too young.

But Bonin got angry, telling Miley he was involved now and had to because if he didn't, Bonin would kill one of Miley's brothers. It was enough to scare Miley into participating; he didn't doubt that Miley would go through with his threats. They take turns sodomising the boy and having him perform fellatio on them. Macabe never stopped crying. Bonin tells him to relax. It will all be over soon. The poor kid thought he was going home. Bonin told him to get dressed. Macabe told Bonin he wouldn't tell anyone, and Bonin said yeah, I know you won't.

Bonin returned to the driver's seat, drove to the end of Pomona freeway, and pulled off at a construction site near a trash bin. He got into the back and told the kid to lie on his stomach. Miley got on his back and pinned his arms down while Bonin was kneeling near his head, putting a shirt around his neck and starting to twist as the kid tried to yell and struggle until he was still. Bonin then flips Macabe over and, with a crowbar, starts to push down on the front of his neck with strength from both hands until he hears the bones begin to crack, but this time, the force spilt his neck open; they knew he was dead. They carried him out of the van, accidentally dropping him on his head, picking him back up and tossing him in the trash bin. Bonin then pauses for a moment before telling Miley that he didn't want to kill the child, but it had to be done. They took the kid's money and tossed all his other ID out the van's window as they drove back along the freeway. Bonin dropped Miley home and told him to keep his mouth shut. Bonin went back to jail the next day for previous charges, none relating to murder. But Miley didn't know how long it would take.

James Macabe was found in the industrial area where he had been left in the area of Walnut, 30 miles away from downtown LA. James Macabe was the youngest known victim.

Photos by KEVIN P. CASEY / Los Angeles Times

Anna Macabe lost her 12-year-old son James. "You know that country song about 'No future in the past'?" says Macabe. "There isn't.'

93MacWilliams, Bryon. "Glen Norman Barker: Sandy Haired Boy Grew up without a father "The Orange County Register.

Victim 16 Glen Norman Barker

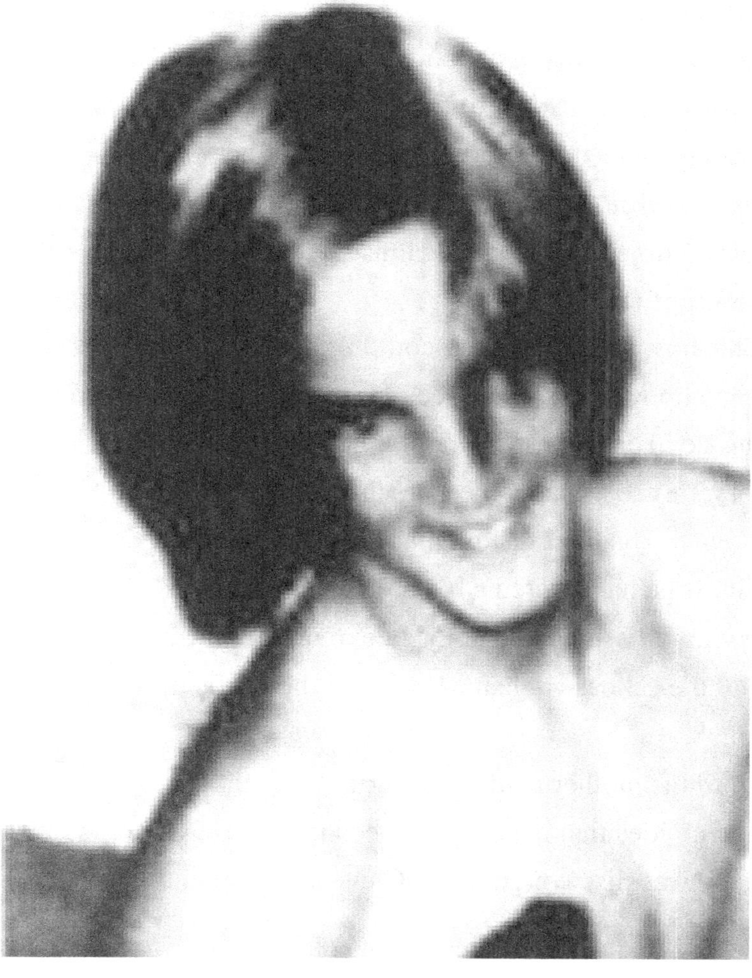

*Image SEQ Image * ARABIC47 Glen Barker (IMDb, n.d.-c)*

In the sprawling cityscape of Los Angeles County, a boy with sandy hair and a stature towering beyond his years came into the world on May 2, 1965. His loving mother, Sharon Rodgers, named him, a name that would echo through the corridors of time long after whispers of his presence faded. His father, Norman Barker (1944-2007), a shadow from a past best forgotten, he had been married at least 6 times and was a bigamist had left them to face the winds of fate alone.

This boy, whose laughter could fill the sun-drenched streets, grew up with the resilience of a young sapling reaching for the sky. His story, woven into the fabric of California's history, turned towards the stars on March 21, 1980, in Orange County. His final resting place remains a mystery; most likely, he has created a blank page in the annals of time, inviting those who hear his tale to ponder the depth of life and the echoes we leave behind in the hearts of those we touch.

Until his mother read the description in the newspaper, she had no idea that her son had been murdered. Glen's ravaged body was discovered in the Cleveland National Forest by hikers.

Sharon and her close friend Susan met at the Peeks family mortuary, where the family friend Susan Maits identified Glen's ravaged body.

Glen's mother had given him money for the bus fare to school on Friday, March 21. Still, he spent the money on something else and hitchhiked from the city's Westmont Elementary School, where he was in eighth grade.

Glen called his mother between 2:30 and 3:00 p.m. He was staying at a friend's house that night. He wore a brown ski jacket trimmed with yellow and blue corduroy pants and white tennis shoes. Police believe Glen was picked up on Beach Boulevard between 3:00 and 5 p.m.

Glen Barker was raped, beaten, and strangled to death; Glen's body, unlike the other victims, had numerous cigarette burns on his body. Glen was murdered as he attempted to hitchhike from school.

For three days, young Glen lay in the morgue as a John Doe; he had a small homemade tattoo of a blue lightning bolt on his right shoulder, his teeth were crooked, and he had birthmarks on each hip. As well as cigarette burns all over his body.

Glen's mother, Sharon, had reported Glen missing, and the police were very aware of the freeway killer. Sadly, by that day's end, Glen Barker and another boy had been sexually assaulted and murdered. [93] Glen used to collect cans and glass for recycling to help his family financially since his father abandoned them when Glen was young; Glen's grandmother recalls that the family never had anything nice.

Her daughter Sharon raised the kids on her own, and what she did get was given to her.
Havoc also visited Sharon Barker at the worst possible time. Diagnosed with cervical cancer that was in remission after treatment, the Huntington Beach woman was blindsided in March 1980 by the murder of her son, Glen Norman Barker, a 14-year-old Huntington Beach boy. The divorced mother juggled her job at a Kmart to attend Bonin's trial in Orange County.
"It didn't help her very much with the cancer," said her father, Elza Rodgers. "It was a strain on her."
Six years after Sharon identified her son at the morgue, Sharon died of cervical cancer (1942-1985), and her last wish was to view Bonin being executed. Unfortunately, she never got her dying wish.

On March 21, 1980, Bill Bonin and William Pugh had a busy
Day, only one week after being released from jail and killing Ronald Gatlin, Bonin still wanted to do a double murder.
So, Bonin and Miley went about murdering two teenage boys, Glen Barker, 14, and Russel Rugh, [15]
During Bonin's 1980 December confession interview with OC Sheriff's Homicide Detectives Bernie Esposito, James Sidebottom, LAPDs Sgt Jigsaw John and Mellecker, LA

Sheriff Sgt David Kushner, Kristi's and Malmberg from the San Bernadino Sheriff's department, he began to talk about the double murder after denying he killed Lundgren.

Bonin: I can tell you two right off the bat.

Esposito: okay

Bonin: I know, and it was Russell, uh, Rouge.

Esposito: Rugh, R-U-G- H

Bonin: and Glen Barker

Esposito: Barker.

Bonin: Barker

Norris (Deputy DA): Why don't you tell us about those two?

Bonin: I picked up Glen, yeah. I propositioned him, and he went for it.

Detective Kushner: Who's this Glen?

Esposito: That's Glen Barker.

Bonin then proceeded to tell the story to the detectives.

"I picked him, and he went for it. I got him in the back of the van. I tied him up. I didn't have any sex with him; no, I did. I sodomised him, yeah, I sodomised him. I was alone. I drove around looking for another person to pick up while Glen was in the van while he was alive. Uh, a couple of people said they didn't need rides. I gave another guy a ride. I told him that Glen was my cousin, and he was asleep. I told Glen that when somebody got in the van, he should be quiet and not say anything because I would look for somebody else to take his place. I would let him go, and he would have to go if I couldn't find anybody. He goes where, and I say I'd take you out of state to a homosexual slave ring where I sell people; this was a cover story. He went for it and kept quiet.

When I finally pulled up and stopped, this guy wasn't going for anything; he didn't want to get in the back of the van; in fact, he got out, so I drove off, and I finally came around to Russell. He wasn't going for it either, but I said, "Okay, I'll drop you off. And I pulled up and stopped the van. I reached over and grabbed him and pulled him towards me, but he got scared. He said OKAY, I'll do whatever you want, you know. In other words, I told him I wanted to give him head. I took the knife and held it to his throat. I drove across the street from where I was. He got in the back of the van with me, and I tied him up. I had both of them then."

Bonin's documented admission provided a far more intricate account. The subsequent excerpt of his confession is from Vonda Pelto's work, "Without Redemption."

"I offered Glen Barker $50 to get him in the van, and he said OKAY. I started by asking him if he hitchhiked much and if he got good rides. I asked him if he got picked up by many gays, and Glenn said yes, especially on Beach Blvd. I asked him what he thought of gays, and he replied they were okay as long as they left me alone; a couple of guys offered ten or $15. My offer is $50.00 for a head job. What do you say about that? I asked him. I reached over and rubbed him, and he was already hard as a rock. It looks like you will go for it, right? Sure, it's your money and your mouth, he told me. I found a place to park, and we got into the back of the van. I told him to take his pants off. He took them down to his knees, and I told him to take him completely off. he said no, you can suck me just like this. I told him OKAY. I went to get some tissue, came back with the knife, and told him to roll over. I tied his hands, telling him that if he didn't do what I instructed him, he wouldn't see another birthday. I got his shirt off and tied up his feet, then I pulled out my dick and said, "Now it's in your mouth. Suck on this punk. Glen started sucking, then acted like he was gagging and said, "I think I'm going to throw up. I told him if you do, it will cost you your life well, since you can't keep my dick in your mouth, it goes up your ass. I fucked him. Afterwards, I told him I was taking him out of state and selling him to a gay farm that he was only worth $10,000, which was a low price as he couldn't handle giving head. Then I got on the road to find someone else. Finally, after a few people turned me down, I spotted a kid worth at least $25,000. I told Glenn I don't need you anymore, so keep your mouth shut when he gets in because he might get away, and if he does, I'll kill you

Victim 17 Russell Duane Rugh

In the sun-kissed land of Garden Grove, amidst the orange blossoms of California, a tale began with the birth of Russell Duane "Rusty" Rugh on March 18, 1965. The son of Sandra Masters (1946-2013) and Russel Rugh, Rusty's life was a canvas of vibrant hues, even as the shadows of his parents' divorce in 1970 cast a sombre tone upon his youthful days.

Rusty, a boy with a heart as wide as the Pacific, navigated the complexities of family ties with the companionship of his sibling, Kristine (1966-2002). His fifteen springs blended laughter and growth, and dreams spun under the vast Californian sky.

As the narrative of his life reached an early epilogue on March 22, 1980, in Orange County, Rusty's spirit found its sanctuary within the peaceful embrace of Westminster Memorial Park. There, among the whispers of the past and the silent promises of eternity. 94

Affectionately known as Rusty to those who held him dear, Russell was last glimpsed by his kin on that fateful afternoon as he departed for the 4:07 p.m. bus. His destination is Brewsters Roosters, where he dedicates five days each week. He worked to create a future where music and his dreams intertwined, where he could spin records and spirits alike as a disc jockey.

In the quiet aftermath, amidst the sorrow and the search for meaning, a stack of Rusty's schoolwork revealed a hand-

94 https://www.findagrave.com/memorial/203273903/russell-duane-rugh

written autobiography. It was an assignment but also a window into his soul. Rusty stood firm against the tide of retribution; he believed in redemption over retribution, in understanding over vengeance.

With a heart heavy with loss, Sandra clung to Rusty's words. He believed that anyone who killed someone should be able to rehabilitate, she said. As she grappled with her own turbulent emotions, she harboured a hope deep within—that Rusty could extend his forgiveness to her, even as she wrestled with her desire for justice against Bonin, who had taken so much from them.

Russell's mother pondered with a heart laden with grief, "Had he foreseen the darkness of his end, perhaps his convictions would have wavered." With a soul inclined to see the best in others, Rusty held firm to the belief that those who commit such grave acts were not lost to their inner turmoil, more needing healing than harm. He advocated for compassion, for the possibility of rehabilitation over the finality of the gas chamber or electric chair—methods he considered cruel and inhuman.

His mother, now reflecting upon the harrowing depths of cruelty one human can subject another to, could not help but feel that Rusty's generous spirit might have reconsidered its stance on capital punishment. She mused that the stark reality of such brutality might have challenged even his most deeply held beliefs about the potential for redemption. [95]

95 Ellingwood, Ken. "The Other Victims of William Bonin." Los Angeles Times (Online), 19/2/1996 1996. https://www.latimes.com/archives/la-xpm-1996-02-19-mn-37703-story.html.

In the wake of unimaginable loss, Sandra found herself adrift in a sea of sorrow, seeking solace in the numbing embrace of alcohol and the quieting effect of antidepressants. The moment the detectives arrived with the harrowing news, marking the end of a two-day search for her beloved son, she reached for a drink to steady the tremors of shock that threatened to overwhelm her.

As the days unfolded, the silence within her family's walls became deafening, starkly contrasting the camaraderie in the local bar's dimly lit corners. There, after the gruelling days in court, she found a haven for her grief, a place where she could unburden her heart and share Rusty's story with those who would listen.

Each morning greeted her with the haunting emptiness of her son's bedroom—a space filled with dreams unfulfilled, and a life halted too soon. They had just begun to settle into their new home, a home that Rusty never truly got to experience. Amidst her anguish, Sandra grappled with the cruel order of the universe, where a mother outlives her child, a pain so profound it once drove her to the brink of joining him in the beyond.

The shadow of Bonin loomed over their lives, a dark cloud obscuring the sun's warmth. Yet, Sandra held onto the belief that with justice served, the sun would break through once more, heralding a day when the weight of her grief might lift if only just a little.

The ripple effects of tragedy touched every corner of Sandra's life, including her younger son, Steven Miller. At the tender age of 11, he found himself drawn into the vortex of the case, meticulously chronicling the names of those claimed by Bonin's dark deeds in a solemn notebook. Rusty's name, a stark number 32 on that list, became a symbol of a vow—an unspoken promise to seek justice.48

Years later, in a candid 1996 interview, Sandra reflected on the turbulent aftermath that her children endured, a path marred by substance abuse, a shadow of the chaos sown by Bonin. Yet, through the turmoil, a story of resilience and recovery emerged. "I understand their problems because I had the problems. And Bonin created most of our problems," Sandra shared her voice, a testament to a year of hard-won sobriety. "He created real havoc in our world," she admitted. Yet, her strength and the strength of her children shone as a beacon of hope amidst the havoc—a testament to the enduring human spirit.

In the dim confines of the van, Glen lay motionless, feigning sleep, clinging to the fragile thread of hope that Bonin had spun—a promise of freedom if another could take his place. With bated breath and a heart heavy with silent pleas, Glen awaited his fate.

Meanwhile, Russell, carefree and unaware of the lurking danger, walked along Beach Boulevard when Bonin, a hidden threat, approached with an offer of a ride to Westminster Boulevard. Despite the tempting proposition, Russell firmly declined, his refusal a silent act of resistance. Concealing his true intentions, Bonin pointed out a market ahead, suggesting he would drop Russell off there under the pretence of running errands. He then manoeuvred the van, parking it tightly against the wall to prevent the doors from opening—a subtle yet sinister tactic in a chilling game of deception.

Bonin then yanks Russell towards him and says, "You mother fucker, I am going to give you some head" Bonin shoves Russell into the back of the van where Glen was still tied up, Rolled him on his stomach and tied his hands and feet with a long extension cord, Russell was forced to give him oral copulation. Bonin told him to remove his clothes. Bonin pulled up Russell's shirt and caressed his hands across the boy's smooth, hairless chest. Bonin tried to kiss him, but he turned his head away. Bonin got agrivated, told Russell to Kiss him, and then reached down and pulled Russell's pants down, revealing his erect dick. Bonin turned to Glen and said, "Hey, this kid got a little hard-on." Bonin then turned Russell over and, without warning, rammed his dick into Russell's rectum. Russell started screaming, and Bonin's dick slipped out; this Bonin was furious and lashed out at Russell, knocking him unconscious. Bonin grabbed Russell by the shoulders and shook him vigorously until he groggily regained consciousness. "That's what happens when you don't do what I say" he then dragged him over to Glen, making them kiss and forcing Glen to give Russell oral copulation. Bonin leaned in close to Russell, his voice steady but firm. "Listen, Russell," he said, "you're taking Glen's place at the homosexual farm now."

Bonin drove up to Ortega Highway, claiming he would drop Glen off there. The tension in the air was palpable as he navigated the winding road, his mind racing with thoughts of what lay ahead.

While Bonin was stopped at a set of traffic lights, he could not help himself, so he reached through the back of the van to squeeze Russell's nuts. Bonin's foot slipped off the brake, causing the car to lurch forward and crash into the vehicle in front. The sudden impact jolted him, and he cursed under his breath, realizing the situation had become even more complicated. Bonin's heart raced as he panicked. He quickly told the lady in the car, "I'll pull into the station up ahead so we can exchange information." "Don't talk to each other," he ordered the boys, his voice tense with urgency. However, when her car wouldn't start, he seized the moment and sped off. Bonin noticed Glen mouthing something to Russell. Furious, he pulled the car over abruptly, climbed into the back seat, and, without hesitation, drove his knee into Glen's jaw, silencing him instantly. "If I catch you talking to him again, I will fucking kill you instead of letting you go" Bonin resumed driving, but the facade he had been maintaining finally crumbled. He had reached his breaking point, unable to keep up the pretence. His grip tightened on the steering wheel as he muttered under his breath, "I've had enough of this." both are going to die.

Glen got upset and said to Bonin, but you said I could go free. Bonin replied, "But you didn't do as you were told, "so now you both have to convince me you should live. Russell suggested to Bonin you should kill Glen, but Bonin asked them both if they would help him kill the other, and both, now begging to survive, agreed to help Bonin kill the other. Bonin had now reached the final destination at the lower campgrounds below Ortega highway and intently listened to them curse each other. Just then, a car approached, and Bonin cranked up the radio, hoping the blaring music would drown out any calls for help. After telling them, the first one to say a word was the one who died. When the car left, he told Glen, "You get to go free, but I am going to strangle you until you pass out. Then I shall dress you and put you out".

Bonin had just choked the life from Glen and told Russell he was going to let him go, but he needed to do the same to him, but only till he was unconscious. Russell knew he was going to die; Russell, feeling the weight of the situation, began to pray softly, seeking solace and strength amidst the chaos as Bonin slowly twisted the shirt around his throat until he, too, was dead. Bonin stripped them both of all their clothes and possessions and dumped their naked bodies.

Russell's body was found near Glen Barkers in Cleveland National Forest in Southern California. Just off Ortega (74) highway. [2] 96

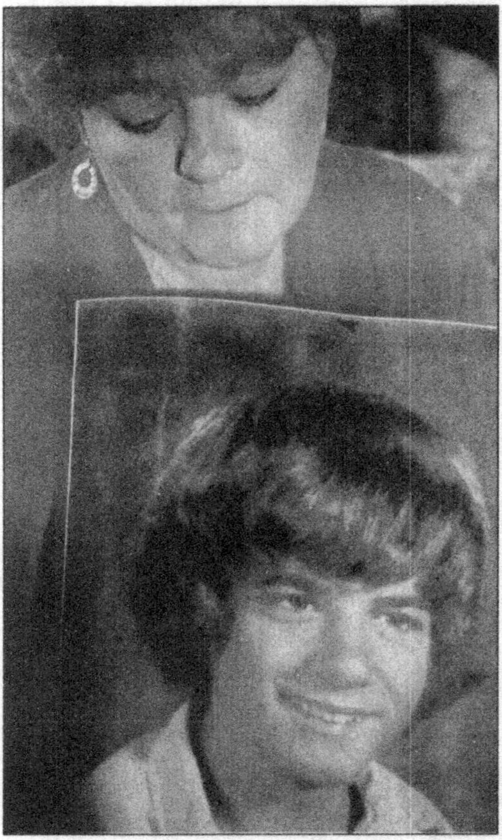

"I had the perfect happy family," says Sandra Miller, who holds a picture of her son Russell Duane Rugh, murdered at age 15.

96 MacWilliams, Bryon. "Russel Rugh: Teen-Ager Opposed Death Penalty in School Essay "The Orange County Register, 1996.

*Image SEQ Image * ARABIC49 Barker and Rugh Crime Scene screen-shot (Dark Reality, 2022) Image SEQ Image * ARABIC50 Crime Scene Screenshot (Dark Reality,2022)*

Victim 18 Harrv Todd Turner

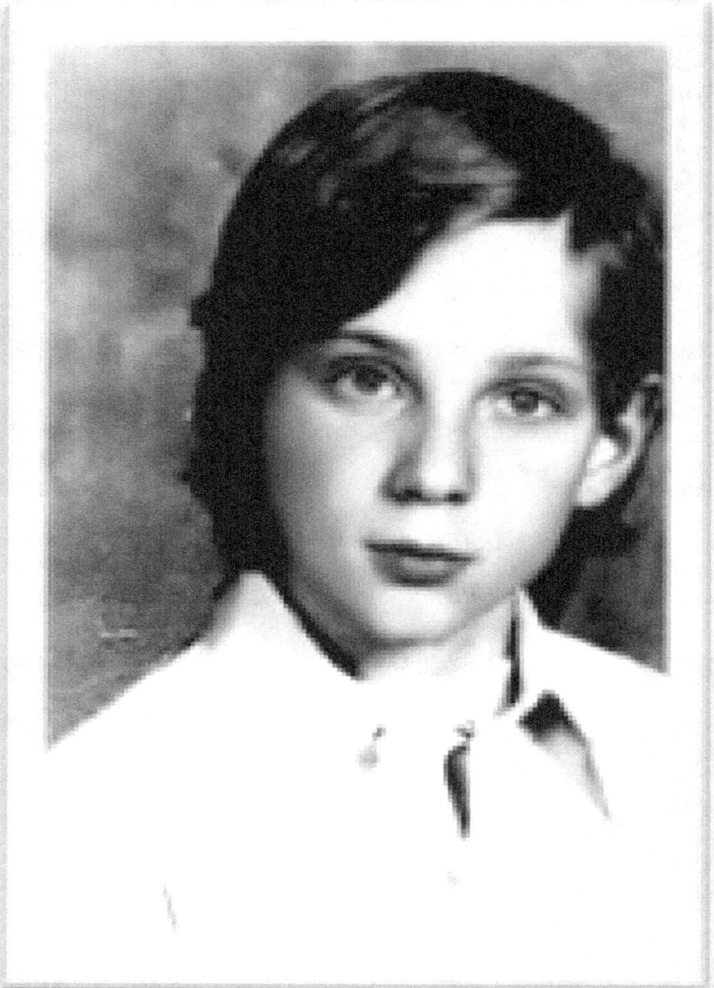

*Image SEQ Image * ARABIC51 Harry Turner (Wiki, n.d.)*

Harry Todd Turner's life began on a summer's day, July 12, 1964, in the sun-kissed environs of Orange County, California. He was the son of Harry Milton Turner (1934- 2001) and Lillie M Dobbins (1939- 2024) It is hard to track his siblings as his sister Cheryl, Tamala and Julie and Pamela and him were separated at a young age and placed into care with Pamela also not living a full life (1958-2001).
His journey, however, was heartbreakingly brief. Harry's future was abruptly stolen at just 15 when most youths are poised on the cusp of life's boundless possibilities. On March 24, 1980, in the sprawling cityscape of Los Angeles, his life was extinguished by the infamous 'Freeway Killer'. In the aftermath, it is believed his parents did not care with the void left by his untimely departure, the particulars of his final resting place remained elusive. It is believed that Harry may have been given to the flames, as no records detail a burial place, leaving those who cherished him to memorialise him in their hearts and memories.
On March 24, 1980, a tragic event unfolded in Hollywood. Harry Todd Turner, a 15-year-old boy, was picked up by William Bonin and William Ray Pugh. Harry recently ran away from the Optimist Home for Boys in Highland Park, California.
Harry's life was abruptly and tragically cut short that day. He fell victim to the notorious 'Freeway Killer', William

Bonin. Despite the case's high-profile nature, details about Harry's life remain scarce.

The following events are based on notes and interviews conducted with Vonda Pelto, and some of the information provided is based on available resources. There might be more to the story that has yet to be uncovered. These accounts offer a chilling insight into the tragic circumstances surrounding Harry Todd Turner's premature death. 17

William Bonin and William Ray Pugh had their first encounter on that fateful night. They were introduced to each other by a mutual acquaintance, Scott Fraser. They connected instantly, finding common ground in their shared interests.

Upon learning that Pugh had spent time in juvenile detention, Bonin engaged him in conversation about their respective experiences within the prison system. This dialogue, disturbingly, included discussions of sex and violence.

Bonin quickly realised that he couldn't harm Pugh, as they had been seen together publicly. Moreover, Bonin began to see the potential in Pugh, recognising an opportunity to manipulate him into becoming an accomplice in his horrific crimes. Bonin had offered Pugh a ride home, and he worked his cruel, manipulative magic.

After Bonin had managed to sexually arouse Pugh, they set out in search of a release. Pugh was under the impression that they were looking for a girl. However, Bonin had a different plan and was determined to see it through. Around midnight, the pair made their way to Hollywood. Bonin led the way, steering them towards an area he knew to be frequented by male hustlers. His intentions were clear, and he was unyielding in his pursuit. This began a chilling series of events that would unfold in the hours to come. Within minutes, Bonin points out a young lad with his thumb out, trying to hitch a ride. Harry Turner had been accustomed to hustling since he ran away, so he settled into the gap between the front seats. He was headed to AJs, a famous Hollywood, Santa Monica, and Highland coffee shop. They all introduce themselves, and Bonin asks him how business was tonight; why Turner says are you a cop? He asks suspiciously, no, Bonin replies, but do you want to earn 30 bucks? Let me give you a head, well, why not? So, Bonin finds a place to park, and he and Turner get into the back.

Turner pulls out his penis, and Bonin gets down to business while Pugh keeps a lookout in the front of the Van. Once Pugh confirms all is safe and no one is around, Bonin retrieves his erect penis and demands that Turner "suck his dick" Hey, that's not what we agreed. I don't give head, Turner says defiantly; within a second, Turner feels the force of Bonin's fist against his jaw. Hearing the commotion, Pugh locks down the Van and closes the curtains.

Bonin screams at Turner to roll over and tells Pugh to get a piece of ass; Pugh replies that he would prefer to receive head, so Bonin demands that Turner suck Pugh off. While Pugh was lying back receiving the oral copulation, Bonin took in the view and then got the idea to get in on the action as well. Pugh, who was also enjoying all of this, pushed turners head further onto his penis, telling him to suck harder, obviously pleased with the power. Still, Turner began to gag, and Pugh was worried that he was going to throw up on him and yelled at him not to; at this point, Bonin was ready to join in and told Pugh to wait a minute before resuming, I guess so Pugh was not accidentally bitten when Turner was painfully sodomised, after a few minutes Bonin was done. Still, Pugh wasn't. He pushed Turner's head down even harder, but Turner couldn't and choked; Pugh got him up on his knees and, with a closed fist, punched Turner in the face. Bonin once again told Pugh to get a piece of ass, and this time Pugh agreed and took his turn, with Bonin watching on with satisfaction. When he was finished, Bonin got back into the driver's seat, looking back at the tortured boy, but they were not finished; Bonin told Pugh to work him over, so while Bonin drove east towards downtown LA, Pugh continued to relentlessly hit the boy, Pugh then realising how much blood was everywhere, stopped to assess the situation, but Bonin was unhappy that Pugh had stopped, so he once again found somewhere to park and showed Pugh a way to torture someone without releasing blood,

Bonin placed Turner into a position that gave him free rein to deliver blow after blow to his abdomen, chest, and lower back. How Turner was still alive at this point is unbelievable, but with lack of oxygen and mind-numbing pain, he doubled over; Bonin then reached for his testicles and squeezed so hard Turner released a blood-curdling scream, which Bonin got excited over. Bonin got back into the driver's seat and told Pugh to continue, Turner tried to protect himself, but it was impossible; in another moment of cruelness, Pugh told Turner it was over; his battered body attempted to relax before Pugh also squeezed the boys' testicles and striking him in the face. At this point, Bonin tells him to stop and drag Turner up to the gap between the seats; it's getting light, and Bonin needs to finish the job. Bonin pulled up around the corner from the gas station and told Turner to take off all his clothes; while Turner was obeying, Bonin whispered into Pugh's ear, we will fuck him first, no squeezing of the nuts after he's weak. You hold his hands, and I will strangle him. Okay, Pugh replied, not even hesitating; Pugh's decisive moment had arrived. Rape and assault were one thing but murder. They both mercilessly beat him until Bonin gave Pugh the cue to hold his hands. At the same time, Bonin tied the boy's shirt around his neck, inserted the tyre iron and began to twist as the noose tightened. Turner's breath weakened until he had no breath left; as his lifeless body lay there, his bowels released all over the carpet in the Van.

As morning set in, they began to panic as they still had to dispose of Turner's body; it was getting risky; they drove around downtown LA and found an alleyway behind some commercial properties with a lot of dumpsters; Bonin briefly stopped the Van; and they pushed the limp body out and drove off making sure no one had seen them. Harry Todd Turner was found later that morning in the alley just off South Bonnie Brae Street. The ligature marks were evident on the neck, and there was no identification. Still, they knew this boy was another victim of the freeway killer; Turner's Penis and shoulder showed signs of being bitten, but who bit him remains a mystery. It had only been five days since Turner had decided to run away from the Optimist Boys' home, hoping to find a better path for himself.

Victim 19 Steven Jay Wood

Steven Jay Wood's narrative begins on September 18, 1963, in the vibrant heart of Orange County, California. His journey, woven into the fabric of the Golden State, was one of youthful dreams and aspirations. His parents Barbara Ellis

(1938-) and Thomas Wood (1936-) had three children Steve Carl (1959-1989), and Pamela

Tragically, his story was cut short at 16 in Long Beach, Los Angeles County, California, on April 10, 1980. The details of his final resting place remain a mystery, leaving an open chapter in the book of his life.

His parting words to his mother, "See you later, alligator," met with her affectionate response, "In a while, crocodile," echo through time—a poignant reminder of their bond.

Steven, with his slight stature, standing at 5 feet 2 inches and weighing a mere 88 pounds, bore the heart of a dreamer. To the world, he may have seemed but a child of 12, yet within him burned the fierce ambition to race with the wind as a jockey. Undimmed by his physical form, his spirit sought to soar upon the backs of thundering steeds, chasing horizons yet unseen.

In the Colombus High Yearbook, Steven was remembered by Tara Furnish and other classmates with a poem.

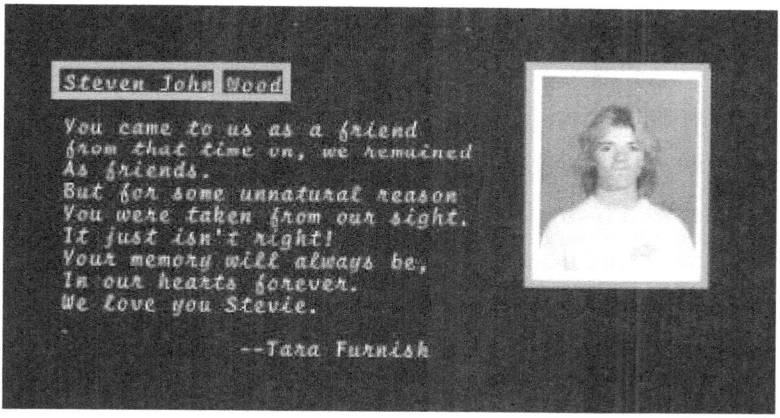

*Image SEQ Image * ARABIC53 Steven Wood (Year: 1980)*

*Image SEQ Image * ARABIC54 Steven Wood (Year: 1980)*

The 16-year-old victim of serial killer William Bonin. Steven disappeared on April 10, 1980, as he was walking from a dentist appointment back to his school. His body was found the next day in Long Beach Alley.

He had been picked up by Bonin in Los Angeles. Steven's nude body was found the following day in an alley behind an industrial complex near the Pacific Coast Highway and Long Beach Freeway. He had been beaten, sodomised and strangled by ligature. 97

Steven's mother caught her last glimpse of him in the soft morning light at approximately 9:30 am. It was a routine farewell as she left him at the school gates, a tender exchange marked by the passing of a ten-dollar bill—a modest token for the day ahead. With that, she turned towards the day's labours.

That afternoon, upon the conclusion of his school day, Steven embarked on a journey from the dentist's office nestled on Rosecrans Avenue. With the day still ripe with possibility, he made his way to his driver's education class at Columbus High School, transitioning from one learning environment to another, each step a stride towards his burgeoning independence. In the waning hours of the afternoon, Steven alighted from the bus at the intersection of Rosecrans and Woodruff. With purpose in his stride, he proceeded northward on foot, each step carrying him forward to his driver's ed class; his journey that day was confirmed

97 Executed Inmate Summary - William George Bonin - Capital Punishment. https://www.cdcr.ca.gov/capital-punishment/inmates-executed-1978-to-present/william-george-bonin/

by the observant eyes of a clerk at Manny's Liquor Store. The clerk, familiar with Steven from his time working there, recognised him as he passed by, marking this spot as a waypoint on Steven's last known route.

Bonin lived nearby and happened to be driving past and not wanting to miss an opportunity, offered Steven a lift; Steven accepted the lift but declined Bonin's proposition. Bonin tried again, this time offering an incentive of 100 dollars if he would let Bonin suck him off. Steven just looked at him and did not say anything; Bonin, not wanting to let this one go, pulled over the car near a self-service car wash and said let's talk for a minute. Trying to convince Steven it was all legitimate, the proposition was legit, and he was safe. Steven was not in danger as Bonin lived really close. He again offered Steven 100. "Just let me suck you off, then I will drop you at school for your lesson. It will take me less than 15 minutes to ejaculate." Steven replied, "It's just a blow job, nothing else, right?" "Right," Bonin said, "right then," Steve said. They got into the back of the van, and Bonin got Steve hard. Still, just before he was ready to ejaculate, Bonin announced he didn't like swallowing the cum, so he went to the front to get tissues; while there, he also grabbed his rope and knife. Bonin put the knife to Steve's throat and told him to roll over. Getting him to put his hands behind his back, Bonin tied him up, and then I took off his pants, shoes, and socks and tied his legs; Bonin fucked him for a while but couldn't be bothered to ejaculate. Bonin took his trusty chain, made a loop and put it around his neck, then casually asked Steven where he lived; Steven said he lived ¼ quarter of a mile from where they were, but coldly, Bonin announced that that was too bad, as he was never going to see his family again, confused and trembling Steve realised what was happening, Bonin twisted the chain until it was snug around Steven's throat, and watched the horror come over Steven's face when Bonin cooly announced he was the freeway killer. Steven was dead within minutes. Bonin untied him, laid him across the back of the van, covered him, drove home, parked the car, and went inside to make phone calls. Bonin got a break with a job interview but got in his van that very afternoon. He headed to the job interview; after the successful interview, he went to his brother's pizza place and hung around there for a while, remembering distinctly that day as the fire department was nearby for a fire. It was getting dark and time to dump the body, finding a desolate alley. He unloaded his latest victim. Barbara Stevens's mother got home from work at about 11.45 pm that night and checked on the kids, expecting to find them all asleep in bed. However, Steven's bed was empty. Barbara felt a little uneasy when Steve was out; he usually wore his jacket, which was still in his room. Barbara began to make some calls and couldn't locate her son.

At 7:40 am the following day, he was found 15 miles from Downey in an alleyway behind 740 West Esther, an industrial section in Long Beach.

The heartache of losing a child is an unimaginable sorrow, and the impact on the family can be profound and enduring. The grief experienced by Steven's mother, Barbara, was compounded by the subsequent loss of her other son, Carl, who tragically succumbed to his own battle with depression. The family's decision to move away from their home in Bellflower to seek solace in Arizona reflects their need for a fresh start and a quieter life, away from the memories that may have haunted them. [46]

The shadow of a profound tragedy lingered over Carl Wood, casting a pall on his young life from when he learned of his brother Steven's fate. At the tender age of 20, the discovery of Steven's body in Long Beach on that fateful day of April 11, 1980, marked the beginning of Carl's descent into an abyss of sorrow. His mother's words paint a picture of a soul adrift in the aftermath of loss, unable to find his way back to the surface. For nine long years, Carl grappled with an undercurrent of grief, a silent struggle that remained largely unseen but deeply felt. It was a testament to the enduring pain that the loss of a loved one can inflict, leaving scars that time alone cannot heal.

Biehn recounted that Carl, among the three children who remained, descended into a vortex of substance misuse and deteriorating mental health, culminating in auditory hallucinations. "The final days were sheer horror," she expressed. The nadir of his desolation manifested on January 8, 1989. Carl pedalled to a local discount outlet, procured a shotgun along with shells, and ended his life within the confines of a companion's carport. Biehn speculated that the timing, coinciding with Bonin's birth anniversary, was likely serendipitous. Yet, she remains persuaded that his downward spiral was a direct consequence of the murder. It did not help that Carl felt guilt over the fact that he too knew Bonin and had once introduced Bonin and Steve. It was too much for Barbara to bare when she was informed of Carls death, she could not bring herself to ID the body instead calling Jigsaw John in hysterics asking him to confirm the identification of her son.

The compounded tragedy rendered Biehn untethered in her sorrow. The once familiar sights of Steven's school, his place of employment, and the now grown-up friends with families of their own became unbearable reminders of what was lost. Seeking refuge from these painful memories, she and her husband, Don, a professional car tester, sought solace in the seclusion of Arizona. Guarded and cautious. Biehn's existence is intimately entwined with the sanctuary of her well-kept abode. Carl's remains are enshrined within a brass urn adorned with his likeness in the tranquillity of the bedroom. A vibrant, sizable portrait of Steven graces the

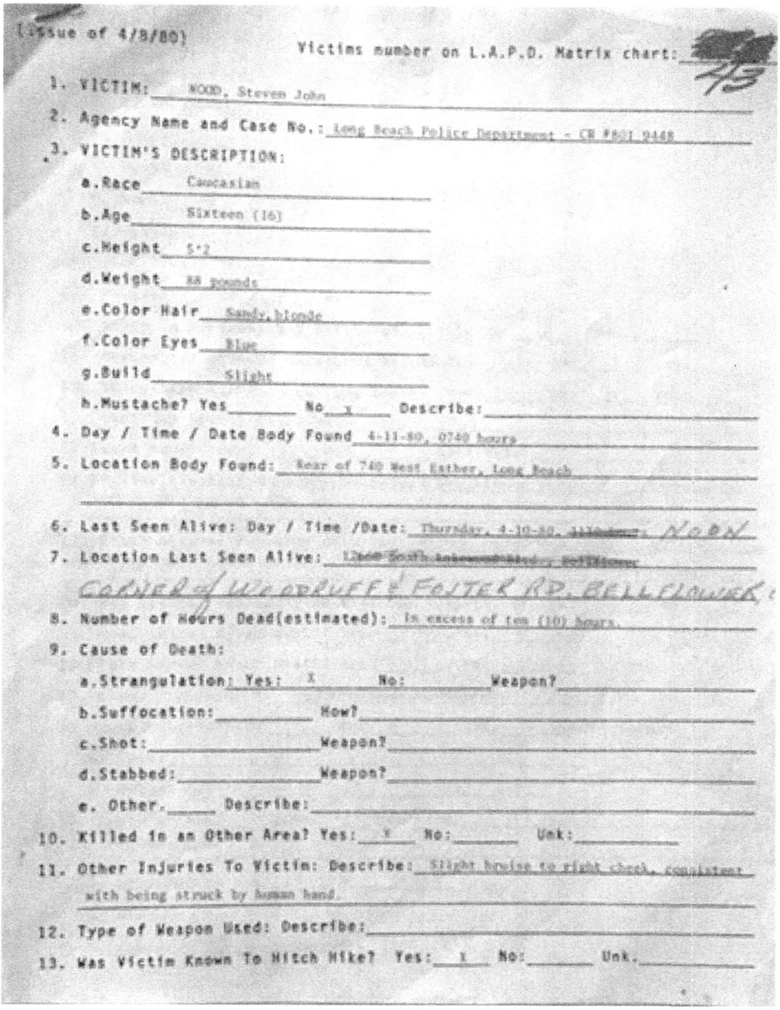

(Issue of 4/8/80)

Victims number on L.A.P.D. Matrix chart: 43

1. VICTIM: WOOD, Steven John
2. Agency Name and Case No.: Long Beach Police Department - CR #80I 9448
3. VICTIM'S DESCRIPTION:
   a. Race Caucasian
   b. Age Sixteen (16)
   c. Height 5'2
   d. Weight 88 pounds
   e. Color Hair Sandy, blonde
   f. Color Eyes Blue
   g. Build Slight
   h. Mustache? Yes____ No x Describe:____
4. Day / Time / Date Body Found 4-11-80, 0740 hours
5. Location Body Found: Rear of 740 West Esther, Long Beach
6. Last Seen Alive: Day / Time /Date: Thursday, 4-10-80, ~~[illegible]~~ NOON
7. Location Last Seen Alive: ~~[illegible]~~ CORNER of WOODRUFF & FOSTER RD, BELLFLOWER
8. Number of Hours Dead(estimated): In excess of ten (10) hours.
9. Cause of Death:
   a. Strangulation: Yes: x No:____ Weapon?____
   b. Suffocation:____ How?____
   c. Shot:____ Weapon?____
   d. Stabbed:____ Weapon?____
   e. Other.____ Describe:____
10. Killed in an Other Area? Yes: x No:____ Unk:____
11. Other Injuries To Victim: Describe: Slight bruise to right cheek, consistent with being struck by human hand.
12. Type of Weapon Used: Describe:____
13. Was Victim Known To Hitch Hike? Yes: x No:____ Unk.____

wall of her craft room. She immerses herself in the therapeutic arts of crocheting and adorning trinkets in this space.

*Image SEQ Image * ARABIC55 The spot where Steven Wood was found Screenshot (Dark Reality 2022)*

Victim 20 Lawrence Eugene Sharp

*Image SEQ Image * ARABIC57 (Lawrence Eugene Sharp* ***(1962-1980) - Find a Grave. . ., 1962)***

Lawrence Eugene Sharp was born in Oklahoma, USA, on November 3, 1962. He was the son of Lloyd Sharp (1939-2011) and Carol Voetee (1943-). Lawrence had two sisters, Cheryl (1960-) and Candy (1965-2006) Tragically, Lawrence passed away at the youthful age of 17 on May 12, 1980, in Orange, Orange County, California, USA. He was laid to rest at the Forest Lawn Memorial Park in Long Beach, Los Angeles County, California, USA. His short life left a lasting impact on those who knew him. 98

Larry Sharp's passion for baseball was as boundless as the skies over Dodger Stadium, where he watched his beloved team play with sincere devotion. The sermons and hymns at church nurtured his spirit, and his imagination soared in the magical realms of Disneyland. The rhythms of rock 'n' roll fuelled his youthful exuberance. Yet, his father's companionship captured his heart during their cherished fishing excursions.

Lawrence, as his mother tenderly called him, was last seen on May 11, 1980, within the comforting embrace of their Long Beach home. With a modest $2 nestled in the folds of his Velcro-sealed cloth wallet, he set out, unencumbered by possessing a car. His journeys were often spontaneous, marked by the hum of bus engines or the kindness of truckers offering a lift. Despite the distance, Lawrence's sporadic check-ins were a beacon of reassurance, a son's silent prom-

98 Place: Orange; Date: 18 May 1980; Social Security: 568043848

ise to his family that he remained safe in the vast tapestry of America.

In a poignant twist of fate, Larry's sister Candy reflected on their heated exchange on that fateful day. In the heat, she summoned their other sister, Cheryl, whose anger manifested in physical blows upon Larry. With a heavy heart and firm resolve, Larry gathered his belongings and departed with a prophetic farewell, declaring they would never lay eyes on him again. The weight of those parting words would come to bear a profound burden of guilt, for his ominous prediction came to pass—they never saw him again. The gravity of that final encounter, marred by conflict and unresolved tensions, left an indelible mark on the fabric of the family, weaving a narrative of loss and remorse that would linger in the silence of his absence.

As a journalist, Lopez testified that Bonin had confided in him about a past intimate connection with Larry Sharp, describing their bond as having been 'intimately profound.' Bonin recounted experiences shared with Larry, including visits to Knott's Berry Farm, and at one point referred to their connection as that of "lovers." Bonin's account was rich with details about their initial encounter and the depth of their acquaintance despite the short-lived nature of their relationship.

It was also mentioned in the documentary on the Lost Murder Tapes that a co-worker of Bonin's, one day, was working with Bonin. They went to northern California together to pick up a truck. On the way back, the co-worker's vehicle broke down, so Bonin suggested he stay behind with the car. The co-worker took the truck and got back to the yard (the city of industry) roughly 10 minutes after Bonin, and apparently with him was a young man described as a late teen with an injured upper lip sandy coloured hair. It was Larry Sharp, but the co-worker did not know his name then. The co-worker did not see Bonin again for a few weeks. When finding out about the death of Larry Sharp, it really shook him up, as he recognised him as the young lad with Bonin. Still, he did not realise that the man he sat next to and had invited back to his home was the killer.

Bonin was familiar with Larry, which was particularly noticeable when their paths crossed again in Eric's company. When probed about the motive behind Larry's murder, Bonin's chilling response was: "One day, I simply awoke with the realisation that I was weary of his presence. The thought of him became burdensome, and it led me to the conclusion that I should end his life." This declaration suggests a calculated intent to commit murder despite Bonin's admission of not having encountered Larry for some time.

17, [99] On May 18 1980, the body of Lawrence Sharp, 17, was found in a trash bin behind a service station in Westminster. He, too, had been beaten, sodomised, and strangled. [100]

Regarding the incident, Bonin stated: "I reached a point where I simply grew weary of him. The idea of him being around became too much, and I decided he had to be eliminated." This remark implies a deliberate decision to commit the act, even though Bonin mentioned that Larry had been absent from his life for some time

Once Lawrence entered the van, Bonin said he recognised him instantly but could not remember his name. He asked for his name again and asked Eric to drive, and Bonin got in the back with Lawrence. Bonin asked if Lawrence wanted to get it on, but that night, Lawrence was not in the mood. Bonin offered him fifty dollars, and he changed his mind.

99 "The Mother and Two Brothers of Convicted Freeway Killer." United Press International (online), January 18, 1982. https://www.upi.com/Archives/1982/01/18/The-mother-and-two-brothers-of-convicted-Freeway-Killer/4056380178000/. 100 Bonin v. Calderon, 59 F. 3d (Court of Appeals, 9th Circuit 1995).

Larry got undressed, and Bonin told him to get it hard, so he started to masturbate. Bonin reached up front, grabbed the knife, and placed it at Lawrence's throat. Lawrence shouted," Hey Bill, what's happening" and Bonin told him to shut the fuck up and do as he was told, and he would be fine.

After Eric parked somewhere safe, he also got in the back. And Bonin instructed him to put the knife back in the front of the van. Bonin accused Larry of not satisfying him last time at Knotts Berry Farm. And now he wanted his dues. Bonin got on top, getting his piece by fucking him as hard as he could. Bonin then told Eric to go ahead and get some. The semen from both of them would mix together, making it impossible to get DNA from them.

Eric was then told to give Bonin Larry's T-shirt so he could put it around his throat. Bonin really wanted to fuck with him. Bonin asked Larry why he was a hustler, to which Larry replied to easy money. Still, Bonin said he hated hustlers, so he got the tyre iron, placed it in the shirt and began to twist until it was snug against Larry's throat. Bonin then said to Eric he really felt like killing him. Still, they would get into trouble, so he would leave Larry like that for a few minutes while Eric and Bonin got in the form to talk privately. Bonin claims that he asked Eric if he could handle the situation, and Eric said Yes, so Bonin gave him instructions on what to do next. Bonin took on the role of

strangling him and told Eric to squeeze his testicles really hardbut Eric said he was worried about Larry screaming. Bonin convinced him that Larry could not make any noise. Within a few seconds, they were both in the back, Bonin strangling him and Eric squeezing his testicles. Eric then used his free hand to start hitting Larry in the face and body … After a brief time, Eric pulled his hand up and exclaimed the mother fucker pissed on me, which Bonin replied they do that when they lose consciousness. Once they were done, they untied him and drove around looking for a place to dump him off. They dumped him behind the Mobil gas station on Westminster Boulevard, and Bonin dropped Eric home. At a place in Leffingwell and said he would call him later, Bonin mentions something he thought was funny that Eric had said, "he wasn't very good looking. I didn't get turned on that much from him", to which Bonin replied, well next time I will try and find you a sweet youngster for you, to which he replied yeah do that, then Bonin feeling exhausted went home.

It was not till Sunday the 18th when Jon Hagey while throwing away some trash, saw a pair of legs sticking out between two cars; while trying to hold back from vomiting, he rushed to call the police but found the mechanic who worked there had already called it in. Larry's naked body was leaning against the left front tyre of a Chevy truck. No evidence was found at the scene.

The LA coroner, though, had more luck and found semen and fibres; the fibres were similar to those found on three other victims: Russell Rugh, Glen Barker and Dennis Fox. The Deputy Coroner at the time, Lendith Lee, estimated that the time of death was around 2 am on May 18.
Bonin was charged with this murder and had confessed to the reporter Lopez. Still, for reasons no one will ever know, Eric, while being arrested at a later date, was later released as they say he was not a part of any of the murders, even though in one of Bonin's accounts, Eric was clearly involved.

Victim 21 Darin Lee Kendrick

Image 59 Darin Lee Kendrick (1961 - 1980)
Find a grave.com 1961

Born on January 31, 1961, in Seattle, King County, Washington, USA, Darin was the cherished son of William L. Kendrick (1936- 2007) and Patricia A. Hickok (1935-). He grew up alongside his brothers, Steve and Troy (1963-), in a household filled with camaraderie and support.

A proud 1979 graduate of Pacifica High School in Garden Grove, California, Darin's youth was filled with the typical joys and aspirations of a teenager. His life was cut short at 19 in Los Angeles County, California, USA. His passing left an indelible mark on his loved ones and the community that knew him.

Darin's final resting place is at Westminster Memorial Park in Westminster, Orange County, California, USA, where he is remembered for the vibrancy of his life and the warmth, he brought to those around him. [101]

Though tragically brief, Darin Lee Kendrick's life was marked by his family's love and his achievements.

In a poignant testimony before the court, Patricia, Darin's mother, recounted the distressing circumstances surrounding her last encounter with her son. She vividly remembered that fateful day when Darin vanished without a trace. He had been diligently performing his duties as a bagger at the local supermarket. The mystery of his sudden disappearance while on the job only added to the family's anguish. [102]

"Bob Edwards, a colleague of Darin's, spoke highly of him, describing him as a dependable employee. Edwards, who is

101 https://www.findagrave.com/memorial/213194869/darin-lee-kendrick 102 UPI. (1981, November 6). Victim identified in Freeway Killings. The Gazette.

believed to be the last person to have seen Darin alive, recounted during an interview that on the evening in question, Darin was assigned to retrieve shopping carts at 9 p.m. However, when he was urgently required back inside the store at 9:15 p.m., he was conspicuously absent and could not be located. 103

It was the evening of April 29. Around 9:00. Bonin was driving around Long Beach. He was agitated and needed another kill. He ended up driving down Katela Ave. At the same time, Darin was rounding up the shopping carts at Lucky's supermarket. After cashing his $200 pay check, Darin felt rather good! Bonin caught sight of Darin and began to drive slowly after him as Darin made his way back towards the store. Finally, pulling up, Bonin asked him if he wanted to buy weed. How much Darin enquired? Forty-five an ounce. Sounds good. What kind is it? Bonin told him to hop in. He would drive around the back and let him smoke a sample. He just needed Darin to get in the van. Darin glanced furtively around, ensuring no one from the office was watching him. With a sense of anticipation, he opened the door and slid into the passenger seat of the spacious van. Bonin parked the van behind the store, switching off the engine and extinguishing the headlights." And he didn't hesitate." pulling out the knife and placing the sharp edge against Darin's throat. Are you the Freeway Killer? "Darin's voice shook with fear, and his eyes widened in shock as he asked. "I don't know what you're talking about, "Try anything, and you're dead, motherfucker, though Bonin was interested in what Darin had learned about the Freeway killer. So, he inquired, Hey, what's this freeway killer shit all about? With a calculated gaze and a nod of feigned interest, Bonin leaned in closer, eager to catch every word that spilled from his lips. The game was afoot, and he was but a player on Bonin's stage, pretending to be engrossed, hanging on to the edge of his narrative. The anticipation was palpable as he sought to unravel the tales he had been weaving with such casual deceit. Darin continued to tell him it was a guy who was going around picking up guys, raping them and killing them. Bonin pretended to be disgusted. Look, I am not gay, and I don't kill people. I just rob people, but don't get me wrong, do what I tell you, or I will kill you. Bonin demanded Darin get into the back of the van and told Darin he was going to tie him up, take his money and drop him off somewhere. He bound the boy's hands and feet with electrical tape. Demanding to know how much money he had, which was about two hundred as he had just been paid, A quick search of his pocket yielded about one hundred eighty and some coins. Bonin couldn't believe his luck. This was the most significant amount of cash he had found on someone. Bonin then realised he hadn't seen Butts for a while. So, he decided now was a fun time to see him. Butts had moved from his apartment on Imperial Highway and moved to 7310 Dinwiddie Street in Downey. His new pad was back from the street as the property was divided into two small structures, one house and the other the converted garage. Bonin hadn't been to his new dwelling, so he pulled down the driveway and brought the van right up to Butts door. And turned back to Darin. You better shut up and not say a word. If you do, you will die. He said before getting out of the van. Bonin knocked on the front door, butts Answered. He was shocked to see Bonin. But also, the van was parked on his doorstep. "Hey, visitors are supposed to park outside the drive. They have to park on the street." But Bonin didn't know that and didn't want to wrestle with the kid on the street. Alright, meet me at the van, he said. Even though Butts had company, wait just two minutes, he said. Alright, hang on. And Bonin reversed the van back onto the street and waited for Butts. Bonin stood next to the van, playing the radio, thus preventing Darin from hearing anything they said. "This better be good," Butts said. "Look, I have a live one in the van and wanted to use your house." Butts knew all too well the words. "Use your house" meant He was already in too deep. As he had already committed five murders with Bonin, was Butts. Ready to let a murder happen in his house. Butts told Bonin, "I cannot. I have friends over." "Fuck get rid of them," Bonin yelled at him. "Look, the kid has money. I'll give you some. Alright." Give me 5 minutes. So, while Butts was getting rid of his visitors.

Bonin told Darin once he got into the house. He isn't to say a word.

This was a new game. That Butts and Bonin like to play. Bonin would tell the kid to be quiet. And Butts would try to make him talk. But the kid knew. If he spoke. Bonin was going to hurt him. Butts was allowed to try any tactic except touching him.

After Butts, friends left. Bonin backed the van into the driveway. And they both hustled Darin inside and dumped him on the living room floor. And while Bonin took the car back down to the street. Butts started the game.

The kid was too scared to talk, even with butts, to threaten, to put his foot in his mouth.

Darin is still Tied up on the floor and frightened as hell. Bonin cut the restraint on Darin's feet.

He helped him up and led him to the bedroom, where he laid him face down on the bed. Bonin Removed the shoes and socks, setting up the scene. He then restrained his legs back up.

Then, cutting off. Darin's work apron. Pants and underwear. "He's a good-looking kid." Bonin and Butts commented. While viewing his prey Bonin got undressed. He was telling Darin to copulate with him orally. While butts got undressed, then, they switched places while Bonin brutally sodomised. Darin. While Vern got orally copulated. Sadistic and punishing, just the way Bonin treats his victims. Butts was getting excited. "This kid gives good fuckin head." He said with delight. "Yeah, you should try this end," Bonin answered back. With disgusting pleasure, "I will", Butts replied as soon as Bonin finishes sodomising Darin. Butts took his turn. Once they were both done. They put him down on his knees. Butts whispered to Bonin that he had some chloral hydrate solution. That they could use. Butts had obtained it from his friend and mentor, James Meurer. Who had gotten it from a friend. It was commonly known as a knockout drug. Chloral hydrate is a prescription drug. Used as a short sedative in hospital procedures, Bonin was aware of its properties. They decided to use it and slowly began feeding Darin the Chloral Hydrate. After a few minutes, he was pretty drowsy and stunned. He commented that he couldn't feel his mouth. Darin began to throw up a thick substance, most likely blood due to the Chloral hydrate, causing gastric haemorrhage. This was not enough torture. Butts now wanted to try a different solution and tried to feed it to Darin. Butts was keen to see what would happen next. The second substance burned his lips, chin, chest and face. It was some poison like caustic soda, otherwise called Lye solution, as Chloral Hydrate doesn't burn, the coroner had reported; the second liquid was not swallowed; they never found any in his mouth or throat. Darin commented that he was tripping. He was entirely out of it. Butts called Bonin out of the room for a quick chat. Standing in the other room,

Butts told Bonin he wanted to try the Ice pick trick. Bonin said, "Go ahead, go and get one." Butts went and grabbed an ice pick and a small hammer, and they went back into the room. Darin was totally out of it. Bonin tied an electrical cord around his neck. Tying a loop in the back and began to twist. When Darin was unconscious, Bonin moved him into a position so Butts, could you do his ice pic trick? Bonin didn't want any noise, so he also gaged Darin as a precaution. Bonin then held down Darin's head.

Butts were getting ready to drive the ice pick through Darin's ear when Bonin shouted stop, wait, it was going to be messy, but it was too late; the ice pick was slammed into the cervical section of the spinal cord, and Darin let out a high pitched scream and then went silent blood was gushing out of his ear even while the ice pick was still in situ, Bonin tried to pull the ice pick out. However, the handle broke off and would have to stay there, still impacting his brain. They placed a plastic bag over his head and moved him into the shower; after a considerable attempt at cleaning everything up, they double-bagged all of Darin's clothes and secured another bag to Darin's head with elastic to try and prevent any blood from leaking out as they placed Darin onto the floor of the van. The only item left out was Darin's wallet, and that may have been accidental, but Butts saw it and kept it as a souvenir. The last body they dumped together was over 100 miles on the outskirts of Baker's field, and it was already late. Butts really didn't want to go for another long drive, but Bonin assured him it would only be a short drive. So, he went along with Bonin. Darin's lifeless, bloodied body was left 15 miles away in the city of Carson and left near a construction site. Butts was dropped home around 1:00 a.m., and Bonin drove home.

It was April 30 when Darin was found; it was determined that the icepick and strangulation were the cause of death. Darin was the 9th Victim dumped in LA county, others being three in Orange County, four in San Bernadino, one in Riverside, one in San Diego and one in Kern County.

Bonin later told tv reporter and journalist David Lopez that Darin was killed ritualistically, but that was not true; it was just another coincidence that Butts was inadvertently dragged into Bonin's schemes yet again, but this was the last time Butts participated in any murders with Bonin.

Victim 22 Sean Paige King

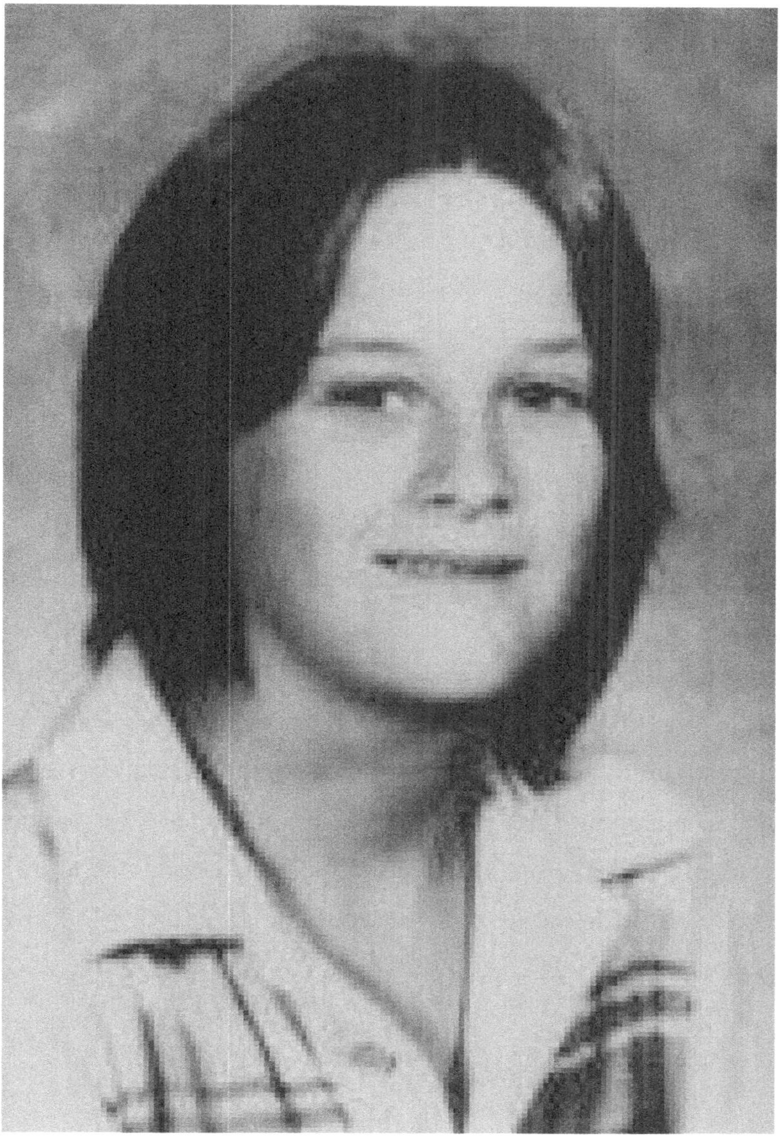

*Image SEQ Image * ARABIC60 Sean Paige King – (Wikimedia Commons, 1980)*

Sean Paige King was born on February 1, 1966, in Los Angeles County, California, USA. Tragically, his life was cut short at the age of 14, passing away on May 19, 1980, in Yucaipa, San Bernardino County, California, USA. His burial details remain unknown, though it is most likely that he was cremated.

Sean was the beloved son of Richard Lee King (1934-1999) and Lavada Weaver (1936-2002. He grew up with many siblings: Brook (1961-2009), Ricci (1955-), and some others whose names are unknown. His parents had several marriages each.

Ray Carbajal, a youth pastor at South Gate, Foursquare church in 1980, said kids always come to him for help. He remembers Sean King attending youth group in May 1980. Ray will never forget the last time that he saw Sean. Ray was turning off Firestone Boulevard when he spotted Sean. They quickly chatted about his positive transitions, starting over at a new junior high. Ray noticed he was walking and asked if his mum had dropped him off at the corner… no he replied I took the bus, so Ray said to have a good day and drove off; little did he know it would be the last time he saw Sean.

*Image SEQ Image * ARABIC61 This is the last place Ray saw Sean. Screenshot (Dark Reality, 2022)*

Ray remembers that when he got home later that day, he received a call from Sean's mum. She sounded worried as she mentioned that Sean hadn't arrived home yet. This struck Ray as strange, so, feeling concerned, he decided to go for a drive to look for Sean. Without success, Ray called all the kids to track Sean down.

Then they see Breaking News, a 14-year-old boy disappears in a suspected kidnapping, and they all realise it may be Sean.

5 foot 6 inches tall. Slender, with dark hair, a fair complexion and green eyes. Sean King, an exemplary student at West Middle School in Downey, excelled academically. Passionate about the water, he devoted himself to swim-

ming and surfing. Last summer, he and his friends frequently shared rides to the beach, embracing the sun and the waves.

Sean's mother, Levada, cautioned her son: "*As you and your friends set out for the beach this summer, make a promise to steer clear of hitchhiking.*" Sean gave his word, assuring her with confidence, *"I won't. I know better than that."*

*Image SEQ Image * ARABIC62 Blue Chevette like Bonin's* ***(Wikipedia contributors, 2024b)***

On May 19, 1980, Bonin set out in his blue Chevette, visiting Butts in hopes of convincing him to join a hunting trip. Although Butts declined the invitation, he agreed to give their friend James Meurer a lift home. Bonin, still optimistic, had Butts accompany them, hoping to change his mind during the drive.

After getting home from school, Sean left in the early evening to take the bus to his girlfriend's house. He wore blue OP shorts, a white T-shirt, white slip-on tennis shoes, and a blue sweatshirt jacket. On his way back to drop off Butts, Bonin noticed young Sean waiting at a bus stop. Bonin wanted to pick him up, but Butts refused, saying he didn't want to get involved.

Despite Butts' reluctance, Bonin stopped the car and initiated a conversation with Sean. He asked Sean for directions to Atlantic Boulevard. Unaware of Bonin's intentions, Sean helpfully replied that it was a mile or two down the road.

"Are you waiting for the bus?" Bonin asked. Sean nodded in response. *"Don't you know the last bus has already been and gone? Where were you headed?"* Bonin continued. *"If it's near Atlantic Boulevard, can I give you a lift?"*

"Alright, cheers," Sean replied, climbing into the Chevette. Butts was not impressed; he couldn't understand how Bonin could reel these kids in so quickly. Sean settled into the back seat as they drove south of First One Boulevard. Butts, knowing what was likely to happen, demanded to be dropped home first. He did not want to be a part of it. Bonin dropped Butts home and told Sean to wait in the car. He needed to grab something from inside; he collected a blanket, rope and a steak knife from the kitchen. Bonin had not used the Chevette in a murder before, so the vehicle never contained his murder kit.

Setting off again, Bonin starts to put his plan into action, beginning with the usual questions about meeting gay people and then offering money to allow Bonin to perform fellatio on him. Sean wasn't interested in that, so he politely declined. Now feeling unsafe, he asked to be dropped off. Bonin, however, detoured onto a side street and found an empty lot to park in. When Sean tried to get out, he discovered the door was locked. Bonin swiftly pulled out the knife and held it against Sean's throat. Panic set in, and Sean began to cry, begging not to be hurt. Bonin told him all he wanted was for Sean to perform fellatio on him, *and if he did what he was told, he would be fine*. Bonin put the knife away, but Sean was still too scared to move. Bonin demanded Sean put his hands behind his back so he could tie him up. Bonin then proceeded to remove Sean's shoes and socks, tied his legs, and was free to begin fondling Sean. Embarrassed about his size, Sean remarked that he was not big, but Bonin said it did not matter. He pulled out his own and shoved it into Sean's mouth.

Bonin was not getting aroused or in the mood, so he stopped and gave Sean a deep, passionate kiss using his tongue. He then, still feeling nothing, redressed himself, reclined the seat Sean was in, covered him with a blanket, told him to pretend to be sleeping, demanded that he not make a sound and enforced his threat, *"If you try to get anyone's attention, I will kill you."*

The following words have been paraphrased from the notes and files Vonda Pelto accessed and published in the book Without Redemption, co-authored with Michael D. Butler.

Bonin decided to call Eric. Since Larry did not turn Eric on last time, he thought Sean might. He drove down Firestone Boulevard, found a phone booth, and made the call.

Eric had visitors, so he could not talk freely on the phone, so Bonin convinced him to meet him at Valley View in twenty minutes. Bonin arrived a few minutes before Eric and found a quiet place to park just north of Imperial to Huffington. He told Sean he would be talking with someone soon and that he had better not make a move. "*You pretend to be asleep; if not, remember what I said. I will kill you, or I may just send you to a farm where they sell sex slaves. Am I clear?*" "Yes," Sean replied.

Eric arrived fifteen minutes later, and Bonin started weaving a new story. He told Eric about the man he had spoken to earlier regarding a job, who now wanted Bonin to prove he could manage the task. The task was to slaughter someone and hide the body well enough so that the body would never be found for at least six months. Bonin continued to inform, "*Eric, I got an adorable kid in the car. I know the kid wasn't your type last time. Still, I reckon this one is right up your alley, so if you really want in on this deal, you will need to help get rid of him*" ... "*Let go,*" Eric anxiously replied.

Eric climbed through to the back of the Chevette, leaned

forward and peaked under the blanket; *"you're right. He is cute; I will enjoy him."* As they drove off, Bonin asked Eric if he wanted Sean in the back so they could get the party started. Eric was eager, so Bonin pulled into Zody's car park. Zody's, an American retail corporation, was known for selling ready-to-wear women's apparel in the 1960s. After parking, Bonin moved Sean to the back seat. He then got on the 605 freeway, heading towards the 10 freeway, and drove towards the Inland Empire of San Bernardino. As Eric and Bonin shared the driving, Sean was forced to take turns performing fellatio on both Eric and Bonin until they ejaculated.

Eventually, they ended up 75 miles east of downtown LA, where Bonin found a quiet country road parallel to some railway tracks; he saw a spot adjacent to a large field surrounded by a bush. He parked and excitedly announced it was time for anal. They took turns sodomising the innocent young man in the back of the car until they were both satisfied. Bonin then motioned for Eric to step out of the car so they could talk.

What do you want to do with the boy now? Bonin asked Eric, knowing what Bonin wished to hear; Eric replied, *"Let's kill him"* Bonin, initiating that he would give the correct answer, handed Eric a steak knife that he had got earlier from Butts place. Bonin told Eric the honour was all his as they returned to the car. They untied Sean and told him to remove the rest of his clothes. Bonin attempted to keep Sean calm and said to him that he was going to choke him until he lost consciousness and would leave him with his clothes nearby for when he regained consciousness, they walked Sean across the field and told him to lay face down on the ground Sean had barely touched the ground when, Bonin grabbed his hands, wrenched them behind his back, held them with all his strength. Eric then wildly began to stab him on each side of his abdomen, then his back and the back of his neck. Blood was everywhere, and the knife started to get slippery. Bonin now excitedly tells Eric where to stab next. Thinking Sean was now dead, they walked away, but they heard noises. They turned to see Sean's legs wildly twitching in the air. Bonin, angry, snatched the knife off Eric and hurried back to the twitching body to finish the job. He yelled at Sean to shut the fuck up. He began to choke the boy with his bare hands, but it did not work, so he flew into a rage and started stabbing; it didn't matter where, as long as he shut up, the final blow went through the side of Sean's mouth. There was silence; the only sound that could be heard was the sound of the woodland cicadas. Bonin and Eric got back into the Chevette and headed to Circle K. They worked up an appetite and were hungry, and the car needed fuel. Bonin still wasn't 100 per cent sure the kid was dead, so he told Eric they should go back and check. Not wanting to get too close, they parked across the street and waited until no other vehicles were around. They rolled down the windows and listened but heard nothing, not even the bugs this time. The silence was tense, and every second stretched out. Suddenly, headlights pierced the darkness—it was a police car patrolling the area. Heart pounding, Bonin started the car, waved at the officer, and slowly drove away, his eyes darting to the rearview mirror, anxiously checking to ensure they weren't being followed. Driving down the 1-10, Bonin tore up all of Sean's ID and tossed it out the window. After Bonin dropped Eric home, he dropped by Butts to pick up a trash bag and give him back his blanket. According to Bonin, Butts greeted him with excitement and wanted to know everything that had happened without him. He wanted the whole sordid details. Butts also told Bonin that he had changed his mind, but Bonin didn't hear him as he called down the driveway when he left.

On his way home, Bonin left around 4:30 a.m. and found a garbage bin at the Kingswood apartments, where he disposed of his clothes.

Victim 23 Steven Jav Wells

Steve was born on September 18, 1961, in Bellflower, California, and sadly passed away at the early age of 18 on June 2, 1980, in Downey, California. Steve was laid to rest at Rose Hills Memorial Park in Whittier, California. He was a part of a large family, with parents James Wells (1933-2006) and Martha Kate Herring (1936- 2012) and five siblings: Denise, Dennis, Dianne, James, and Susan. Steven was six feet one inch tall, around 170 pounds, with sandy blonde hair and blue eyes, just the type of boy Bonin liked. Steven Jay Wells left the apartment in Norwalk, where he now lived with his mother, on June 2. He took a bus to his job at Porter & Griffin Printing Co., a small print shop in Los Angeles. After finishing work, he was on his way to meet his father in Downey, where they were getting fitted for tuxedos for his twin sister's wedding.

Between 8 p.m. and midnight that day, he was murdered. His naked, strangled body was found on June 3, 1980, and dumped behind the Mobil station on the corner of Adams Avenue and Beach Boulevard in Huntington Beach.

Remember at the end of chapter four when Bonin asks Munro the strange and unusual question?

"Hey Munro, how would you like to go out and have sex with a hitchhiker and then take his life?" Munro looked at Bonin like it was a big joke.

So, Munro just brushed it off and forgot what Bonin said, and then they finally arrived back at Bonin's home, went in, and went to bed.

The next day, Munro's life turned for the worse, and there was nothing he could do to stop it. Munro and Bonin spent the day driving trucks for work. Eventually, Bonin told his boss he was tired and wanted to go home. Bonin's boss said, "Okay, see you tomorrow." With that, Bonin and Munro-climbed into Bonin's van and began their journey home. The atmosphere grew tense as they entered Downey on June 2, 1980, around 5:40 p.m. Bonin's eyes locked onto a lone hitchhiker on the opposite side of the road. Without a word, he made a sharp U-turn, the van's tyres screeching against the asphalt, and sped towards the unsuspecting figure. Bonin pulled over his 1974 green van. An 18-year-old man approached and said, "Hi, I need a ride." Bonin asked, "Where are you headed?" The young man replied, "Just down the road." Bonin nodded and said, "Okay, get in." Munro slid open the van's side door, and the young man, Steven, climbed in and shut the door behind him. He settled between the driver and passenger seats, the tension palpable as Bonin began to ask him questions. Bonin asked, "Hey, what's your name?" "Steve," the young man replied.

"Steve, I'm Bill, and this is Jim," Bonin introduced himself, gesturing to his friend. They exchanged brief smiles, a moment of uneasy camaraderie. Then, Bonin leaned in slightly and asked Steve.
"What do you think of gay people? Then Steve smiled and replied, "Oh there, okay, I am bisexual." Bonin said," Oh really, so do you want to come to our house, or shall we come over to yours?" The plan teetered on the brink of failure because Steve lived in an apartment complex where Bonin was unwilling to venture. As tension mounted, Steve unex-

pectedly replied, "Oh, I will come to your house." Relief washed over Bonin as he quickly instructed Munro to drive home. With a sense of urgency, Bonin slipped into the back of the van, the night cloaking their next move in mystery. When they picked up the hitchhiker, Steven Jay Wells, he initially agreed to have sex with Bonin. Later, he allowed himself to be tied up, expecting to be paid for having sex with a friend of Bonin's. 104 It is claimed that Bonin and Munro tied Steven up, took his money, beat him, and then strangled him with his T-shirt.

As Munro prepared to drive down the road, he unfolded a paper map to find his way to the house. With a determined look, he set off, but not before casting a quick glance into the rearview mirror. He saw Bonin and Steve orally copulating with each other. When returning to Bonin's residence, Munro got lost, prompting Bonin to take over the driving. As they finally arrived, Bonin pulled into the driveway, unaware that the Los Angeles Police Department was surveilling his home. The officers watched intently as the van pulled in but claimed they never saw Steven. They watched as Munro reversed out of the driveway.

Meanwhile, Bonin had sent Munro to fetch some hamburgers. "Munro drove out of Bonin's driveway and headed down the road. Suddenly, some 8-track tapes fell onto the van floor. He stopped and bent down to pick them up. Sitting back up, he noticed a Downey police car with its lights on. Munro pulled over, and a police officer approached, asking for his license. Munro explained that he had a Michigan license but not a California one. The officer informed him that he couldn't drive the van without an adult driver and instructed him to go home and wait until he had one. Munro turned the van around and drove back to Bonin's home in Downey."

"As Munro entered the driveway, he overlooked the Los Angeles Police and Orange County Sheriff's Department still stationed outside Bonin's home. Bonin and Steven were inside, unaware of the unmarked police cars, watching their every move. Munro hurried into the house, his heart pounding. Bonin immediately approached him, his eyes filled with concern.

'What happened?' Bonin demanded.

Still catching his breath, Munro replied, 'The Police stopped me. I told them I didn't have a license.'

Bonin's face tightened, but he forced a calm tone. 'Don't worry, we'll go to the store later.'

Bonin then headed towards his mother's bedroom, motioning for Munro to follow. As they entered the dimly lit room, the tension was palpable. Steve looked up from the bed, his eyes narrowing.

'Hi,' Steve said, his voice low and wary.

"Bonin asked Munro if he wanted to join them, but Munro shook his head. 'No thanks, I'm going to watch Happy Days in the living room,' he said. Munro settled on the couch, lighting a cigarette as the familiar theme song played. Minutes later, Bonin emerged from his mother's bedroom, his expression unreadable. He approached Munro and said, 'Hey, come with me.'

Munro stubbed out his cigarette, feeling unease in his stomach. He followed Bonin back into the bedroom, where the atmosphere was tense. Steve glanced up, his eyes flickering with suspicion. The room felt charged, every movement heavy with unspoken words." Steve is lying naked on the bed." Munro stood there, listening intently as Bonin turned to Steve. 'Hey Steve, how would you like to make 200 dollars?' Bonin asked, his voice low and enticing.

Steve's eyes narrowed as he looked at Bonin, curiosity and suspicion mingling in his gaze. 'Yes,' he replied slowly, 'how?'

So, Bonin told Steve he knew a guy who was really into bondage and really got off on tying guys up. Steve glanced at Bonin, a hint of curiosity in his eyes. Munro, however, couldn't tear his gaze away from the two of them, sensing something unusual in the air. As their conversation continued, Steve finally broke the tension. "Okay, I'm game for some fun," he said, his voice steady but with a trace of anticipation.

Bonin's expression remained unreadable as he picked up the phone. Each number he dialled seemed to echo in the room, heightening the suspense. Steve and Munro exchanged a quick, uncertain glance. Bonin spoke briefly into the phone, his words too low to hear. When he hung up, he turned to Steve with a cryptic smile. "Alright, he'll be right over," he announced.

Munro's heart raced as Bonin's gaze shifted to him. "Munro," Bonin said, calm but commanding, "go to the kitchen, open the drawer, and get the rope." The words hung in the air, heavy with implication. Munro swallowed hard, his mind racing with questions as he moved towards the kitchen, the suspense thickening with each step. Munro went out to the kitchen and looked around, confused. So, he returned to the bedroom and told Bonin he could not find it. So, Bonin got up, entered the kitchen, and got the rope. At this point, Steve was lying on the floor of the hallway with his face in a pillow, and Bonin started to hog-tie him while he lay on his belly. Once fully restrained, Steve lay on his side, fear creeping into his voice as he tried to talk to Bonin. "Hey, this isn't your house," he stammered. Bonin's response was cold and direct. "No, we broke into it." Panic surged through Steve. "If you want money, I can write you a cheque. I have $300 in the bank," he offered desperately. But Bonin's expression didn't change. Steve's mind raced, and he started asking more questions, realising he had made a terrible mistake. But Bonin got angry, punched him, and told him to shut the fuck up, or he was going to kill him.

As they talked, Munro stood frozen, unable to comprehend the unfolding events. A sense of dread settled over him; whatever was happening couldn't be good. His mind was a whirlwind of confusion and fear, unable to grasp the full extent of the situation.

Just then, Bonin instructed Munro to enter the bedroom and fetch Steve's clothing. Munro hesitated momentarily, then complied, retrieving the clothes and handing them to Bonin. Bonin immediately began rifling through the pockets, his movements quick and methodical. He pulled out a set of keys and turned to Steve, his eyes narrowing. "What are these for?" he demanded.

Steve's voice trembled as he replied, "They're the keys to my job. I am a truck driver at the Porter and Griffin paint company." The room fell silent, the weight of the situation pressing down on everyone. Bonin looked at Steve and said, "Okay, I will knock you out, put your clothes back on, and leave you on a park bench." As he spoke, Munro moved closer, kneeling beside Steve. His voice was low and trembling as he whispered, "I don't know what this guy is going to do to you, but if he kills you, will you please tell the man upstairs I didn't do it?"

Steve managed a nervous smile and replied, "Okay."
While Munro was asking Steve if Bonin killed him, to say to the man upstairs, meaning God, that he did not do it, He continued to shake his head in disbelief, unable to fully grasp the gravity of the situation. Munro went and stood in the hallway; at this point, Bonin took Steve's T-shirt, placed it around Steve's neck, and started to twist it so tightly that as Steve was lying on his belly, he began to shake. Munro was confused and had no idea what was happening. Suddenly, Bonin barked, "Hold his feet, quickly!" Instinctively, Munro obeyed, thinking to himself that he was somehow helping Steve. He did not realise he had just helped William Bonin commit murder.

It was now too late for Munro. He was trapped and could not escape from what he had now stepped into. When Steve finally stopped shaking as Bonin finished strangling him, Bonin turned him over, reached down, grabbed Steve's testicles in one hand and squeezed until they heard a popping sound. Munro asked why he had done that, and Bonin said it was so the Police knew he had killed him; Munro then noticed that Steve's face was blue. Munro asked Bonin why his face was blue. Is he in trouble? Asked Munro, and Bonin looked at Munro and spoke.
"Munro Steve is dead." And Munro looked at Bonin and said dead; what do you mean he is dead? Bonin said he was dead. So, Munro then asks Bonin what he will do

now, and he tells Munro we will wait until dark and dump him behind a gas station next to the freeway. Munro did not do or say anything, and then Bonin told Munro to go into his brother's bedroom and get the big box. Munro went in there and could not find it, so Bonin went in there and got a very tall, large cardboard box and told Munro to help him put the body in the box.

Munro said I do not want to get into trouble. Bonin told Munro, "Do not worry; you will not get into trouble if we get busted. I will tell the Police you have nothing to do with it, so Munro smiled and said OKAY. "Bonin said we will wait until dark, pull the van up to the house, put the body in the van, and dump it. So, Bonin waited until it got dark. Munro and Bonin carried the body in the box out to the van and covered it with an old stolen tent Munro had, and then they both went back into the house. The whole time, the Police had the house under surveillance. If they had done something sooner, Steven may still be alive.

Well, as they returned to the house, Bonin talked to Munro and told Munro, "Okay, it is time to meet my crime partners. Munro did not understand what he meant but said OKAY. So, Bonin told Munro that he had partners in crime. Their names were Vernon Butts and Gregory Miley, so Munro said OKAY. At about 8 p.m., Bonin and Munro got in the van. They started driving towards the home of Vernon Butts in Downey, California. As they pulled up to the house, Munro asked, "Hey, will this guy kill me, Bonin said, not while he was there.

Bonin knocked on the door, and a colossal man opened the door. He was 6 feet tall, weighed 150 pounds, and wore a Darth Vader costume and a pointy wizard hat. Butts looked very creepy. He introduced himself as a magician. As we went into the house, Bonin introduced Munro to Butts. Bonin said Vernon, this is Munro. Munro, this is Vernon, so they said hello to each other, and then Bonin announced to Butts that Munro was my new crime partner, so Butts smiled. So, then Butts showed Munro a coffin made into a coffee table, and one coffin turned into a telephone booth. Munro did not know what to think.

Then Butts showed Munro a cabinet and opened the door, and six identification cards were inside the door. Munro asked him whom they belonged to, and Butts said those were the people he had killed. So, Munro returned to Bonin and stood there until he told Butts to come outside and see what he did. So, then Butts followed Bonin and Munro out and walked to the van; Bonin opened the van door and showed Butts the naked body of Steven Wells. Butts said, "Oh, how nice you got another one, "and then told them to take the body and "drop it off somewhere." Bonin asked Vernon do you want to come with us? Butts said no, so Bonin told Butts to call him if he heard anything. Well, Munro and Bonin got back in the van. They started down the road, drove to Huntington Beach, California, pulled over, stopped at a McDonald's restaurant, and ordered two hamburgers, cokes and fries using Steve's money. Bonin opened the window while passing through the drive-through window, and an awful smell drifted out. The woman at the window asked him what that horrible smell was, and Bonin told her it was a dead body in the back.

*Image SEQ Image * ARABIC64 The area where Steven Wells was dumped, Screenshot (Dark Reality, 2022)*

He grabbed the burgers and took off before she could call the police. So, as Bonin continued to drive down the road in Huntington Beach, he saw a closed gas station. This is where Bonin dumps Steven's nude body at the rear of the

closed gas station. Steven was found on June 3 at the gas station.
In the documentary "City of Angels, City of Death," episode five, there is a scene around 25 minutes in which Jerry Lefrois mentions that the police had the house under surveillance. It is puzzling why they did not seem to notice crucial details, such as Steven's presence and the movements of Munro and Bonin. Despite being tasked with surveilling Bonin, they failed to follow them when they dumped Steve, which seems like a significant lapse in surveillance for a suspected serial killer.

This is a transcript of the scene in the City of Angles City of Death documentary.
"Robert Souza: John and I have been working on this case for about 36 hours, and we got a call from our Lieutenant. He said the counsellor over Los Padrinos Juvenile Hall. He's got a kid there that's talking about the freeway killer. John and I considered going home to sleep, returning, and talking to him later. But let's go talk to him, I said. This could be something we don't know. So, this kid's name was William Pugh, and he was kind of cagey at first with us because we were really looking for some deal to go easy on him on his auto theft charge.
But then he started opening up a little bit, and he said, well, I've been hanging out with this guy. He is really into the

freeway killer thing. He has all these news clippings in his glove box. And I said, what kind of cars does he drive?
It's a Van.
I said so; what's his name? Bill Bonin
Jami Floyd: Police have looked into a number of mentally disordered sex offenders during this investigation, and one of the things that had come up was William Bonin.
Robert Souza: We looked at each other like this is it?
How well do you know this guy? And he said, well, I've been, you know, around him quite a bit. And I said, is it a sexual thing with you guys, or what's going on? He says yeah, kind of. But there's a lot more to it. I asked if he had ever seen him do anything. Have you ever seen him pick up a kid or anything? He said. Nobody asked me if I wanted to go along with them because he wanted to pick up some young boy.
That was enough for us right then because I was anxious at that point
We have to get somebody on him right now.
So, we rushed back to the station and told our Lieutenant. We had a meeting with the SIS Special Investigations section. They specialise in surveillance, and a very close friend of mine and former partner, Jerry Lefrois. We all called him frog, and I say frog. This is a big one, man.
This son of a bitch is the freeway killer. There's no doubt in my mind.

104 Executed Inmate Summary - William George Bonin - Capital Punishment. https://www.cdcr.ca.gov/capital-punishment/inmates-executed-1978-to-present/william-george-bonin/

RELIEVED — Lavada Gifford, mother of Sean King, one of the boys whom convicted "freeway killer" William Bonin had been accused of murdering, embraces jury foreman John Lang outside Los Angeles Superior Court yesterday after the jury condemned Bonin to death. Although found guilty of 10 murders, Bonin was acquitted of the charge of killing King.

AP Laserphoto

'Freeway killer' sentenced to die

By The Associated Press

LOS ANGELES — The jury that condemned William Bonin to die in the gas chamber for 10 "Freeway Killings" spent a long time going over its notes but decided on the sentence on a unanimous first vote, the panel's foreman says.

Bonin's lawyer said the 35-year-old defendant "had prepared himself for it" and was "emotionless" when the verdict was pronounced yesterday.

The lawyer, William Charvet, said Bonin feels various legal rulings in the case "will cause the Supreme Court to look at this case very closely" and order a new trial in the homosexual torture slayings of young men and boys whose nude bodies were dumped near Southern California freeways.

The jury had convicted Bonin of the 10 murders Jan. 6. He was also convicted of 10 counts of robbery, and it was the special circumstance of murder committed during a robbery that the prosecution used in seeking the death penalty. In California, death can be imposed only when murder is committed under special circumstances that are clearly spelled out.

Lefrois: In the Special investigation section, we were tasked with the surveillance and apprehension of high-felony targets early in the evening of June 2. We were told that a possible suspect drove a 72 Ford van.

When we got to the location, we secured an observation position across the street. About an hour or two later, we observed two individuals come out carrying a large cardboard box.

And then they put the box in the van. And they drove off Broadcasting with our radio was that they had made a U-turn. We're heading out westbound on the Main Street. But they couldn't locate him when the units arrived in that area.

Lefrois: A day or two later, a body had been found behind the gas station.

Joan Renner: It ended up being Steven Wells's body. He was on his way to a job, and he'd been waiting for a bus.

He had been abused so brutally that he was almost unrecognisable.

He was in such a condition. When he is found, this is an enormous escalation from this killer. This kind of violence on the body was bad enough before. It's worse now.

Lefrois: And that's when we started thinking that maybe when they came out of that house, this young man, Wells, was in the box that we saw them bring out and put in the back of the van.

Paul Holes: This is a tough position for this surveillance team to be in because they don't think they can go up and confront Bonin at this early stage during the surveillance just to see what was in the box and possibly kill whatever the investigation was going to benefit from the surveillance. Lefrois: We made several trips that we followed them on, but there was nothing to suspect he had that he'd done any foul play until the night of June 11." [105]

105 City of Angels, City of Death. (2021)1. [Documentary]. Canada: Official release in English.

Suspected Victim 24 (1996) Jamie Trotter

The investigation into James "Jamie" Trotter's disappearance led detectives through a bewildering array of misleading clues. Originally listed as one of Bonin's suspected victims. Reports of sightings of the 13-year-old boy would emerge only to dissipate as quickly as they appeared. Complicating the search, pornographic images of a boy resembling Jamie surfaced, deepening the enigma. In a fervent quest for answers, private investigators scoured the country, hoping to find any sign of the missing teenager.

Seventeen years after Jamie vanished on his way to a school bus stop in Costa Mesa, a hiker in 1990 discovered a horrifying scene in the Cleveland National Forest. The remains, charred and scattered by animals, were obscured by the passage of time and natural decay.

A pivotal moment in the investigation occurred in 1996 when detectives could make a near-certain identification. They meticulously matched Jamie's dental records with the remains found. The chilling correlation of his age, the details of his disappearance, and the remote location of the discovery drew a sinister connection to the victims of the infamous serial killer William Bonin, suggesting that Jamie was another of Bonin's victims.

Justice was slow but eventual for Jamie Trotter's killer. James Crummell, the man behind Jamie's tragic end, was sentenced to death in 2004. However, in a final twist of fate, Crummell took his own life in his cell at San Quentin on May 29, 2012, leaving a trail of darkness and lingering questions. [106]

106 L Romney, K Ellingwood. "There's Still No Closure for Dead O.C Boys Family." Los Angeles Times (online), 1996. https://www.latimes.com/archives/la-xpm-1996-10-10-mn-52479-story.html.

Suspected Victin 25 Jeff Sayre

Arvetta and Denver Sayre of Santa Ana understand that no one will ever face trial for the murder of their teenage son in November 1979. However, Arvetta Sayre took a vacation the week Randy Steven Kraft received a jury's verdict, seeing it as the closest form of justice they might ever get, believing Kraft to be their son's real killer. Your involvement in this case is crucial, and any potential leads or information you may have could be the key to solving this mystery. Fifteen-year-old Jeffre Sayre is among 21 young men in Southern California whose deaths prosecutors have linked to Kraft. However, these cases were not included in his trial. Deputy District Attorney Bryan F. Brown charged Kraft with 16 murders in Orange County, adding eight more during the penalty phase. However, they had accused him of 21 additional murders in court documents. Brown had to exclude these other cases for strategic reasons and to conserve court time.

The Sayres apparently understood. "Dan DiSanto, the D.A. investigator, approached them immediately after the guilty verdict and informed them that their son's case would not be included in the penalty phase," Arvetta Sayre said. "He wanted to ensure we understood the reasons behind this decision, and we truly appreciated his consideration."

But was he really a victim of Kraft's? I genuinely believe he was a victim of William Bonin's. 107 The death of Jeffrey Sayre was one of several in Orange County that could have been included in the guilt phase of the trial. However, delaying the trial would have required another preliminary hearing. The Sayre case faced two significant issues: the only solid evidence linking Kraft to the teenager's death was a notation on a list found in Kraft's car, and Jeffre Sayre's

107 https://www.latimes.com/archives/la-xpm-1989-08-12-me-270-story.html

body was never found. Without a body, prosecutors couldn't demonstrate that he was killed in the same manner as Kraft's other victims, nor could they gather fingerprints or evidence from a death scene.
"The Sayre case was just too thin," said one law enforcement official. "But you can be sure Randy Kraft killed him." Officials are confident because of the notation "Westminster Date" on what they believe is a death list. Sayre had just left his date's house in Westminster when he disappeared and was last seen near a bus stop at Bolsa Avenue and Valley View Street. [108]
Jeffrey was last seen in Westminster, California, on November 24, 1979. He had gone out with his girlfriend and her three siblings to watch the film *And Justice for All*. After the movie, they returned to his girlfriend's house to watch television.

Jeffrey's disappearance is shrouded in unique circumstances. He was last seen in Westminster, California, on November 24, 1979. After a movie night with his girlfriend and her siblings, he left around 10:00 p.m. to catch a bus home. Unbeknownst to him, the local buses had stopped running for the night. He may have decided to hitchhike home instead. Unfortunately, he never arrived and has not been heard from since.

108 Jeffrey Bryan Sayre – The Charley Project. https://charleyproject.org/case/jeffrey-bryan-sayre

Might I add that Bonin likes to pick up victims from bus stops?

At the time of his disappearance, Jeffrey was a sophomore at Saddleback High School. According to his mother, he was uninterested in his studies and wanted to drop out to work full-time. However, she and his stepfather insisted he stay in school until he turned sixteen.

Jeffrey's family life appeared stable. His mother and stepfather described him as a typical teenager with no significant issues at home. They never believed he ran away, as he had no history of such behaviour and wasn't experiencing any problems at home. Additionally, he left without his jacket, money, or identification, which further convinced them that his disappearance was not voluntary.

Jeffrey was a beloved family member, and his sudden disappearance was entirely out of character. His mother and stepfather have always kept hope for his return, continuing to search for answers and passionately believing he did not leave on his own accord.

Authorities believe Jeffrey was a victim of serial killer Randy Kraft, also known as the Scorecard Killer, due to circumstantial evidence and notes related to his crimes. One such note included the date Jeffrey went missing in Westminster, along with another suspected victim, Paul Fuchs, who disappeared in 1976. Neither boy has ever been found.

The Freeway Killer, who targeted young men in the Los Angeles area during the 1970s and early 1980s, is another suspect. William Bonin, also known as the Freeway Killer, operated in the same regions where both boys went missing. Although the exact whereabouts of Bonin at the time of Paul's disappearance are unclear, the similarities in the cases of Jeffrey and an unidentified John Doe Victim 8 suggest a possible connection.

From my small office in Western Australia, I have conducted as much investigation as possible. However, the police departments have the final say. There is always hope that new leads or evidence may come to light, leading to a potential reopening of John Doe's case for DNA testing to determine his true identity.

Jeffrey Missing Since: November 24, 1979
Missing From: Westminster, California
Classification: Missing Person
Sex: Male
Race: White
Date of Birth: August 26, 1964
Age at Time of Disappearance: 15 years old
Height: 5'6"
Weight: 120 pounds
Distinguishing Characteristics:
Caucasian male with brown hair and hazel eyes.

Jeffrey's nickname is "Jeff."

He may spell his middle name as "Brian."

He has a birthmark on his upper left arm.

Chapter 12 Munro Victim or Accomplice?

Bonin and Munro returned to the van, put their boots back on, and took off. As they drove, they listened to the radio and finally arrived back at the Bonin home. As they pulled into the driveway, several police cars watched Bonin pull his van into the driveway. Bonin shut the van off, and the police watched as Jim Munro and Bonin exited the van and talked. Bonin told Munro to run his hands over the van carpet to see if there was any blood. Munro said no, so they closed the van door and entered the house.

As Bonin closed the house door, the phone rang. It was Vernon butts on the phone. Bonin told Munro to quickly turn on the news. Munro did, and it had big headlines as it said the freeway killer had struck again, claiming his 45th victim. So, Munro looked at Bonin and said Hey, that is the guy who is going around picking up hitchhikers and killing them then it hit Munro; he shits himself and is terrified. Munro did not know what to do, so Bonin laughed and said, "Hey, you did not know. Did you? Munro said what? Bonin then told Munro. Bonin looked at Munro and said, "I am the freeway killer." He then entered the living room, sat down, and ate the hamburgers they had bought during the body dump. As he ate, Bonin glanced up at the ceiling and said, "Thanks, Steve," then looked down at the floor and repeated, "Thanks, Steve." Finally, he turned to Munro and, with a twisted smile, added, "Wherever you are," before bursting into laughter. Munro was paralysed with fear. As the night wore on, they entered Bonin's bedroom and lay on their beds. Bonin turned off the lights. The lights had been off for a few seconds when Munro suddenly jumped up and turned them back on. After noticing the abrupt action, Bonin asked, "Hey, what's up, Jim?" Munro said, "Are you going to kill me?" Bonin looked at Munro and said, "You want me to prove to you that I am not going to kill you"? Munro replied, "Yes, how?" Bonin responded, "Let me tie you up." Munro hesitated, feeling he had no choice, and reluctantly agreed, saying, "OK, go ahead." Little did Munro know that he was making a colossal mistake. Did Munro just give his life to a serial killer? What was he thinking? Bonin got the rope, hog-tied Munro, put a T-shirt around Munro's neck and started to apply pressure. Bonin told Munro, "You know I can kill you right now, and you cannot do anything about it" Munro began to cry and asked if he could call his mom and dad and say goodbye.

Bonin reassured Munro, saying, "It's all right.". "I will not kill you right now; "You are too important to me," "But if you run or call the police, I know where your family lives." I will kill you; furthermore, If I cannot kill you, one of my friends will "Munro pleaded for his life, saying, "OK, I… I will never tell anyone." Bonin untied him and let him go. Munro lay in bed, his mind racing, until exhausted, he eventually drifted off to sleep. The following day, Bonin and Munro drove to work. On the way, Bonin stopped to buy a copy of the Los Angeles Times. When they arrived at the office, Bonin hesitated momentarily before loudly announcing, "He has done it again!" The other truckers looked at Bonin and asked, "Who did what?" Bonin said the killer struck again. They all stood up and examined the paper. Bonin and Jim Munro then stepped outside, where Bonin showed Munro the newspapers. Munro glanced at the paper and asked, "Hey, who is that?"

Bonin said that it was Steve, "the guy I killed last night". Munro told Bonin that the photo didn't look like Steve. Bonin explained that it wasn't taken yesterday but was their most recent one. Munro asked, "Now what?"

Bonin instructed Munro not to move. Confused, Munro asked why. Bonin pointed to a white van on the side street and said, "You see that van? It's the police. They're watching us right now, so act naturally."

On June 5, 1980, three days after the murder of Steven Wells, on the 2nd, Bonin, Munro, and some other truckers were en route to the Los Angeles airport to fly to New York to pick up some 18-wheelers. They decided to stop at a McDonald's for a quick meal. While they were waiting in line, several detectives noticed Bonin. One detective even stood directly behind him and struck up a conversation.

The Detectives were there as they had been alerted to a possible robbery. The robbery went ahead, and unbeknown to Bonin, the Detectives were already involved. Without a second thought, Bonin bolted after one of the perpetrators. His heart pounded as he realized he couldn't catch him on foot. Desperation surged as he sprang into his car, tyres screeching, and tore off in pursuit. Wow, the balls on this guy, a serial killer chasing after an armed perp when he just got done murdering someone three days before. Bonin then drove to the airport in Los Angeles, left the car with Munro, and flew to New York. Munro went back to Angel Street, and while Bonin was in New York, Munro apparently hocked some of Bonin's things and drove Bonin's van all over Los Angeles to throw the cops off. Munro had been ordered to do this until Bonin got back. He was not given a choice. He was scared for his own life and did not want to die, so he did precisely what Bonin told him to do, no matter what it was. Until Munro finally got his chance to break free, he ran.

It was June 11, and Munro tried to continue like any other typical day, trying to act like everything was normal. He decided he needed to get the hell out of that place. Munro could not forget the night of the murder. The stench was overwhelming, a nauseating blend of decay and rot. It clung to the thick and suffocating air with a sickly-sweet undertone that churned Munro's stomach. The odour was so potent it seemed to seep into his very pores, leaving a lingering, unforgettable impression. Munro would never forget the smell of that body. It haunted him, lingering in his mind like a dark shadow he couldn't escape. Desperate for comfort, he really wanted to visit his ex, Tammy.

Munro arrived at the trucking company and went into the office., He saw Marion sitting there; she was so beautiful. Blonde hair, big boobs and Munro wanted her. She did not want anything to do with the hired hand. At least, that is what Munro thought because she was in her twenties, and he was only 18. Bonin was dispatched on a truck run, giving Munro the perfect opportunity to escape. Seizing the moment, Munro's mind raced as he grabbed Bonin's keys and sped off towards Long Beach. Every mile felt like an eternity, his mind racing with the fear of being caught. He finally reached his ex-girlfriend Tammy's place, seeking refuge. That night, he partied with her, trying to mask his anxiety with laughter and drinks. But the tension never left him. He knew he could only stay for one night before he had to return and collect his pay, the looming threat of Bonin's wrath hanging over him like a dark cloud.

Chapter 13 The Arrest of William Ray ("Billy") Pugh

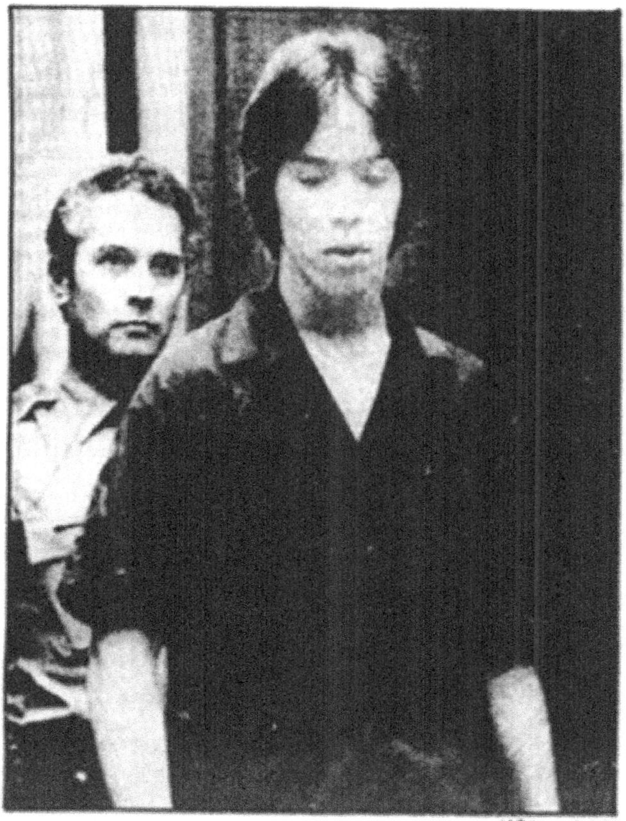

(AP Laserphoto)

*Image SEQ Image * ARABIC66 William Pugh*

This is Pugh's version of events. On March 24, 1980, Pugh met Bonin at a party in California and was around the same age as Munro. After the party, Bonin offered Pugh a ride home. Once Pugh was inside the van, Bonin asked Pugh if he would like to engage in sexual intercourse; at this point, they were already driving, and Pugh had politely declined the offer, but Bonin did not take no for an answer. Bonin moved his hand over to Pugh's thigh. When Bonin stopped at the next set of traffic lights, Pugh tried to jump out, but Bonin quickly grabbed Pugh by his collar and pulled him back in. This was when Bonin started to tell Pugh how he enjoyed picking up young men and teenage boys to rape, torture and murder them. Bonin leaned in close and whispered into Pugh's ear, "If you want to kill somebody, you need to plan and find a place to dump the body before you pick a victim." Bonin then drove Pugh back to his home, knowing that he could not kill young Pugh even if he wanted to, as people saw Pugh get into his van and knew them both. It was also at this time Bonin told Pugh that he liked to kill on Fridays and Saturdays, leaving Sundays free to take his girlfriend skating in Anaheim.

Pugh was reported to have had sandy-coloured hair and braces on his teeth at the time of the murders.

Bonin said it was around 11:00 pm when Pugh announced he needed to get home, so phase one was implemented. Bonin offered him a lift. Bonin then began phase two Bonin began asking Pugh personal questions asking if Scott had given Pugh a blow job, to which he replied no, not yet, but would like some, so Bonin reached across and began to caress Pugh's bulge and asked if he would like Bonin to suck him off, sure why not was apparently Pugh's reply. Bonin parked the van, and they both got in the back. It was a tight squeeze as Pugh had his bike with him still. Pugh was really excited, and Bonin knew, so he asked if they could take the situation further, as he was really horny and on edge as he really wanted to kill again. But Pugh told him that he only received head and did not receive anal sex but was happy to give it. That's not what Bonin wanted, so they stopped, but this was part of Bonin's plan. Bonin put the next step of his plan in motion, asking Pugh if he liked boys, "Sure he said, but I like girls better" Since we are both horny, let us go find a chick, but if we cannot find a chick, we could always pick up a guy. But we do need to get rid of the bike. So, they dropped off the bike and cleared the back of the van for the encounter. Pugh thinking they were looking for a girl, was eagerly anticipating getting his nuts off, but what if the girl doesn't want sex Pugh asked; well, too bad, we will fuck her anyway. We will just take it the same with the guys. We will never know whether Pugh realised that something was not quite right, but he continued with the initial plan. Oh, but what happens if they tell? Bonin asks, planting the seed of his real intent. Pugh's answer was to beat her up and make threats. This is when Bonin starts to reveal his real purpose, nah, we better not take chances. We will just have to kill her. Bonin had worked Pugh so well that he was now

contemplating murder.
It was now May 1980, and Pugh (CDC# C53164) had been arrested and incarcerated for car theft; while in Los Padrinos juvenile hall in Downey, he heard on the radio news that they were searching for the perpetrator of the murders in hopes of making a deal. Pugh quickly confessed to a counsellor that he knew the freeway killer. But he never mentioned that he played a part in some of the murders with Bonin.
This information gave the authorities a suspect, William Bonin.
With that information in hand, Detective Jigsaw John urgently needed to speak with Pugh. Pugh divulged everything he knew, leaving out anything that he was involved in. This was the lead they needed.

It was not until much later that the authorities were informed that Pugh knew more about the murders than he let on.
Pugh was eventually charged with sodomy and the murder of Harry Todd. Pugh was convicted as a juvenile offender and only received a 6-year sentence for voluntary manslaughter, the maximum penalty for voluntary manslaughter at the time; at the time of Pugh's sentencing, Judge Everett Ricks Jr gave him the maximum penalty, but as he had al

ready served 894 days in custody, he claimed he would be out in less than 4 years. [109]

Pugh apparently earned a reputation as a snitch. While Pugh was in prison, he reported to authorities about his conversation with Hampig (Harry) Sassounian. Apparently, Sassounian had confessed to killing a Turkish Diplomat on January 28, 1982. Apparently, four inmates, including Porn star John Holmes was, called to court to testify about the jailhouse conversation where Sassounian allegedly admitted to the killing. [110, 111]

From the information, I managed to source online. Billy also couldn't escape trouble even after he was released.

On October 4, 1994, charges were filed under Health and Safety Code case number XSO NA021871-01 and case number N02187101. These charges, filed on November 16, 1994, were for a felony in Los Angeles, California, under offence codes 1137(A) and H 11377(A).

In Los Angeles, California, Health and Safety Code 11377(a) pertains to the possession of methamphetamine. This law makes it a crime to possess methamphetamine, with penalties varying based on the circumstances:

Misdemeanour: Simple possession for personal use is typically charged as a misdemeanour, punishable by up to one year in county jail and a fine of up to $1,000.

109 'Freeway" Figure Gets Six Years ". Reading Eagle (Online), September 7, 1982, p 70.

110 "Teenager to Stand Trial for Diplomats Murder" Times Daily (Online), May 6, 1982, 31. 111 UPI. (1982, May 7, 1982). Young Armenian faces assassination charges. Lodi (Ca.) News-Sentinel.

Felony: If you have prior convictions for certain serious offences or sex crimes, possession can be charged as a felony, carrying a sentence of 16 months, two years, or three years in state prison.

Billy pleaded guilty on November 16, 1994, and was sentenced to 32 months in state prison. [112, 113]

In 2009, he was arrested on March 16 by the LASD-IRC OPS, WAD, CLASS, DA MESS CNTR, under booking number 1839134, for a misdemeanour.

In Los Angeles, misdemeanours are offences less severe than felonies but more serious than infractions. Here are some critical details about misdemeanour charges:

Misdemeanours can result in a county jail term of up to one year and a maximum fine of $1,000

Common misdemeanour offences include petty theft, driving under the influence (DUI), public intoxication, simple assault, disorderly conduct, trespassing, and shoplifting.

Pugh was released the next day.

On April 24, 2009, Billy was arrested by SUPR CRT-CLARA SHORTBRIDGE FOLTZ, booking number 1885914, for a (M) Misdemeanour, and he was sent to Twin Towers Correctional Facility. Where he spent 20 days being released on May 14, 2009

112 Los Angeles Criminal Attorney. (n.d.) Methamphetamine possession in California1. Retrieved July 26, 2024, from https://www.losangeles-criminalattorneys.com 113 Will I go to jail for possession of a controlled substance in Los Angeles? (HS 11350) - Southern California Defence Blog. https://www.southerncaliforniadefenseblog.com/2013/03/will_i_go_to_jail_for_possessi.html

2010 Billy was arrested by the KERN COUNTY Sheriff's Department on October 21, 2010, Prison ID S01919208
He was sent to the Lerdo Pretrial facility.
The crime type or offence was not specified, but he was offered bail of 25,000,00. Unfortunately, I couldn't find specific details about Pugh's 2010 case outcome in Kern County.

2011 Disturbing the peace case number RIM1108901PUGHWILLIAM620925 offence code l415(2) PC
Charges were filed on July 8, 2011
The charge of disturbing the peace under California Penal Code 415(2) PC typically involves making loud, unreasonable noise that disturbs others. This can include actions like playing loud music, shouting, or causing a commotion in public spaces.
In Pugh's case, the specific details of what led to the charge aren't provided. Still, it likely involved behaviour that disrupted the peace and quiet of the community.

In 2011, Billy was charged under case number RIM1113984, with the crime type and offence not specified. The charges were officially filed on October 7, 2011.

In 2012, Billy was charged under case number 644770WP-PUGHWILLIAM620925, with the crime type and offence not specified. The charges were officially filed on March 9, 2012.

On July 1, 2018, he was arrested for an unspecified crime. He spent two months in prison and was released on September 1, 2018, with credit for time served. [114]

114 Spy Fly. (n.d.). People search, phone search, property search. Spy Fly. Retrieved July 26, 2024, from https://www.spyfly.com

Chapter 14, The Arrest of Vernon Butts

N.Y. Stocks

Los Angeles Times

Late Final

2 Jailed in Freeway Killings

LATE NEWS

U.N. Sets Nov. Deadline for Israeli Pullout

Dow Hits 3-Year High

Sihanouk Quits Cambodia Fight

Salvador ...ts Raided

Trucker, Magician Accused

CARRIER MIDWAY, SHIP COLLIDE; 2 SAILORS DIE

3 Soldiers Die in San Diego Fireworks Blast

*Image SEQ Image * ARABIC67 LA Times front cover (Freeway Killers Arrested in 1980. . . - RareNewspapers.com, n.d.)*

While investigating William Bonin, the authorities asked people if they knew who Bonin's friends were. During these inquiries, someone mentioned Vernon Butts. With this information, they found Butts' address and went to his house to interview him.

"Yeah, Yeah," he said, "I know who William Bonin is. I sometimes drive his van." Butts went on to tell the Police officers that they sometimes drove at night and picked up hitchhikers; at this point, the police officers realised that they were speaking to an accomplice. Butts started to describe to the police how he would drive the van, and Bonin would get in the back and pull the curtain. Vernon said he could sometimes hear things going on, sometimes screams, occasionally sexual activity; Butts was trying to downplay his involvement. The police were stunned by Vernon Butts' confession. Following his admission, detectives promptly arrested him. They recognised his crucial role in the prosecution. They offered him a deal: they would not seek the death penalty in exchange for his testimony against Bonin and complete cooperation. Vernon also revealed the involvement of several others: James Munro, Gregory Miley, and William Pugh.

Vernon Butts was Bonin's primary accomplice, often serving as his driver. Munro aided Bonin with the last murder, while Greg Miley was coerced into killing several times. The most surprising accomplice was Billy Pugh, the young man who first revealed Bonin's name to the police.

Dr. Vonda Pelto is a clinical psychologist who gained significant insights into the minds of serial killers during her tenure at the Los Angeles Men's Central Jail from 1981 to 1985. She was responsible for preventing the suicides of high-profile inmates, including notorious serial killers like William Bonin (the Freeway Killer) and Kenneth Bianchi (the Hillside Strangler).

Pelto's experiences are detailed in her book Without Remorse: The Story of the Woman Who Kept Los Angeles' Serial Killers Alive. In it, she describes the psychological profiles of these criminals and the complex dynamics of her interactions with them. She notes that many of Bonin's accomplices had exceptionally low IQs and were heavily dependent on him, often manipulated into taking part in his crimes.

Pelto's work provides a unique perspective on the psychological manipulation and dependency that can exist between a dominant criminal and their accomplices. Her insights highlight the tragic reality that many of these individuals were victims themselves, coerced into committing heinous acts under the influence of a more dominant personality.[115]

Butts boasted to other prisoners about holding an axe to a friend's throat after being caught for murder. He claimed that he, Bonin, and the others carved satanic symbols into their victims. However, Butts was exaggerating to intimidate others, as none of their victims bore such marks, and there were no satanic murders in the area. Razook later informed the police that Butts was studying paganism and would not harm anyone.

When Vernon Butts was arrested. He was housed in the Los Angeles County jail in dorm 6000 in a single cell, and when he went to court, he was bound over for trial. Vernon Butts

115 Without Remorse: The Story of the Woman Who Kept Los Angeles' Serial Killers Alive by Vonda Pelto, Ph.D. | Without Redemption: Creation & Deeds of Freeway Killer Bill Bonin, His Five Accomplices & How One Who Escaped Justice. https://withoutremorsebook.com/without-remorse-the-story-of-the-woman-who-kept-los-angeles-serial-killers-alive/

committed six murders associated with William Bonin, but in 1981 before he went to trial, Butts committed suicide; he left a note saying that he could not let his parents find out what he had done to those boys with Bonin.

In a San Bernardino newspaper, Vernon Butts revealed that Bonin forced him to obey "like a puppy dog" during a series of homosexual murders, threatening to kill him if he refused. Butts mentioned that he and Bonin were friends, and he hadn't noticed anything amiss until the first murder he was involved in. Unfortunately, he felt trapped; "Bonin had associates, and I was too scared of him." Bonin had made threats to kill him and his fiancé Cati Razook. [116] Butts didn't dare go to the police. However, once in custody and knowing Bonin was behind bars, he revealed everything: "I was a scared little puppy dog. If Bonin said jump, I jumped." Bonin and Butts would drive around, luring young victims with promises of drugs or sex, with Butts usually behind the wheel. Butts claimed he did not participate in the murders. Regarding Sean King, Butts stated he was with Bonin when King was picked up but was dropped off at home before Bonin killed him.

Butts even moved to escape Bonin, but Bonin suddenly showed up and said, "Let's go." It was either to comply or become the next victim. Butts also expressed that he believed he was a victim too: "I am one of those few that remains alive – Miley, Munro, and I, and the other guy." The

116 AP. "Freeway Killer Defendant Links Bonin to Slayings." San Bernadino Sun (online), 19 October 1980, 11.

"other guy" he referred to was the young male Bonin was sodomising the night he was arrested.

Butts said fear had dominated him over the past year. This fear persisted even after he was placed in the jail's protective unit. One day, he found himself face-to-face with Bonin in the lawyer's visitation room. Overwhelmed, Butts began screaming for the guards and was quickly removed from the room. Vernon Butts struggled significantly with fear during his time in jail. Despite being placed in the protective unit, his fear persisted. Butts' fear and anxiety were so overwhelming that he ultimately took his own life. He was found strangled with a towel in his jail cell, a death that was officially ruled a suicide. 117

Vernon Butts, who had confessed to his role in the gruesome Freeway Killer murders of young men and boys, was found dead in his cell under chilling circumstances. With a towel twisted tightly around his neck, he had strangled himself by kneeling before the towel rack in his solitary hospital room cell. This death bore an unsettling resemblance to the torture-sex slayings he was accused of orchestrating. Sheriff's officers were quick to label it a suicide, but shadows of doubt loomed large. Butts, just 23 years old, was the state's pivotal witness against William Bonin. His attorney, Joe Inger, cast a sceptical eye on the suicide ruling, noting that Butts had been in a surprisingly positive frame of mind after a recent court hearing, showing no signs of the despair

117 "Freeway Killer Accomplice Gets 25 Years to Life Sentence." Lodi News-Sentinel (Online), February 4, 1982, 29

that might drive one to such an end. Inger offered no alternative theory, leaving the true nature of Butts' death cloaked in mystery and raising the haunting question: was it really suicide or something far more sinister? [118] The prosecution was at a loss; they desperately needed Butts' testimony to secure a conviction against Bonin. Without it, their case was in jeopardy. How could they continue now? Forced to reevaluate their strategy, they had to dismiss some of the murder charges. Reluctantly, they decided to put the other accomplices on the stand despite their concerns that individuals with low IQs might make unreliable witnesses.

Vernon Robert Butts was born on August 29, 1957, in Lynwood, Los Angeles County, California. Vernon's life was cut short on January 11, 1981, at the youthful age of 23. He now rests peacefully at Rose Hills Memorial Park in Whittier, Los Angeles County, California.

118 UPI. "Vernon Butts, Who Confessed to Taking Part in The." United International Press (online), January 11, 1981. https://www.upi.com/Archives/1981/01/11/Vernon-Butts-who-confessed-to-taking-part-in-the/1950348037200/.

Chapter 15 Arrest of Bonin

*Image SEQ Image * ARABIC68 Bonin in chains (Blanco, n.d.-b)*

The pivotal moment in the investigation occurred when a young man, detained for car theft, offered to provide information on the Freeway Killer in exchange for leniency in his own case. Despite William Bonin never confessing his identity as the Freeway Killer to him, apparently. The young man, Pugh, harboured suspicions. His doubts were fuelled by the discovery of numerous newspaper clippings about the Freeway Killer case stashed in Bonin's glove compartment, hinting at a connection to the notorious crimes. They had a solid lead with Pugh's information and information given to them via a hotline number. The head detective, John St John, and the task force began to look into William Bonin, and they found it horrified them. It was then that the police decided to place William Bonin under surveillance. They knew they needed to catch him in the act to secure a conviction. The tension was palpable as surveillance began on June 2, 1980, with every moment potentially bringing them closer to stopping a killer.

On June 11th, 1980, on the ninth day of police surveillance, the team followed Bonin in his 1973 Ford Econovan to the Hollywood area. Bonin was seen talking to five different young men standing on street corners.

Munro tells me then that when Bonin returned to the trucking company after a run, he found that Munro had stolen his car; Bonin had to get a lift from his Boss, Ed Delomer, back to his house in Downey. Bonin was angry that he got in his death van and drove to Hollywood to look for Munro, the people he stopped to speak with. He was asking if they had seen Munro. But no one had seen Munro.

While Bonin drove up and down the road, getting extremely frustrated, he eventually pulled over. He picked up a young man for tension release. The police saw some sort of transaction take place. The young man, 17-year-old Harold Tate, gets into Bonin's van. They drive to an isolated area in a vacant lot on Santa Monica Boulevard. After a while, the van starts to shake; despite Harold's resistance, the defendant, William Bonin, orally copulated him. The surveillance team had a dilemma; they did not want to blow their cover but did not want to give Bonin a chance to murder anyone else. They decide to move, walking over; they bang on the van and slide the door open. They find the young man tied up and handcuffed. They then realised that the young man was being sexually assaulted. He was seventeen, which meant they now had a reason to arrest Bonin. They could charge him with a Lewd and Lascivious act against a minor. The challenge begins: They need evidence linking him to the freeway killings.

The police found a length of white nylon cord and three knives in the van. They hoped to match the shag green type carpet in his van to carpet fibres found on some of the other victims; they also were cord, pliers, a car jack and tyre iron blood splatters and a rape kit.

They found newspaper clippings of the murders in the glove box, and the van doors had no handles inside, preventing anyone from escaping the Death van. [119] It was exceedingly early in the case when they arrested Bonin and charged him with the rape of the seventeen-year-old boy. He had only been charged with the rape, he had not yet admitted to any murders, and everything that they found did not belong to him. Still, all he would say was he knew who the killer was, and he was forced to help against his will. They could not risk releasing him back onto the streets.

119 Executed Inmate Summary - William George Bonin - Capital Punishment. https://www.cdcr.ca.gov/capital-punishment/inmates-executed-1978-to-present/william-george-bonin/

The police needed a confession, and Detective "Jigsaw John" St. John had a plan. One afternoon, he returned to interview Bonin, hoping to elicit his empathy, if any existed. Sitting across from Bonin, John slid an envelope across the table. Bonin reached for it, opened the envelope, and read the contents. After reading, he placed the paper down and looked at the detective. The letter, supposedly written by one of the victim's mothers, begged for information about her son's whereabouts. In a stunning revelation, Bonin opened up and confessed to Detective John St. John that he had raped and killed 21 young men and boys. Bonin later retracted this statement.

*Image SEQ Image * ARABIC70 Items found in the house, Screenshot (Dark Reality, 2022)*

*Image SEQ Image * ARABIC71 Screenshot (Dark Reality 2022)*

*Image SEQ Image * ARABIC72 Screenshot (Dark Reality, 2022)*

Chapter 16 The Arrest of James Munro

In the late afternoon of June 12, 1980, everyone at Dependable Driveaway learned of Bonin's arrest. Bonin's girlfriend had reportedly called to inform them that he had been taken into custody in connection with the Freeway Killer case. The news of his arrest sent shockwaves through the company as employees grappled with the revelation that their colleague was implicated in such a notorious series of crimes. 120 Munro had only worked at Dependable Driveaway briefly before the arrest. He was hired on May 27, while Bonin had been there for 11 weeks. They often drove to work together and discussed the news stories about the 'Freeway Killer.' Munro didn't arrive at work until noon to pick up his pay. When he realised Bonin was not at work, he became nervous and was reportedly chewing his nails. When the call came through, company owner Ed Demier instructed the staff not to tell Munro yet, as they wanted to see if he knew anything. Eventually, Ms. Perkins, Ed Demier's daughter, told Munro they had just caught the Freeway Killer to see his reaction. In reality, the police had only suggested there might be a connection with the Freeway Killer. Bonin had been arrested for sodomising an underage male in the back of his van.

Ms. Demier recounted that Munro had asked if Bonin had been arrested. When she inquired why he thought that,

Munro replied, 'Well, he was in Hollywood last night and has a van.' Munro then turned on the radio to listen for updates about the Freeway Killer

Munro asked for his pay check. He had already stolen Bill's blue Chevette sedan and taken off to his ex-girlfriend Tammy's on June 12, seeing this as his chance to escape Bonin for good. While still at Tammy's, he called Bonin's mother. She mentioned that she had heard her son was arrested as a suspect in several murders and told Munro, 'I do not want to talk about Billy. He is an extremely sick little boy.' Munro informed her that he had Bonin's blue Chevette. Alice responded that she had called the police and reported it as stolen. Munro said, 'Hey, I have the vehicle, so tell the cops it has not been stolen.' Alice agreed to call them back. Munro replied, 'OK, I will leave it at a store with the keys in it,' she said, 'OK.' Munro left the car. Munro stayed at Tammy's from June 11 to June 17. While there, he asked if the police wanted to talk to him. So, he called Los Angeles Police Robbery Homicide and asked if they wanted to talk to him, and they said yes, come in, so Jim came in and sat down. A Robbery Homicide Detective by the name of Kirk Mellecker came up to him and started asking him questions. Jim began to get scared. So, he decided to lie and get out of that police station, go on the run and leave his ex-girlfriend's house in Long Beach. That night, Munro took off running down the road, knowing he

James M. Munro

was now a wanted man and needed to get out of California as quickly as possible. As it got dark, he started hitchhiking, hoping to get rides from truckers—the fastest way out of the state. Ride after ride, Munro moved further east, drifting away from California. He decided to call the Los Angeles Police to see if they were looking for him. The detective investigating the Freeway Killer case confirmed they wanted to talk to him, so Munro hung up. He had no intention of returning to the police station. That's when the wanted posters went up.

Around the 4th of July, Munro arrived in Nashville, Tennessee. He stopped at a country music restaurant, sat, and ordered food. He looked dishevelled, with dirty hair from running through the desert, as if he hadn't bathed in days. He wore an old Army green shirt, blue jeans, and hiking boots. Munro carried a large, sharp hunting knife capable of slicing a bear, wearing it openly for everyone to see. After sitting for a while, Munro went to the back of the restaurant and used a pay phone to call his ex-girlfriend in Los Angeles. He asked if the police were looking for him, and she said no, so he hung up.

Munro returned to his seat, ordered coffee, and smoked a cigarette. After a while, he decided to move on again. He got up, walked out of the restaurant, and started hitchhiking again, determined to get as far away as possible.

From Texas, Munro arrived in Georgia. He came to a small town around midnight. Munro walked into the open small store, where two girls with hair still looking stunning under the dim lighting were working. The small store exuded a cozy and inviting atmosphere. Soft, Dim lighting cast a gentle glow over the wooden shelves lined with an eclectic mix of items. The air was filled with a subtle, pleasant scent of vanilla and lavender, creating a calming effect as soon as you walked in. The first thing Munro noticed was One of the girls had huge melons, and one thing Munro was into was a chick with big breasts. They both looked at each other, and she let Munro know she wanted to fuck him with her eyes, so she took him to the back of the store, where Munro penetrated her with his cock; upon her request, also engaging in other sexual activities instigated by the young woman, Munro noting the pleasure her enormous breasts had given him. Munro was so hard that he did not want to stop. Still, he had to, as A Georgia state police officer entered the store to check on his 18-year-old daughter and ensure everything was fine. Munro, unaware that the girl's father was a police officer, was frightened. As Munro appeared from the store's backroom, the officer asked him for identification. Panicking, Munro, who was on the run, provided a false name. Munro's heart raced while the officer stepped aside to verify the false identity. He knew he had only moments before the officer discovered the truth.

Munro glanced around, spotting a side exit near the back of the store., Munro headed to Michigan.
Munro finally arrived back in Michigan in the late afternoon of July 23, 1980. Exhausted, he sat down next to a store, drank a cold beer, and smoked a cigarette, contemplating his next move. Eventually, he found an old friend in his hometown of St. Clair. Munro recalled that his name was Tim "Rocky" Snider, and he helped Munro hide in a trailer park. For the first time in a while, Munro felt safe. He spent time with Tim's family, who had no idea that Munro was wanted for murder.
One late afternoon, Munro walked into a store and got a surprise. He saw his mother behind the cash register. A flood of emotions hit him—relief, guilt, and overwhelming sadness. He had been on the run for so long, and seeing his mother brought back memories of a simpler, happier time. She took one look at him and broke into tears. She had never seen her adopted son looking so bad; Munro looked like he hadn't eaten or showered in weeks. He felt like he had just left a warzone. The sight of his mother's tears made him feel a deep sense of shame and regret for the life he had been leading.
After a brief, emotional encounter, Munro left the store and headed down the road. As he walked, his cousin Cindy spotted him and pulled over. Seeing his dishevelled state, she offered him a ride to her apartment. Grateful for the help,

Munro accepted, hoping to find solace and a plan for his uncertain future.

When they arrived, Munro sat down and lit a cigarette. His cousin asked, "Where the hell have you been?"

"A fucking war zone," Munro replied with a weary smile. "You will never know."

She had no clue that Munro was a wanted man on the run. It was July 31, and Munro was sitting there, eating a peanut butter and jelly sandwich, when he made a phone call. He asked his cousin Cindy Porter if he could call and reverse the charges. She agreed, so he called his old girlfriend in California.

Tammy answered the phone, and Munro was on the line.

"Tammy, are the cops looking for me?" he asked.

Tammy replied, "Oh, but can you call me back in 5 minutes?"

Munro agreed, hung up the phone, and kicked back, smoking a cigarette while he waited. Unbeknownst to him, Tammy immediately called the Los Angeles Police and informed them that James Munro had just contacted her and would call back in 5 minutes. The police instructed her to keep him on the line so they could trace the call.

When Munro called her back, Tammy answered and started talking to him. She began discussing intimate topics, telling him she still loved and wanted him back—anything to keep

120 AP. "Freeway Killer" Suspects Were Co-Workers, Pals." Santa Cruz Sentinel (online), August 3, 1980. https://www.newspapers.com/article/14885531/freeway-killer/.

him talking. Meanwhile, the police traced the call to Michigan.

Very soon after Munro hung up, the Michigan State Police, the FBI, and detectives from Michigan arrived at Cindy Porter's home in Port Huron. There was a knock on the door. Cindy answered it.

"Yes, may I help you?" she asked.

The police displayed their badges and asked if they could come in. Munro started to panic. He had to move fast. Was there a way out? No chance, so he decided to play it safe.

As the officers began talking, they asked Cindy for her name. "Cindy Porter," she replied. Then they turned to Jeff and asked, "Who are you?"

"Jeff Porter," he answered.

Finally, they looked at Munro. He momentarily put his hand on his knife, then took it off. The police asked, "Who are you?"

"Jim Munro," he said.

The officers checked the description and confirmed that Munro was the man they were looking for. He was promptly arrested; they grabbed him and handcuffed him.

Cindy was shocked and had no idea what was happening.

He was surprised when they took Munro outside: TV cameras were everywhere, filming the arrest. Hundreds of people stood behind a police line, watching as the Michigan State Police and detectives brought Munro out.

While Munro sat in the police car, Cindy yelled at him, "Who the hell did you kill? It's all over the state, and on our capital news, you are all over the news." Munro just stared at her, unable to say anything. The police drove him to the Port Huron police department.

At the police station, Munro confessed to what Bonin had done, unaware he was being recorded. As he began to speak, a torrent of emotions surged within him. Fear, guilt, and a profound betrayal gnawed at his conscience. He felt trapped, knowing his words could seal his fate, yet he couldn't hold back the truth.

Every detail he recounted brought back vivid memories of the horrors he had witnessed and participated in. His voice trembled as he spoke, each word feeling like a weight lifted off his chest, simultaneously adding to his guilt's burden. He was torn between the need to unburden himself and the fear of the consequences that awaited him.

Munro was horrified at the thought of his parents sitting down for their evening meal, watching the Channel Seven Action News every night, and seeing their son's face plastered across the screen. The shame and regret he felt were almost unbearable. He imagined their shock and disappointment, and it made his heart ache. The realization that he had brought such pain to his family was a torment he couldn't escape.

"Eighteen-year-old James Michael Munro from St Clair Michigan has been arrested in connection with the Californian freeway killings – 45 young men and boys were murdered. Their nude bodies were dumped along the freeways in southern California." [121]

On August 1, 1980, neighbours recalled James Michael Munro as a shy boy who had lived in Port Huron. They remembered Munro cutting lawns in the summer and shovelling snow in the winter. The news of his arrest shocked them; they couldn't believe that the sweet, shy boy they knew could be responsible for what the television news was reporting. To them, Munro was just an innocent kid with a few tattoos who had hitchhiked from Michigan to the West Coast and, unfortunately, met the wrong person.

Munro was booked into the county jail, awaiting the arrival of California detectives. The Los Angeles and Orange County Robbery Homicide police departments were notified of his arrest. They scrambled a jet to head to Michigan and extradite Munro to California.

Munro was sent upstairs and placed in a cell. He sat there until the following day when the Los Angeles and Orange County Robbery Homicide divisions arrived. Munro was

121 James Munro | Accomplice of The Freeway Killer | William Bonin. https://wickedwe.com/james-munro/

brought downstairs and saw Kirk Mellecker, the head of the robbery-homicide department. When Munro entered the room, he asked why he had been arrested.

Mellecker replied, "Because, Munro, you did not come back to talk to us."

Munro sat down, and Mellecker read him his Miranda rights. Mellecker asked, "Do you understand your rights as I read them to you?" Munro responded, "Only if I can go home."

Mellecker said, "Well, we will talk about that."

Munro then sat there for hours, being drilled on the murder. Despite the intense questioning, Munro did not admit to killing Steven Wells; he insisted that Bonin had done it, but he was there. Munro finally left the jail and flew back to California. On August 3, 1980, he arrived in California and was booked into the Los Angeles County Men's Jail at 441 Bauchet Street. He was issued booking number 5788-561. The robbery-homicide detectives escorted Munro to his new cell in dorm seven thousand, hospital room number 7005, single cell status.

As Munro entered the dimly lit room, he looked around and saw a steel sink, a bed, and a toilet. The reality of his situation hit him hard, and he sat down, breaking down in tears. He had no idea how much trouble he was in.

Munro stayed there until Monday morning when he was taken to the Municipal Court. He went before a female judge, and as he sat there listening to all the charges laid against him, he realised all he could do was stand up and enter a not-guilty plea.

Munro was appointed a pregnant female attorney. Her name was Madelyn Gale Kopple. Munro thought she was very nice-looking and appeared to be in her thirties. Madelyn and Munro discussed the case, and she reassured him, telling him not to worry and that she would do her best to represent him.

Munro was charged with first-degree murder with exceptional circumstances and faced the death penalty. He was overwhelmed and didn't know what to think.

Munro pleaded not guilty in court with the support of his appointed attorney, Madelyn Gale Kopple. Despite the mounting evidence against him during the preliminary hearing, she was a kind lady who believed in Munro. By the end of the hearings, a female judge told the defence attorney, "I know that boy is not guilty, but it is a sad case." Had the court stood by this belief, Munro would have been free. Instead, Munro was bound to the superior court in Los Angeles to stand trial.

Munro arrived in superior court in department 120 before Judge Everett Ricks. The judge looked at Munro, fired his attorney, and appointed James Goldstein in her place. That night, Goldstein visited Munro in jail and threatened him, saying that if he didn't plead guilty, he would arrange for Munro to be killed. Munro was terrified and didn't know what to do.

Under immense pressure, Munro pleaded guilty to fifteen years to life, not fully understanding that he had just agreed to a life sentence.

When Munro went to court as a witness for the prosecution, he entered William Bonin's trial. Bonin stared at Munro, trying to gauge what he would say. Bonin's gaze was intense, like two cowboys in a standoff, ready to shoot each other down.

Munro took the witness stand and testified that William George Bonin was the Freeway Killer responsible for 21 murders in Southern California. As Munro recounted the murder of Steven Wells, the jury was visibly shocked. They were ready to deliver a guilty verdict without delay.

Once Bonin's trial ended, Munro faced the judges for his sentencing. He tried to withdraw his plea and fire his attorney, but the court refused. Munro was sentenced to 15 years to life and sent off to state prison, unaware of what awaited him. He entered the California Department of Corrections.

On February 26, 1996, William Bonin was executed. The night before, James Munro watched the execution live. Munro wanted to call and see if Bonin had any last words and if he could reveal the locations of more bodies to give the families closure. Bonin told everyone, "You will never get closure; you will see that the death penalty will not bring them back and that it sends the wrong message." He also advised that if anyone thought about committing a crime, they should go to a quiet place and think about it before acting.

All Munro could do was shake his head in disbelief, wishing he could go back and change everything, but it was too late. His fate was sealed.

Munro now sits behind prison walls, hoping for release someday. He says he was a target for abuse, having no family or friends in prison. The California Department of Corrections allowed the violence he endured. He was beaten and raped several times. Munro hopes that by sharing his story, someone might support him and believe in his innocence. He longs for a loyal friend to provide friendship, funds, and moral support to the once young man whose justice failed.

Chapter 17 The Arrest of Gregory Miley

*Image SEQ Image * ARABIC73 Gregory Miley*

The authorities finally caught up with Miley in Houston, where he lived. On August 22, 1980, 19-year-old Gregory M. Miley was arrested in Texas and waived extradition on charges of murdering Charles Miranda and James Macabe, along with two counts of robbery and sodomy. On October 29, 1980, Orange County raised the stakes, charging Vernon Butts with the murders of Mark Shelton, Robert Wirostek, and Darin Kendrick, plus 17 other felony counts, including conspiracy, kidnapping, robbery, sodomy, oral copulation, and sex perversion. Greg Miley was also charged with another Orange County murder and seven related felony counts. By December 8, suspect Eric Marten Wijnaendts, a 20-year-old Dutch immigrant, had been added to the roster, charged with complicity in the murder of Harry Turner. 122, 123 In August 1980, Gregory M. Miley admitted his participation in the sexual assaults and murders during a recorded telephone conversation with a friend. To avoid the death penalty, Miley pleaded guilty to first-degree murder and was sentenced to 25 years to life. He was received by the California Department of Corrections and Rehabilitation on February 16, 1982, from Los Angeles to serve life with the possibility of parole for first-degree murder. 124

On November 11, 1983, Miley faced additional charges for another murder in Orange County. He was again sentenced to life with the possibility of parole. Miley's crimes were part of the horrific spree committed by William Bonin, the "Freeway Killer," who, along with his accomplices, terrorized Southern California by abducting, sexually assaulting, and murdering young boys and men.

In both cases, Gregory M. Miley was convicted for his role as an accomplice to William George Bonin, known as the "Freeway Killer," in the murders of two boys, ages 14 and 12, in Los Angeles and Orange counties. Bonin and his accomplices, including Miley, were responsible for a series of brutal crimes that terrorized Southern California between 1979 and 1980.

122 Filkins, Dexter. "Clues From a Condemned Man Past." Los Angeles Times (Online), 1996. https://www.latimes.com/archives/la-xpm-1996-02-18-mn-37484-story.html. 123 Serial Killer Calender.Com." William George Bonin, N/A, accessed 1/10/2023, 2023, https://www.serialkillercalendar.com/William%20BONIN.php. 124 Inmate Death at Mule Creek State Prison is Suspected Homicide - News Releases. https://www.cdcr.ca.gov/news/2016/05/26/inmate-death-at-mule-creek-state-prison-is-suspected-homicide/

The victims, mostly young boys and men, were sexually assaulted, tortured, and murdered, with their bodies often dumped along freeways.

Miley was convicted of callous and vicious crimes. According to the Orange County District Attorney's Office, he has continued to commit criminal offences in prison, resulting in 26 rule violations, including nine attempted sexual assaults. The DA's office stated, "If released from prison, he would be an incredible risk to society." 125 Officials at Mule Creek State Prison (MCSP) are reviewing the death of inmate Gregory Miley as a suspected homicide.

The incident occurred at approximately 7:25 p.m. on Monday, May 23, when another inmate attacked Miley during the evening yard program. Miley, who was serving two life sentences for his role as an accomplice to the "Freeway Killer" William Bonin, was escorted to the prison medical facility. He was evaluated and medically cleared to return to his housing unit.

However, Miley returned to the prison medical facility and became unconscious at approximately 9:07 p.m. A medical emergency was declared, and he was transported to a nearby hospital. On Wednesday, May 25, at 4:10 p.m., Miley was removed from life support and pronounced dead.

There was an investigation into Miley's death. Officials examined surveillance footage, interviewed witnesses, and conducted forensic analyses to determine the circumstances

125 Orange County Da S Office to Oppose Parole for Double Murderer." Daily News (Online), 30 November 2011. https://www.dailynews.com/2011/11/30/orange-county-das-office-to-oppose-parole-for-double-murderer/.

surrounding the attack. The identity of the inmate who attacked Miley had not been disclosed, and authorities did look into whether Miley's past crimes or behaviour in prison could have been motives for the assault.
According to Munro, Miley was constantly bragging about what he did and claimed to have enjoyed the murders. Munro couldn't understand how Miley was not ashamed of what he had participated in. Miley's death was an accident. It was meant to be an attempt from another inmate to gain points so he would not be moved.

They have a point system. If you were good, you had low points, and the inmate known as Heavy D was about to be moved as he had a low level of points. He had pretty good behaviour. The plan was to assault Miley to get more points so he wouldn't be moved. Miley was chosen as the victim of the assault as he had been raping his cellmate. They thought he deserved the beating. But it went wrong, and he died. Heavy D was charged with Miley's murder.

Miley's prison record was marred by continued criminal behaviour. According to the Orange County District Attorney's Office, he incurred 26 rule violations while in prison, including nine attempted sexual assaults. These violations highlighted his ongoing threat to society, even while incarcerated. Miley's convictions included the murders of two boys, ages 14 and 12, and he had been serving his sentences since 1982.

Miley's death marks a violent end to the life of a man involved in some of Southern California's most heinous crimes. His convictions were part of a series of brutal acts committed by Bonin and his accomplices, who terrorized the region between 1979 and 1980. [126]

126 Ancestry.com. U.S., Cemetery and Funeral Home Collection, 1847-Current [database online]. Lehi, UT, USA: Ancestry.com Operations Inc, 2011.

Chapter 18 The Arrest of Eric Wijnaendt

*Image SEO Image * ARABIC74 Eric Wiinaendts arrest*

LARRY BESSEL / Los Angeles Times

Eric Marten Wijnaendts, 20, is led from court by deputies after arraignment in strangling case.

One of 'Freeway Killer'

Boy Sentenced

Eric Marten Wijnaendts initially faced charges of intoxication and battery on a police officer when he encountered William Bonin, a registered sex offender accused of violating parole, during their time in jail. Behind bars, an unexpected and twisted connection formed between them—a sexual relationship that would have dire consequences Upon their release, Bonin and Wijnaendts continued their dark alliance. It is believed that together, they took the life of Harry Todd Turner, a runaway from the Antelope Valley desert area. Wijnaendts faced severe charges related to the strangulation death of Turner. Turner's nude body was discovered on March 25, 1980, in an alley near 1610 S Bonnie Brae St, leaving a trail of grief and horror in its wake. Wijnaendts was not suspected of any other killings; Wijnaendts was arrested when he appeared voluntarily to submit to questioning. [127] Bonin covered for Eric Wijnaendts, who apparently committed two murders with him, for three fundamental reasons. First, due to their relationship, Bonin had a special place in his heart for Wijnaendts. Second, Bonin saw it as a "two-for-one" bonus; by implicating Wijnaendts in the Turner case, he hoped to gain leverage, something he might not have done if Wijnaendts hadn't helped him. Lastly, Bonin knew that Detectives, who had extensive interviews with him, believed Wijnaendts was involved but could not definitively prove it.

Bonin dangled the possibility of Wijnaendts' involvement until it was clear that doing so would not help him avoid the death penalty. Letting Eric skate allowed Bonin to thumb his nose at the system. In part, this led Bonin to spill his guts to detectives in December 1980 to get out from under the Turner murder charges. While the interviews were kept secret for three months, this decision changed everything.

March 24, 1980, was a pivotal day when Bonin, Wijnaendts, and others crossed paths. If any of those paths had changed slightly, the following events would have been dramatically different. Reporter J.J. Maloney broke the Free-

127 UPI. "Eric Marten Wijnaendts, a Dutch Bonin Youth Who Met The "United Press International (online), December 9, 1980. https://www.upi.com/Archives/1980/12/09/Eric-Marten-Wijnaendts-a-Dutch-bonin-youth-who-met-the/8654345186000.

way Killer story with his articles, which shocked the public and put detectives under intense pressure.

Eric Marten Wijnaendts did not live long; whether he got away with murder or was a scapegoat, he passed away on April 24, 1989, leaving behind three young children. According to the Orange County Sheriff's Department coroner record, Eric's death was ruled a suicide, but the circumstances were strange. The cause of death was eerily reminiscent of the way Bonin had murdered most of his victims. Eric was found with a ligature around his neck, consisting of a red insulated electrical appliance cord. A second cord-like ligature was also loosely applied around his neck. Similar material was found binding his hands behind his back, though it was loose and not restricting his wrists.

After his release from prison, Wijnaendts struggled to rebuild his life. He faced significant challenges, including societal stigma, the psychological impact of his time in prison and his association with Bonin. Despite these difficulties, Wijnaendts attempted to reconnect with his family and find stability. However, his past continued to haunt him, and he remained under scrutiny from law enforcement and the public.

Wijnaendts' tragic end left many questions unanswered. His death, mirroring the method used by Bonin on his victims, fuelled speculation about whether it was indeed a suicide or if there were darker forces at play. The investigation into his

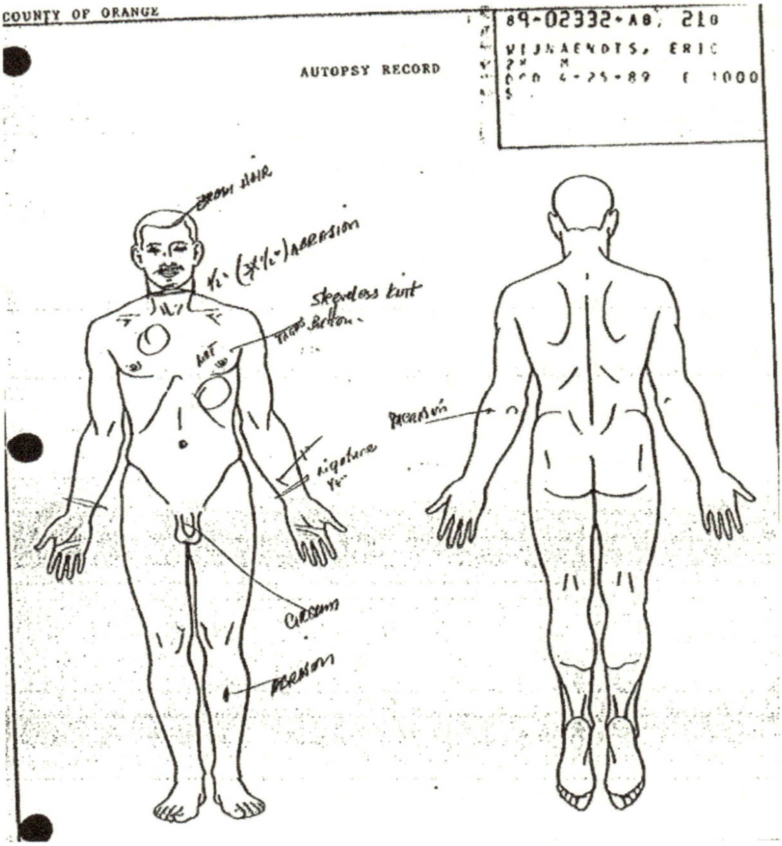

death did not conclusively determine if foul play was involved, leaving a cloud of mystery over his final days. 128 According to the Orange County Sheriff's Department coroner record, Eric Marten Wijnaendts' death was ruled a suicide under strange circumstances. . He was discovered wearing only a sleeveless white knit shirt.

128 Ancestry.com. U.S., Find a Grave® Index, 1600s-Current [database online]. Lehi, UT, USA: Ancestry.com Operations, Inc., 2012.

Eric's toxicology report showed traces of ethanol, opiates, and codeine. He died of asphyxiation, but was it suicide, or a sex adventure gone wrong? Either way, it shows that Eric had some secrets. Was he a deviant like Bonin, or another victim Bonin lured into his twisted life? Was he really involved with the crimes mentioned? Could he no longer bear the guilt? We know that he was engaged with Bonin and had been a suspect in the crimes at one time or another.

Chapter 19 Trial of William Bonin

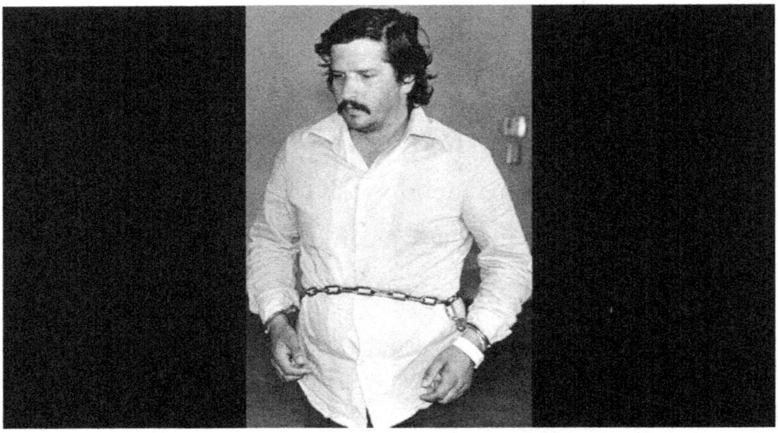

*Image SEQ Image * ARABIC76 William Bonin Screenshot (Dark Reality, 2022)*

During the trial, William Bonin's mother, Alice, testified that she and Bill would argue constantly about his same-gender attraction. At one point, he even married because Alice was insistent on him leading a heteronormative life.

On January 2, 1981, William Bonin was charged with the murders of Donald Hyden, David Murillo, Robert Wirostek, Darin Lee Kendrick, Sean King, John Doe, Marcus Grabs, Thomas Lundgren, Charles Miranda, James Macabe, Ronald Gatlin, Harry Todd Turner, Steven Wood, and Steven Wells (Pen. Code, § 187). He was also charged with robbing all the persons named above except for Wirostek, King, and "John Doe" (id., § 211); sodomising Grabs (id., §

286, subd. (b)(1), c); and committing mayhem on Lundgren (id., § 203)

On October 19, 1981, William Bonin was acquitted of the murders of Sean King and Thomas Lundgren, of sodomising Marcus Grabs, and of committing mayhem on Lundgren. However, he was otherwise found guilty as charged. All the special circumstance allegations were found true, except for the felony-murder-sodomy exceptional circumstance. Allegation.[38] [129]

William Bonin was brought to trial in Los Angeles County on November 5, 1981, charged with the murder of twelve of his victims whose bodies had been found within the county. Deputy District Attorney Stirling Norris, the prosecutor, sought the death penalty for each count of homicide Bonin was being tried for. In his opening statement to the jury, Norris declared, "We will prove he is the Freeway Killer, as he has bragged to several witnesses. We will show you that he enjoyed the killings. Not only did he want it and plan to enjoy it, he had an insatiable demand, an insatiable appetite—not only for sodomy but for killing. [130]
The prosecutor also highlighted Bonin's disturbing habit of grooming young men, whom he referred to as "people of low mentality," especially compared to Bonin, who was

highly intelligent. This manipulation was an essential aspect of Bonin's predatory behaviour.

During the trial, both Gregory Miley and James Munro testified against Bonin. Miley, who was 19 at the time and one of Bonin's sexual partners, testified that Bonin was responsible for the deaths of Charles Miranda and James Macabe.

The trial proceedings were intense and emotional. The prosecution presented detailed evidence of Bonin's crimes, including testimonies from surviving victims and forensic experts. The jury heard graphic descriptions of the torture and murder methods Bonin used, which included ligature strangulation and sexual assault. The defence attempted to argue that Bonin's confessions were coerced and that he was not solely responsible for the murders, but the overwhelming evidence presented by the prosecution led to his conviction.[69]

Miley said that he was with Bonin driving a van he owned on the night of February 2, 1980; Bonin picked up Miranda in Hollywood in the early morning hours of February 3 and consensually sodomised him in the back of the van; Bonin whispered to Miley, "The kid's going to die," and then started to tie up the youth; Bonin asked, "What does your dad want for you? How much do you think we can get for ransom? Maybe a couple thousand?," and Miranda responded, "I don't think that I can get that much"; defendant asked, "How much money do you have?," and Miranda replied, "About $6"; Bonin told Miley to take the money, and he complied; Miley said, "Well, why don't you let the kid go?," and Bonin answered, "No, man, he'll know the van and he'll know us"; with Miley's help Bonin proceeded to beat Miranda, to strangle him with a shirt and to crush his neck with a jack handle. Bonin and Miley dumped Miranda's nude body in an alley and disposed of his clothing in various locations.

After murdering Miranda, Miley quoted Bonin saying, "Well, I'm horny again. I need another one," Miley responded, "Oh, man, no way. I don't want to do it anymore. I want to go home." Still, Bonin went ahead and eventually picked up Macabe in Huntington Beach in the early afternoon of the same day, February 3, 1980. Not long afterwards, Bonin and the boy engaged in consensual sexual activity in the van; the trio then drove on; again Bonin and the boy engaged in more sexual activity soon however, Bonin started to tie up Macabe; he asked, "What could you get for ransom?," and stated, "This is a kidnap". Macabe tried to fight back with Miley's help Bonin proceeded to beat Macabe and to strangle him with a shirt and to crush his neck with a jack handle. Bonin and Miley dumped Macabe's fully clothed body onto the side of a road and took money from his wallet; Bonin then threw Macabe's wallet out of the van's window. 131

129 Mosk, J. (1989)1. People v. Bonin. Supreme Court of California2. Retrieved fromhttps://scocal.stanford.edu/opinion/people-v-bonin-30907 130 William Bonin | Found a Grave. https://www.foundagrave.com/grave/william-bonin/

Munro, who—like Miley—was also a sexual partner of Bonin and about 19 years old at the time relevant here, demonstrated that it was Bonin who was responsible for the death of Wells. "He mentioned that on June 2, 1980, he was with Bonin, who was driving his van. During their drive, Bonin picked up Wells, who was hitchhiking." and participated in mutual consensual oral copulation with him in the back of the van. The trio eventually arrived at Bonin's home in Downey; there, Bonin and Wells continued their sexual activity. "Soon, Bonin convinced Wells to let himself be tied up. Bonin then took $10—the entire contents of Wells's wallet—along with various identification items." With Munro's help, Bonin then beat Wells and strangled him with a T-shirt, disposed of his clothing and other property, and eventually dumped his body behind a gasoline station; Bonin told Munro that he was the "Freeway Killer" that Miley was one of his partners in crime, and that he had committedabout 14 murders in the course of his activities.

*Image SEQ Image * ARABIC77 David Lopez Screenshot (Dark Reality, 2022)*

Another controversial witness was David Lopez, a reporter for the Los Angeles television station KNXT. Lopez conducted a series of interviews with Bonin so that nothing would be repeated. Bonin was incredibly open with Lopez about his crimes. Lopez ultimately testified that Bonin had confessed to killing 21 young men, even though he was only on trial for half that number.

Bonin also told Lopez that he only revealed the location of Sean King's body to the police because they offered to buy him hamburgers. Scott Fraser and Ray Pendleton testified that Bonin had admitted to them, while driving his van, that he picked up Markus Grabs and killed him during sexual intercourse. Jailhouse informers also testified to other pertinent facts Bonin had shared with them, noting that he often said he would not leave any witnesses alive.

131 People v. Bonin (1989): Supreme Court of California Decisions: California Case Law: California Law :: US Law :: Justia. https://law.justia.com/cases/california/supreme-court/3d/47/808.html

Bonin was physically linked to several victims through DNA and forensic evidence, including blood, semen stains, hair, and carpet fibres. Forensic evidence showed that six of the homicides for which Bonin was charged were committed using a unique 'windlass' strangulation method, referred to as 'Bonin's signature trademark.' This was Bonin's modus operandi.

William Bonin incited significant public outrage. As James Munro sat in court, the list of victims Bonin was accused of killing was read out:

- Mark Shelton
- Markus Grabs on August 6, 1979
- Donald Hyden on August 27, 1979
- David Murillo on September 9, 1979
- Robert Wirostek on September 13, 1979
- Walter Tanner on November 14, 1979
- Frank Fox on November 30, 1979
- John Kilpatrick on December 10, 1979
- James Moore on February 1, 1980
- Charles Miranda on February 2, 1980
- James Macabe on February 3, 1980
- Ronald Gatlin on March 14, 1980
- Glen Baker on March 21, 1980

- Russell Rugh on March 21, 1980

The list continued, and the public demanded justice as more victims' names were read:

- Harry Todd Turner on March 21, 1980

William Ray Pugh was charged and convicted for this homicide. He received a manslaughter sentence and was released after six years. In contrast, James Munro, who did less, received a life sentence. The victims continued:

- Steven Wood on April 11, 1980
- Darin Lee Kendrick on April 29, 1980
- Lawrence Sharp on May 18, 1980
- Sean King on May 20, 1980
- Steven Wells on June 2, 1980

As the court listened to the names being called against William Bonin, James Munro wondered what he had gotten himself into and how he would get out of it."

"The jury reviewed each victim, homicide by homicide, calling them out one at a time as Bonin sat there. They declared, 'We, the jury, find William Bonin guilty of the homicide of:

- Markus Grabs
- Donald Hyden
- David Murillo
- Frank Fox

- Charles Miranda
- James Macabe
- Ronald Gatlin
- Glen Barker
- Russell Rugh
- Harry Turner
- Steven Wood
- Darin Kendrick
- Lawrence Sharp
- Steven J. Wells.'

"The jury took several hours to read all the verdicts. The victims' relatives in the courtroom were crying and yelling, prompting the judge to ask for silence. Outside, people cheered joyfully in the streets, celebrating that justice had been served against the serial killer.

Next, the jury had to decide Bonin's second fate: death or life in prison without parole. They ultimately decided that William George Bonin must die in the gas chamber for his crimes against society. Bonin was sentenced to death, transferred to the California Department of Corrections, and delivered to San Quentin State Prison. He was placed on Death Row until his execution by lethal injection, following California's change from gas to lethal injection."
Surprisingly, Bonin was not murdered in prison. According to Lloyd Carlo Douglas, Bonin showed him newspaper

articles about 'the little boys I got a hold of.' Douglas quoted Bonin as saying he did not recognise the photo of his nephew, Lawrence Sharpe, whom Douglas had not seen since early 1970 when Sharpe was around 7 or 8 years old. It was not until after Douglas pleaded guilty to charges of voluntary manslaughter and second-degree burglary that he informed the authorities about what Bonin had told him. Douglas also claimed that he and Bonin had a sexual relationship while in the high-security section of the Los Angeles County Jail between June and August 1980. Bonin would regularly orally copulate with Douglas through the bars of his cell. Bonin also mentioned that not all the bodies had been found and most likely never would be. [132] After Lloyd Carlo Douglas revealed Bonin's confessions and their interactions in prison, Bonin continued to await his fate on Death Row.

*133 Image SEQ Image * ARABIC78 Bonin at Orange County Court Screenshot (Dark Reality, 2022)*

132 Blake, Gene. "One of the Freeway Killer Victims Was His Nephew, Witness against Bonin Reveals "Los Angeles Times (online), 1981, 16. https://www.newspapers.com/article/68731355/the-los-angeles-times/. 133 People v. Bonin (1989): Supreme Court of California Decisions: California Case Law: California Law: US Law: Justia. https://law.justia.com/cases/california/supreme-court/3d/47/808.html

Chapter 20 James Munro's Trial

Munro was now facing the Los Angeles County court system, with the deputy district attorney's office headed by Sterling E. Norris, a man in his 50s with white hair. In 1980, Munro refused to testify against Bonin. Norris then devised a plan to change Munro's mind. He instructed his secretary to get close to Munro and pretend to be romantically interested in him, hoping Munro would do anything she asked. Munro fell for her and even proposed marriage. She told Munro she would ask her daughters.

Desperate to win his freedom since his arrest, Munro tried everything. When he refused to testify, the DA was furious, and the secretary cut ties with Munro, despite Norris violating every rule in the book to get Munro to testify."

Munro sat in a single cell at the Los Angeles County Jail. The police department gave him a radio to help pass the time, given his situation of being locked up for a crime he did not commit and being forced to plead guilty, which would result in a life sentence. What kind of justice is it when young, mentally challenged individuals who cannot afford an attorney are thrown away? Who would fight with everything they had to get Munro free?

In 1980, the municipal court judge, the Honourable Judge Brown, stated, 'I know that boy is not guilty, but it is a sad case.' Her hands were tied, and justice was impartial, leading to mentally challenged young kids being sent to prison."

*Image SEQ Image * ARABIC79 James Munro (Wiki, n.d.)*

Steven Wells's father was furious with the district attorney's office for doing everything possible to appease Munro and secure his testimony against Bonin. They went to great lengths, even breaking bar laws, to obtain Munro's testimony. Sterling Norris committed prosecutorial misconduct, as outlined in a letter from Steven Wells's father, James Wells. If you read the letter carefully, it suggests that the District Attorney's Office was setting up James Munro to be killed.

James Wells' letter stated that on March 11, 1982, Senior Judge Ricks was the Judge in James Munro's Trial.

Our son Steven Wells was murdered on June 2, 1980, by William Bonin and James Munro. We sat in court and heard Sterling Norris repeat the lies told by James Munro about the circumstances of Stevens's death. When he had finished parroting one of Munro's Eight confessions of not having committed any crimes on his own and being a mere victim of circumstances, our son was made to look like an ignorant homosexual who willingly joined two men he never saw before having sex with them and allowed himself to be tied up and tortured and murdered. Mr Norris made a point to say that no force was needed. We are not criticising Ernie Norris in any way. He had a job, so he insisted that James Munro was an innocent bystander who would not have committed any crime on his own and was a victim of circumstances. However, we cannot find the words to tell you

134 "Retarded Youth Meted 15 Year Sentence ". Eugene Register-Guard (Online), March 16, 1982, 5.

how painful and disgusting this was. We kept silent because we were told that James Munro's testimony was vital to convicting William Bonin and would do anything to accomplish that. Sterling Norris made and led us to believe that when James Munro was sentenced, he would go directly to state prison and be put in the regular population, which was the general mainline population, with no special treatment. Now, we find that this has all changed.

That was a letter everyone could understand from a parent, and James Munro understood this; however, James Munro almost landed in the same fate when Bonin tied James Munro up, and Munro pleaded for his life also.

We must now cater to Munro. If he were put in state prison, he would have to be isolated and unable to earn any money for cigarettes. This would be cruel and unjust. We wonder if everyone has forgotten where Steve is right now.?

The key to this letter was Sterling Norris, who believed that James Munro was himself a victim and ignored the statement made by Channel 2 television reporter David Lopez. Lopez claimed that Bonin held Steven's head. At the same time, Munro tried to kill him by hitting him in the throat, which never happened, according to court records and Munro's testimony. Bonin only punched Wells in the chest. Munro held Wells down while Bonin killed him, but the documents show that Bonin tied up Wells and Munro was forced to hold Wells's feet, not kill him.

So, we cannot stand by any longer and see James Munro patted on the back. We are asking you to help. The only Innocent bystander was our son Steve. He was a contributing human being who supported himself by honest work and goals. He was not a street kid. James Munro earned his punishment.

Munro sat in the courtroom, facing his fate in the defendant's chair. He kept staring at the Judge, trying to figure out what was happening as the first witness came to testify against him. It was Jigsaw John. He testified that Munro was with William Bonin when Bonin strangled Steven Wells. However, he admitted that there was no semen in the anus, making it hard to charge Munro with a sex crime. Munro listened to lie after lie as his attorney, Madelyn Kopple, was winning the case.

However, after the Los Angeles Coroner testified that Steven Wells was strangled, things took a turn for the worse for Munro. He still did not understand what was happening. The Judge then bound him over to the superior court to stand trial for first-degree homicide with special circumstances attached. If a jury found Munro guilty, Munro would be executed. "In the California criminal justice system, it seems that unless you're wealthy, famous, or a former president, you'll likely end up in prison.

On March 15, 1982, James Munro faced sentencing before Judge Everett Ricks Jr. At the time, his trial attorney, James

Allen Goldstein, had pressured him to plead guilty to avoid the death penalty. Consequently, Munro wanted Goldstein removed from his case, but Goldstein refused.
During the sentencing, Goldstein addressed the court, saying, 'Your Honour, Mr Munro has written a letter requesting my removal as counsel and asking to withdraw his guilty plea to proceed on the original charges, which included special circumstances making him a candidate for the death penalty.' Judge Everett Ricks Jr. responded, 'Okay, all those motions are denied; they are unfounded. If Mr Munro continues to waste the court's time and bother me, I might just let him go to the death penalty trial.'

Ultimately, James Munro was sentenced to 15 years to life."[134]
When reviewing the April 2, 1982, transcript, a crucial document in Munro's case, several mentions were made of Munro's letter to the court. One request was to withdraw his previously entered plea. Munro wanted to proceed to a jury trial on the original charges, a constitutional right, and to have Mr. Goldstein relieved of his position as Munro's counsel. The court responded that the motions were denied and deemed ridiculous, so they were rejected.

The court further stated that Munro should pray every few seconds that he is not going to the gas chamber with Bonin, as the court would have no problem sending him there. Munro was also denied the opportunity to address the court, as the Judge believed he would only irritate him and provoke the Judge to do something he already wanted: send Munro to the gas chamber. However, due to the plea deal, the Judge warned that if Munro irritated him enough, he would withdraw the plea and let the case go to a death penalty trial.

How could Munro get a fair trial and sentencing when the Judge encouraged him and allowed him to be represented by poor counsel who clearly did not advocate for his client? Poor legal representation can have severe consequences for a defendant, including:

Inadequate legal representation can lead to wrongful convictions, where an innocent person is found guilty.

Defendants may receive harsher sentences than they would have with competent representation.

Poor representation can result in missed opportunities to appeal or challenge evidence, making it harder to overturn a conviction.

Defendants may experience significant stress, anxiety, and a sense of injustice, which can affect their mental health.

Legal fees and the costs associated with a wrongful conviction or unfair sentencing can be financially devastating.

A conviction, especially a wrongful one, can severely damage a person's reputation and future opportunities.

I am not saying that Munro did not deserve to be punished for his participation. He most certainly did. He received a 15 to life sentence. It has now been a staggering 46 years since he was incarcerated. Has he been punished enough? The time he has already served is significant, especially compared to others who have committed more serious crimes and received more lenient sentences. Many complicated circumstances were attributed to Munro's Trial and sentencing. Munro was also a victim of William Bonin, according to a probation report statement provided by a probation officer to the court.

Munro endured a profound injustice. Regardless of their circumstances, every individual must be granted a fair trial. Several vital factors should be considered to ensure Munro received a fair trial and sentencing.

It is imperative that an independent body thoroughly examine Munro's counsel's performance to ascertain whether they provided adequate representation. A new trial with competent defence counsel should be strongly considered if lacking.

The Judge's conduct should be scrutinised to ensure impartiality. If the Judge is found to have encouraged or allowed poor representation, they should be recused from the case.

Munro should be granted the right to effective legal representation. This includes ensuring that his counsel is adequately prepared and capable of advocating for his interests. Munro should be allowed to appeal his conviction and sentencing based on the grounds of ineffective assistance of counsel. This could lead to a retrial or a review of the case, offering a ray of hope for justice.

A public inquiry into the handling of Munro's case could help identify systemic issues and ensure accountability for any misconduct by the Judge or counsel. It could also lead to reforms in the legal system to prevent similar injustices.

MR. GOLDSTEIN: Your Honor, Mr. Munro has requested that he be allowed to address the court.

THE COURT: Well, Mr. Munro can address me if he wants to, but I think it would be better for him to be quiet because the only thing he's going to do is irritate me and make me do something that I would like to do if we hadn't agreed otherwise for his testimony against Bonnin, and I just don't like Mr. Munro's attitude anyway. I think everyone has bent over backwards to be nice to him. He was given a break in this matter because his testimony was needed against Bonnin. So, why he acts with a chip on his shoulder I just can't comprehend at all.

If he irritates me enough, I might withdraw the plea and let it go to a death penalty trial in the matter.

MR. GOLDSTEIN: I have warned Mr. Munro of that, Your Honor.

THE COURT: Mr. Norris just may not object to that.

MR. GOLDSTEIN: We would submit it.

MR. NORRIS: We submit it, Your Honor.

THE COURT: All right. Due to Mr. Munro's cooperation in testifying against Mr. Bonnin and the plea negotiation previously entered into in this matter, and also it should be noted from the probation report that the defendant has no prior criminal background at all. This is his first involvement in criminal activitv of any type. The probation report states in mitigating the defendant ha^d no apparent predisposition to do this. He was induced by others to

5

*Image SEQ Image * ARABIC80 Munro Court documents refusing jury trial*

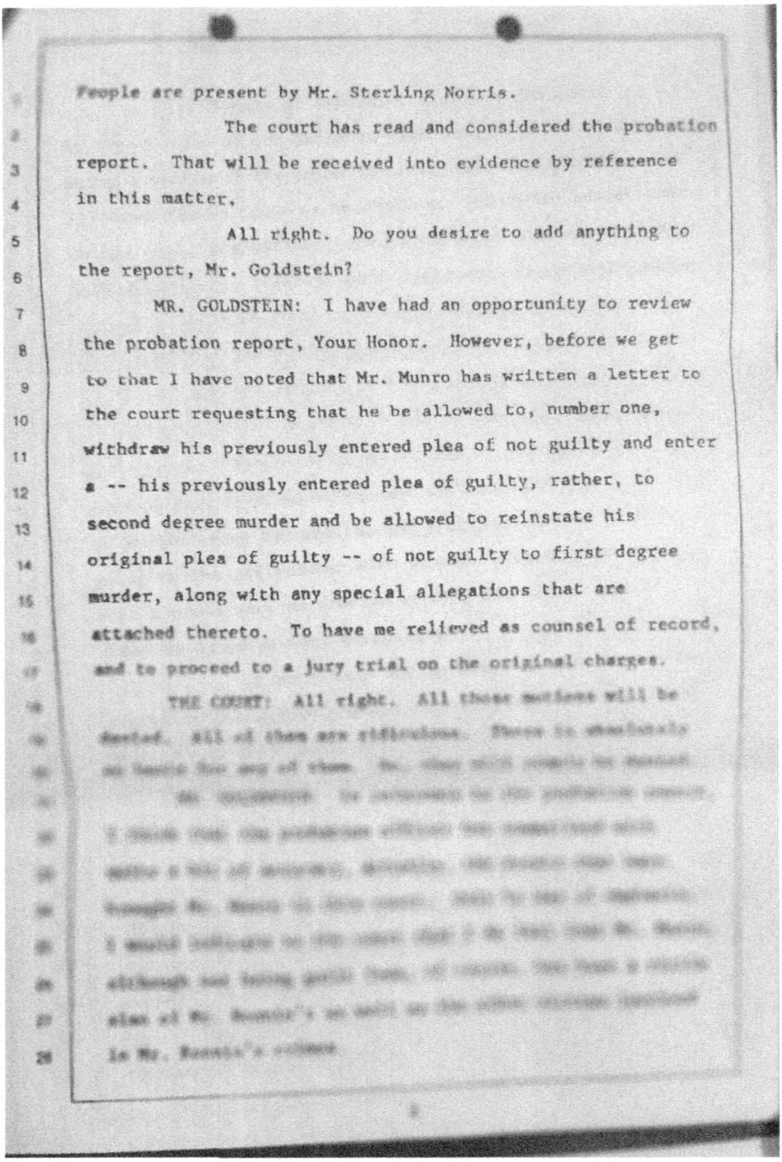
People are present by Mr. Sterling Norris.

The court has read and considered the probation report. That will be received into evidence by reference in this matter.

All right. Do you desire to add anything to the report, Mr. Goldstein?

MR. GOLDSTEIN: I have had an opportunity to review the probation report, Your Honor. However, before we get to that I have noted that Mr. Munro has written a letter to the court requesting that he be allowed to, number one, withdraw his previously entered plea of not guilty and enter a -- his previously entered plea of guilty, rather, to second degree murder and be allowed to reinstate his original plea of guilty -- of not guilty to first degree murder, along with any special allegations that are attached thereto. To have me relieved as counsel of record, and to proceed to a jury trial on the original charges.

THE COURT: All right. All these motions will be

*Image SEQ Image * ARABIC81 Munro court documents denying new lawyer*

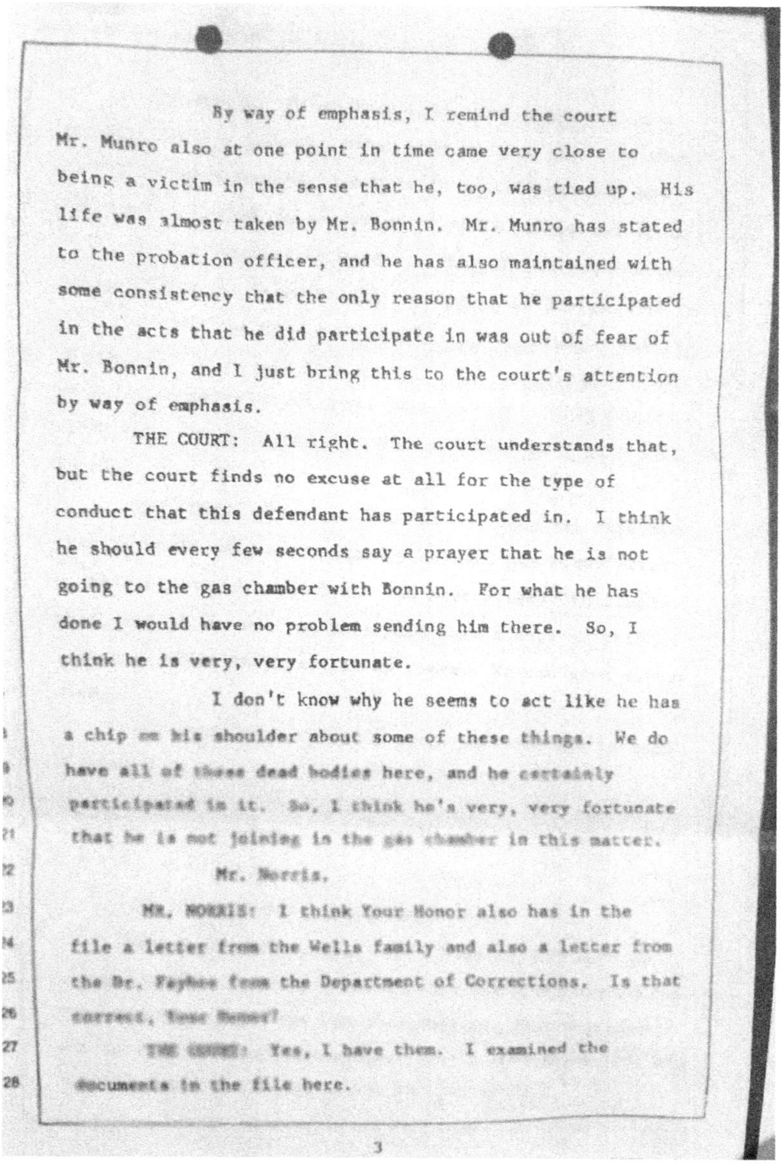

By way of emphasis, I remind the court Mr. Munro also at one point in time came very close to being a victim in the sense that he, too, was tied up. His life was almost taken by Mr. Bonnin. Mr. Munro has stated to the probation officer, and he has also maintained with some consistency that the only reason that he participated in the acts that he did participate in was out of fear of Mr. Bonnin, and I just bring this to the court's attention by way of emphasis.

THE COURT: All right. The court understands that, but the court finds no excuse at all for the type of conduct that this defendant has participated in. I think he should every few seconds say a prayer that he is not going to the gas chamber with Bonnin. For what he has done I would have no problem sending him there. So, I think he is very, very fortunate.

I don't know why he seems to act like he has a chip on his shoulder about some of these things. We do have all of these dead bodies here, and he certainly participated in it. So, I think he's very, very fortunate that he is not joining in the gas chamber in this matter.

Mr. Norris.

MR. NORRIS: I think Your Honor also has in the file a letter from the Wells family and also a letter from the Dr. [illegible] from the Department of Corrections. Is that correct, Your Honor?

THE COURT: Yes, I have them. I examined the documents in the file here.

3

*Image SEQ Image * ARABIC82 Court documents*

participate in the crime, and the defendant has no prior record whatsoever.

The factors in aggravation, the court finds the crime involving the taking of a life in a vicious callous manner.

Two, the plan in which the crime was carried out indicates premeditation in the matter. Therefore, pursuant to plea negotiation previously entered into, the defendant will be sentenced to the state prison for 15 years to life. He will be givencredit -- we continued this thing so many times now. It was originally 544 days. Do you have the figures?

MR. GOLDSTEIN: I think that was from January 29th, Your Honor.

THE COURT: That is what I thought. We started to continue from January 29th. So, that will be until March 15th.

MR. GOLDSTEIN: An additional 46 days, I believe, Your Honor.

THE COURT: Is that about what you calculate?

MR. NORRIS: That would be approximately right, I think.

THE COURT: All right. The defendant will be given credit for 590 days time actually served, 295 days good time or work time.

I calculate 885 days. Is that right? That sounds like a lot of time. Has he been in that long?

MR. GOLDSTEIN: He has been in actually almost 500 --

6

*Image SEQ Image * ARABIC83 Court Documents*

what was it, 590 days.

THE COURT: Right. 295 good time work time. So, a total of 885 days is the calculation.

MR. NORRIS: Whatever that would calculate; whatever Your Honor's calculations are added to the actual time in custody.

THE COURT: Right, actual time in custody.

All right. The Department of Corrections -- it will be noted for the record that the court feels this defendant should stay in state prison the rest of his life, or a very, very substantial time of it. He is easily led and participates in heinous type activity.

The Department of Corrections is ordered not to release this defendant without notifying the district attorney's office of the date of release and also notifying the Wells family in this matter. Mr. Norris will provide them with the address of the Wells family in this matter.

I think that covers everything. Anything else?

MR. NORRIS: Satisfactory, Your Honor.

THE COURT: Mr. Goldstein.

MR. GOLDSTEIN: Satisfactory.

THE COURT: All right. Thank you. Good luck, Mr. Munro. I hope you realize the break you have gotten in this matter, even though you don't seem to realize it.

All right. The defendant will be remanded.

(Proceedings concluded.)

*Image SEQ Image * ARABIC84 Court Documents*

SUPERIOR [illegible] OF CALIFORNIA, COUNTY OF LO[illegible]NGELES

5-5-98

DEPT 120

May 3, 1999

TERRY A GREEN — Judge

M LEJEAL — Deputy Clerk

NONE — Bailiff

NONE — Reporter

(Parties and Counsel checked if present)

PEOPLE OF THE STATE OF CALIFORNIA

A361090 vs

Counsel for People
DEPUTY DISTRICT ATTY

Counsel for Defendant

01 MUNDO, JAMES MICHAEL — NON APPEARANCE MATTER

187 A 01 CT

NATURE OF PROCEEDINGS

EXPARTE ORDER REM

THE COURT HAVING READ AND CONSIDERED THE DEFENDANT'S (PLAINTIFF'S) PETITION FOR EXECUTION BY LETHAL INJECTION,, MAKES THE FOLLOWING ORDER:

"MOTION DENIED. THE RECORD REFLECTS THAT DEFENDANT WAS CONVICTED OF 187 (2ND DEGREE) ON 4-6-881. THIS IS NOT A CAPITAL OFFENSE AND THEREFORE DEFENDANT CANNOT BE SENTENCED TO DEATH."

A COPY OF THIS MINUTE ORDER IS ORDERED SENT TO

JAMES MICHAEL MUNRO C-44535
B-7-201-LOWER
P. O. BOX 409000
IONE, CA 95640

MINUTES ENTERED
5/5/99
COUNTY CLERK

REMANDED

*Image SEQ Image * ARABIC85 Court documents*

*Image SEQ Image * ARABIC88 William Bonin and his mother Alice before execution in 1996 (Dr Theodore Kaczynski, 2021)*

William Bonin was executed on February 23, 1996, in the execution chamber at San Quentin State Prison. He was the first inmate in California to be executed by lethal injection since the state resumed executions in 1996, following a halt in 1967. Bonin shares a grim record with Robert Alton Harris, who was the first to be executed in the gas chamber at San Quentin in 25 years. The state of California had deemed the gas chamber to be cruel and unusual punishment, leading to the adoption of lethal injection as the new method of execution. 136, 137

135 Executed Inmate Summary - William George Bonin - Capital Punishment. https://www.cdcr.ca.gov/capital-punishment/inmates-executed-1978-to-present/william-george-bonin/

Before his execution, Bonin spoke to a radio host just 24 hours prior. He mentioned that he had made peace with God and expressed his only regret: not having the chance to become a professional bowler. When asked if he had any message for the victims' families, Bonin said, "They feel my death will bring closure, but that is not the case. They are going to find out."

Warden Arthur Calderon solemnly ordered the execution to begin at 12:09 a.m., and Bonin was pronounced dead at 12:13 a.m. Bonin spent his last day in quiet contemplation, visiting with friends. Around 6 p.m., he was escorted to the death watch cell. Bonin requested two large pepperoni and sausage pizzas, three pints of coffee ice cream, and three six-packs of regular Coca-Cola for his last meal. During the evening, he was visited by the warden and the Catholic chaplain. At 11:30 p.m., he gave his final statement to Warden Calderon.

"The death penalty is not the answer, and I feel it does not address the problems at hand. It sends the wrong message to the country's youth. Young people act as they see others acting instead of as they are told to behave. I suggest anyone considering serious wrong doing go to a quiet place and consider it seriously.

Chapter 21 William Bonin Execution

*Image SEQ Image * ARABIC86 San Quentin Screenshot (Dark Reality, 2022)*

William George Bonin, notoriously known as the "Freeway Killer," carried out a series of brutal crimes between 1979 and 1980. He abducted, robbed, raped, and murdered 14 teenage boys with the help of his co-defendants, who were young men aged 17 to 21.

In 1982, Bonin was sentenced to death for ten murders in Los Angeles County. About a year later, he received another death sentence for four additional murders in Orange County. He was also suspected of other killings in Kern, Riverside, San Diego, and San Bernardino Counties. Still, he was not prosecuted for these crimes. 135

With the assistance of four co-defendants—Vernon Butts, William Pugh, James Munro, and Gregory Mathew Miley—

William Bonin kidnapped, robbed, raped, and murdered ten teenage boys in Los Angeles County between 1979 and 1980.

Bonin was eventually brought to justice and spent 14 years on death row, awaiting his execution. He authored short stories, composed poems and painted during this time. He also corresponded with one of the victim's families, showing no remorse for his crimes. In a particularly callous letter to Sean King's mother, he called Sean a "little screamer."

Bonin claimed that Vernon Butts was the ringleader, although he was the one who directed the others.

*Image SEQ Image * ARABIC87 Robert JR, William Bonin and Paul Bonin before Execution 23 Feb 1996 (Dr Theodore Kaczynski, 2021)*

William Bonin was 49 years old when he was executed. At the time, Governor Pete Wilson stated that William Bonin's execution marked a definitive end to his reign of terror, a poster boy for capital punishment.

The State of California executed William Bonin, known as the Freeway Killer, on February 23. The media's reaction was not shock at the execution itself but rather frustration over the lack of clarity in what they had witnessed. Reporters were unsure if they had actually seen an execution. While in San Quentin, Bonin and three other serial killers—Lawrence Bittaker, Randy Kraft, and Douglas Clarke—would sit and play cards. They were known as the "San Quentin Bridge Club." The club disbanded when Bonin was executed.

Neighbours remember the screams from his house and his attempts to coax their children indoors.

Old-timers recall Bonin offering X-rated movies and free beer to the boys on Angell Street.

Even in the greying grid of 1950s tract homes, a few residents saw Bonin as more than just a hollow-eyed killer, adding a layer of complexity to his character.

Even Dolly Sanders, who tends a bar at the Ric Rac, a neighbourhood pub, recalls a different side of Bonin. She remembers the time in 1979 when Bonin sat with her at the hospital the night she thought her son was going to die. "He

136 "William George Bonin." Clark County Prosecuting Attorney, http://www.clarkprosecutor.org/html/death/US/bonin322.htm. 137 Last Words Spoken by Famous Criminals https://www.thoughtco.com/[illegible]-before-execution-970951

didn't want to leave me alone," she said. Sanders also remembers the night Bonin strolled in with a young boy. She was at Bonin's house, playing cards with his mother. "I just got this funny feeling," Sanders said. "Something wasn't right. He was too young.

When the curtains opened, witnesses saw Bonin lying on the gurney with his eyes closed. His chest heaved once, maybe twice. A few minutes later, officials announced that he was dead and thanked everyone for attending.

Kevin Fagan, a Chronicle reporter, remarked that the event was "less involving than watching a vet put down a dog" and that Bonin appeared as if he "was being anesthetised for surgery." Many witnesses felt the execution was a disappointment, expecting more spectacle. They thought they had paid for a carnival but didn't even see a freak show.

In other words, people wanted more drama from the death penalty. But for those who wanted Bonin's' last moments to be painful, According to Court records, several executed inmates in California may have been conscious, or partially conscious, during the administration of chemicals that would cause significant pain for a period. He points to the California execution logs of William Bonin as one example, which contained indications that there were problems associated with the administration of the chemicals that may have resulted in Bonin being conscious during portions of his execution.

Letter to Vonda from Bonin in San Quentin

"3"

a medical Isolation Room all by myself. At least up at San Quentin I had a T.V. and could talk to people down the row. I would have had yard privileges shortly and been able to go every other day or so for like 4 or 5 hrs. Here at Orange Co. I can't even get Roof time. I hope Bill (my attorney) is successful in getting a roommate for me. They have a bunk bed in this room now. It would help to keep the atmosphere sane.

They do supply the daily newspaper. It helps. It's not the L.A. Herald Examiner.

Well Doc. I'll close for now. I wish you the best of luck in finding those trends and similarities.

By the way, it is Vonda, right?

Take care and keep the research going. It will help someone in the end.

Your Loving Friend
Bill

Chapter 22: The Lost Homicide Tapes.

*Image SEQ Image * ARABIC89 Screenshot (Dark Reality, 2022)*

In 2022, 40 years after the original interview, Tapes were discovered of an interview with William Bonin discussing the crimes. [138] Bonin confessed to 21 homicides; these tapes had been sealed for over 40 years, were never used in trial, and were never meant to be seen or heard by the public. Bonin spoke at this interview on the proviso; nothing he said could be used against him. [139]

LACDAO: Where did you stab him?

BONIN: I stabbed him in the side on both sides and in the upper left part of the back.

LACDAO: How did you muffle his screams?

138 Keel, Anna. "The Freeway Killer Lost Murder Tapes ", 1.24minIMDb Pro, 2022. TV Series 139 LACDAO refers to the Los Angeles County District Attorney's Office, which identifies who Bonin is talking with on the Lost tapes.

BONIN: I stabbed him in the mouth.

BONIN, I know a couple of times, to make sure somebody was dead, I would scratch the eyeball with the knife.

BONIN: The ice pick was inserted into his left ear and both nostrils.

LACDAO: Why?

BONIN: I will put it this way: it was a compulsion. It was a drive.

LACDAO: When you picked him up, did he happen to say where he was going?

BONIN: He said he was headed down through Mexico toward South America. We started heading south, and I started talking to him about whether he had met any gay people and everything. And he told me he was gay himself, and that's when I asked him if he liked to get it on, and he said yes. So, I turned around and headed north. I parked, and we got in the back and started getting it on, and that's when I stabbed him in the arm. I stabbed him in the left arm. I stabbed him again and then again and again. I pulled him out of the van, and, umm, he was still alive. So, I just kept on stabbing him.

LACDAO: Was he nude or was he ….

BONIN: he was nude

LACDAO: OK, what did you do with the clothes?

BONIN: I threw it out with him

LACDAO: When you say you strangled him with this pipe, how did you do that? Did you lay it across his neck?

BONIN: Across his neck, and you apply pressure downwards.

LACDAO: But it was your idea to use the ice pick? Uhm, for what purpose?

BONIN: I can't give you a reason why I used it except for possibly, uhm, making sure that the person was dead. I didn't hear any noise, so I went home.

BONIN: We drove further north on Beach Boulevard and spotted James Maccabe.

I stopped. I asked him where he was going; he said he was going to Disneyland. I said, well, hey, so he got in, drove down the road, pulled off to the side, and I went in the back, and I had sex with Macabe.

I tied him up and put his T-shirt around his neck. That's when the youngster realised what was happening. He yelled three or four times," I won't tell anybody. "He started kicking, and I strangled him. Went back and dumped the body off and then left and went home.

BONIN: I stabbed him in the side on both sides and in the upper left part of the back.

LACDAO: How did you muffle his screams?

BONIN: I stabbed him in the mouth.

BONIN, I know a couple of times, to make sure somebody was dead, I would scratch the eyeball with the knife.

BONIN: The ice pick was inserted into his left ear and both nostrils.

LACDAO: Why?

BONIN: I will put it this way: it was a compulsion. It was a drive.

LACDAO: When you picked him up, did he happen to say where he was going?

BONIN: I believe he said he was headed down through Mexico headed down toward South America. We started heading south, and I started talking to him about whether he had met any gay people and everything. And he told me he was gay himself, and that's when I asked him if he liked to get it on, and he said yes. So, I turned around and headed north. I parked, and we got in the back and started getting it on, and that's when I stabbed him in the arm. I stabbed him in the left arm. I stabbed him again and then again and again. I pulled him out of the van, and, umm, he was still alive. So, I just kept on stabbing him.

LACDAO: Was he nude or was he ….

BONIN: he was nude

LACDAO: OK, what did you do with the clothes?

Don Kilhefner, Ph.D. LGBTQ+ rights Activist historian and co-founder of the LGBTQI Community Services Centre discusses the centre and the freeway killer. The centre provided meals and accommodation for the LGBTQI community. Some young men had no money, so their way of getting around was hitchhiking and sometimes working as prostitutes. Don states that the freeway killer exploited that used that to his nefarious ends. When the LGBTQI community realised that Bonin was hunting and Killing their LGBTQI community, they were angry, shocked and sad. At the community centre, they put signs warning people not to be hitchhiking. At the time of the freeway killings, a law in California was that a man could be arrested for touching another man. The entire community was affected.

*Image SEQ Image * ARABIC90 Screenshot (Dark Reality 2022)*

BONIN: I went to the Gay Community Service Centre this particular day. I talked to him and told him I could give him a place to stay. I believe it was more for the torture and the killing than it was for sex. As time went on, it got so that the torture part was more important than just a feeling of superiority or power.

LACDAO: Where and when did you first see him?
BONIN: I saw him at the bus stop on the corner of Old River School Road and Firestone Boulevard. I asked him where Atlantic Boulevard was, and he told me it was up the road. I said, "Are you waiting for the bus?" he said yeah, and I said the last bus had already run, and I said, "Well, hop in. I'll give you a ride.
LACDAO: what was your intention?
BONIN: I intended to go out and have sex with Sean King and kill him, so I started propositioning Sean, and he said no. He said Well, you can let me out right here sc that when I pulled out the knife, I put my hand around his neck. He didn't try to resist it or anything. He says I don't want to die I tied his hands behind his back, tied his feet, and then took off and headed out towards San Bernadino.
BONIN: I finally stopped on the side of this road. There was no traffic at all, and I sodomised him. Ahhh, then we walked to the place where I dumped him. I used my T-shirt. I was starting to strangle him, but it wasn't working, so I took the knife and stabbed him,
LACDAO: where did you stab him.
BONIN: I stabbed him in the side, both sides, in the upper left part of the back, in the throat two or three times, and in the mouth part. And I started walking away, and this is when I heard some noises coming out of him, and so I stabbed him a couple more times.

LACDAO: Can I ask Mr Bonin about the Turner case? Did you intend to sodomise him after you tied him up?
BONIN: I know I was going to tie him up, and then I guess whatever was gonna come to mind. At that point, I tied him up, and I had sex with him.
LACDAO: Tell me how you strangled him.
BONIN: I believe I would've used his T-shirt
LACDAO: Why did you decide to tie him up?
BONIN: Render him helpless
LACDAO: Why?
BONIN: I guess it made me feel more superior to him if he was scared
BONIN: Where do you want to start, Bernie?
LACAO: Why don't we start with Markus Grab
BONIN: I reached down, and I grabbed hold of his nuts, and I squeezed them, and it hurt, so he broke loose from the bondage, and that's when I stabbed him again and again until he was UH completely sort of like helpless, but he was still alive.
I pulled him out of the van, and he was still alive. I had to talk myself into stabbing him more to kill him. I knew I couldn't leave him there, you know, alive, and I grabbed his ear, and I banged it against the rock that was right there next to where you found him.

Chapter 23 The California Department of Corrections

*Image SEQ Image * ARABIC91 Screenshot (Dark Reality, 2022)*

The homicide detectives who worked in Los Angeles at the time and who were a part of capturing the freeway killer were Kirk Mellecker, John Paul St. John, also known as Jigsaw John, who, by the way, was a world-famous detective hired to find this serial killer, even had a television show based on his work as a detective. Dave Kushner from the Orange County Sheriff's Department and Ernie Esposito. The four detectives were working on a series of killings from 1978 to 1980 when they got their break.

The Los Angeles and Orange counties had put out a curfew. All residents were required to be in by 6 p.m. unless they were working. The entire population of southern California was in a panic, living in fear of this killer.

Stores were closing, schools were on high alert, and parents could not get any help. Anyone who was still trying to hitchhike was arrested if caught. The fear was palpable. The panic was real.

March 23, 1982, James was sent to the California Institute for Men in Chino Street Prison; it was a living hell. He was escorted to a single cell with an old, uncovered mattress and a hole in the ground to piss and shit in. It smelt so bad. James was left in that cell for several days until he was moved to a regular cell, which was not much better. Still, he was given a dirty old mattress, a bar of soap, and at least there was a toilet, even if it was just an old metal one. He sat in that cell every day with bugs crawling all over him. The correctional officers did not care because all prisoners were just numbers. They were not treated like human beings, which is Munro's case. Munros number C44535, Munro, like many others, was left to fend for himself. Eventually, James was moved to the Deuel Vocational Institution Tracy State Prison. Living conditions were better, but still, he only had a mattress and a bar of soap; that is all that was given to the inmates. Inmates were allowed to have a television in their cell if they could afford one. However, as Munro had no family to support him financially, he stared at the walls until he was moved again.

Now Munro sits in a nine-by-12-foot cell looking out a window, wondering if he will ever get out or if society just forgot about him and all the abuse he suffered from his serial killer and the criminal justice system. The system that was supposed to protect him failed him.

In 1984, James was in such a state of anger and resentment towards his parents that he changed his name to Michael Bandit. This act was a way for him to express his desire to retaliate against his parents, particularly his father, for the traumatic experiences he had endured as a child. His decision was a manifestation of his deep-seated emotional turmoil, as he was now in a federal prison, trying to make his father confront the consequences of his actions.

James's journey of self-identity was a tumultuous one. In 1992, he decided to reclaim his original name, James Munro, a symbolic act of reconnecting with his past. Later, he embraced a new identity, Tina, a name that represented his struggle for self-acceptance.

On April 12, 1999, James Michael Munro was in such a state of emotional turmoil that he sought a trial so desperately that he even petitioned Governor Pete Wilson to be executed. James was overwhelmed with guilt for what had happened and wished the Wells family could find closure. He had lost the only family he had ever known and loved and was even willing to sacrifice his own life for a crime he did not commit if it could bring the Wells family closure. However, the Governor's office responded that James's request was not legally possible, and the motion was denied.

James Munro was not alone in his struggle. A fellow inmate who also believed in his innocence petitioned for assistance, showing that even in the darkest times, there can be a glimmer of hope and support.

Freeway Killer Accomplice asked Governor Wilson for execution or parole.

By Charles Roger Jorss August 22, 1998. Ione California.

The accomplice in the freeway killings was James Munro, 37. An inmate in the California Department of Corrections asked Governor Wilson for the state of California to either execute him or parole him. Munro was convicted for the 1980 freeway murder case of Steven James Wells, an 18-year-old from Downey, CA. Munro was sentenced to 15 years to life under a plea agreement, which Munro did not want. The freeway killings were between 1979 and 1980, In which William Bonin and Vernon Butts killed 45 young men. The two main perpetrators of these heinous crimes are as follows: Bonin and Butts would dump their dead victim's bodies along the side of the freeway in the Los Angeles area. In 1979, Munro came to California; Munro was a drifter who travelled from one place to another. The only items Munro had been the clothes on his back. He had no money to provide shelter, which ultimately led to sleeping in the streets of Hollywood, a suburb northwest of Los Angeles, CA. Munro did not meet Bonin until early May of 1980 when Bonin picked up Munro. In Hollywood, CA,

Bonin's potential victims were young males between 18 and 35. His victims were usually Drifters, the homeless and young men who seemed not too bright. Bonin would pursue the weak to feel superior to his victims. Munro's education years were spent in schools whose pupils were considered handicapped or mentally retarded. Munro spent from the time he was five years old (preschool age) to the time he was 17 years old in special education schools for disabled students, which was located in Port Huron, MI. Munro's employment was on and off due to his learning disabilities, which ended his progress in progressing in society and the employment world, which was no fault of Munro's. For the past 18 years, Munro has repeatedly tried to appeal his conviction but came to no avail. Munro has written numerous law firms proclaiming his innocence. To this day, no law firm has responded in taking the case or an investigation into Munro's Innocenc. From day one, the state of California wanted the killer or killers who allegedly committed these heinous crimes. The state did everything it could to obtain a conviction against Bonin, even if it meant convicting an innocent man as an accomplice when Bonin threatened the so-called accomplice and if he (Munro) did not partake in disposing of Stephen James Wells's body. At the municipal court level, Munro pleaded not guilty to the charge of homicide in the first degree. Defence attorney Ms Madelynn Gail Kopple of Santa Monica, CA, represented

Munro, who was forced off the case by Superior Court Judge Everett Ricks, Department 120 of the Los Angeles County Superior Court, Los Angeles, California. After the removal of Ms Kopple. The trial court appointed Mr James Goldstein, attorney at Law out of Van News, California. In or about April 1981, Munro's new defence attorney, James Goldstein, came to the LA County Gaol and threatened Munro by telling Munro, "You will go into court tomorrow and play guilty, or else you are a dead man." Munro pleaded with the trial court several times about a conflict of interest between his defence attorney, James Allen Goldstein, and himself due to the threats that Munro received from Goldstein. The trial Court denied Munro's request for new counsel and a trial by jury. Judge Ricks had also threatened by numbered deaths during the Superior Court proceedings after Munro was bound over from the manipulable court. This statement of a death threat is on record. The present judge, in Department 120, Judge Green of the Los Angeles Superior Court in and for the County of Los Angeles, agrees with Judge Rick's opinion and the death threats. To this day, the honourable Judge Green has denied my Munro numerous requests for his transcripts and a trial, which Munro states he never received. Munro today states." I want a day in court. Munro asked the California Governor, Pete Wilson, for execution or parole. is because of his strong remorse about what happened to the Wells. Son Munro feels that asking Governor Wilson for an execution date would be a fair exchange for his life to be terminated in exchange for Wells's grief for losing their son. Munro asked that the wells forgive him because he was acting out of fear when Bonin made him assist in the disposal of their son's body and the fact that Bonin was going to kill him if he didn't assist in the disposal of the Wells' son. Munro has a BPT (board of prison terms) hearing every two years, and the Wells keep coming up and are protesting that Munro killed their boy when Bonin was the one that murdered Stephen Wells. States Munro, for that reason, that, with only an emotional outcry from the Wells, the BPT has no choice but to deny Munro his parole. Munro asks if there is anyone in society to help him. Please contact him at the listed address at the end of this article. Munro also requests that if any nation-wide attorneys can help him prove his innocence in this case, one can contact him.

FREEWAY KILLER ACCOMPLICE
ASK GOVERNOR WILSON FOR
EXECUTION OR PAROLE

By Charles Roger Jorss
August 22, 1998
IONE, CALIFORNIA - The accomplice in the Freeway killings, James Munro, 37 years of age, an inmate in the California Department of Corrections, asked Governor Wilson, for the State of California, to either execute him or parole him.

Munro, was convicted for the 1980 Freeway Murder Case of Steven James Wells, an 18 year old from Downey, CA. Munro was sentenced to 15 years to life pursuant to a plea agreement in which Munro did not want.

The Freeway Killings were between the years of 1979 and 1980, in which 45 young men were killed by William Bonin, and Vernon Butts, the two main perpetrators in these heinous crimes. Bonin and Butts, would dumped their dead victims bodies along side of the freeway in the Los Angeles area.

In 1979, Munro came to California. Munro was a drifter and traveled from one place to another. The only items that Munro had in his possession were the clothes on his back. He had no money to provide shelter which ultimately led to sleeping in the streets of Hollywood, a suburb, northwest of Los Angeles, California.

Munro did not meet Bonin until early May of 1980, when Bonin picked up Munro, in Hollywood, California. Bonin's potential victims were young males between the ages of 18 to 39 years of age. His victims were usually drifter, the homeless, and young men who seemed not to bright. Bonin would pursue the weak, in which, Bonin could feel superior over his victims.

Munro's education years were mainly spent in schools whose pupils were considered handicap or mentally retarded. Munro spent from the time he was 5 years old, (pre-School age) to the time he was 17 years old in special education schools for the disabled, which was located in Port Huron, Michigan.

Munro's employment was on and off due to his learning disabilities which, hindered his progress in moving ahead in society and the employment world. Which was no fault of Munro's.

For the past eighteen years (18), Munro has repeatedly tried to appeal his conviction but, came to no prevail. Munro has written numerous law firms proclaiming his innocence. To this day, no law firm has responded in taking the case on or investigate into Munros' innocence, which Munro still proclaims.

From day one, the State of California wanted the killer or killers who allegedly committed these heinous crimes. The State did everything they could to obtain a conviction against Bonin. Even, if it meant convicting an innocent man as an accomplice, when the so-called accomplice was threatened himself by Bonin, if he (Munro) did not partake in disposing of Steven James Wells' body.

At the Municipal Court Level, Munro plead not guilty to the charge of murder in the first degree.

Munro, was represented by Defense Attorney, Mrs. Madelyne Gail Kopple, of Santa Monica, California, who was forced off the case by Superior Court Judge Everett Ricks, Department 123, of the Los Angeles County Superior Court, Los Angeles, California.

After the removal of Mrs. Kopple, the
(continued on page 2, column one)

*Image SEQ Image * ARABIC92 Inmate Charles Roger Jorss wrote this part of the letter on August 22, 1998.*

Tina Marie Munro, a shining example of resilience, courage, and self-acceptance, proudly identifies as a bisexual, transgender person.

Arriving in prison, Tina found solace among fellow LGBTQI individuals, yet still grappled with her gender and sexuality. Seeking clarity, she turned to the invaluable support of mental health services, including therapy and counselling. Reflecting on her childhood, raised by her adopted mother and grandmother while her father was in Vietnam, she remembered her early questioning of her body and identity and her sister's supportive role in her journey. [140]
As Tina continued to explore her true self, she consistently wore women's clothing. After moving out and eventually ending up in prison, she learned about gender dysphoria and realized she was transgender. In 2014, Tina was officially diagnosed with gender dysphoria and understood she was a female trapped in a male body. Following treatment, she underwent breast surgery and legally changed her name to Tina Marie Munro in 2019. Since then, she has lived as a female, finding acceptance and support in her community, a testament to the power of community in the journey of self-discovery.

140 Qatar - Mental Health - Expat Focus. https://www.expatfocus.com/qatar/guide/qatar-mental-health

Tina's love for women and, most importantly, her desire for herself is a powerful example of self-acceptance's transformative power, offering others hope and inspiration.

Gender dysphoria is a condition where a person experiences significant discomfort or distress due to a mismatch between their gender identity and their assigned sexual orientation at birth. This sense of unease can be intense and may lead to mental health issues such as depression and anxiety. [141, 142]

People with gender dysphoria often have a powerful desire to live as a gender different from their assigned sex. This can involve changing their appearance and behaviour and sometimes undergoing hormone therapy or surgery to align their physical characteristics with their gender identity.

It is important to note that gender dysphoria is not a mental illness. Still, the distress it causes can lead to mental health problems. Treatment typically involves a combination of psychological support, hormone therapy, and sometimes gender-affirming surgeries, which can include procedures to change the chest, face, or genitalia to align with the person's gender identity.

141 What is Gender Dysphoria? – LIBERTY PSYCHOLOGICAL ASSOCIATION. https://shervanshahhian.com/2023/05/11/what-is-gender-dysphoria/ 142 Transformed - Evangelical Alliance. https://www.eauk.org/news-and-views/transformed

Tina Marie Munro, a shining example of resilience, courage, and self-acceptance, proudly identifies as a bisexual, transgender person.

Arriving in prison, Tina found solace among fellow LGBTQI+ individuals, yet still grappled with her gender and sexuality. Seeking clarity, she turned to the invaluable support of mental health services, including therapy and counselling. Reflecting on her childhood, raised by her adopted mother and grandmother while her father was in Vietnam, she remembered her early questioning of her body and identity and her sister's supportive role in her journey.

As Tina continued to explore her true self, she consistently wore women's clothing. After moving out and eventually ending up in prison, she learned about gender dysphoria and realized she was transgender. In 2014, Tina was officially diagnosed with gender dysphoria and understood she was a female trapped in a male body. Following treatment, she underwent breast surgery and legally changed her name to Tina Marie Munro in 2019. Since then, she has lived as a female, finding acceptance and support in her community, a testament to the power of community in the journey of self-discovery.

SHORTY AND TINA 2023

Chapter 24 Munro Parole Appeal

Inmate Number	Munro, Tina Marie
CDCR Number	C44535
Parole Eligibility date	02/ 1988

August 2029 Parole Suitability Hearing

Date	Action	Outcome
February 12, 2016	Inmate Petition to Advance	Inmates' petition to advance their next parole suitability hearing date was denied.
AUGUST 21,2014	Parole Suitability Hearing	Inmate was denied parole for 15 years
April 09 2014	Parole suitability hearing	Parole suitability was postponed
January 16 2014	Parole suitability hearing	Parole suitability was postponed
July 15, 2010,	Inmate petition to advance	The inmate's petition to advance their next parole suitability hearing date was rejected because they are not eligible to file for the petition at this time.
February 06 2009	Parole Suitability Hearing	Inmate was denied parole for five years
February 09 2005	Parole Suitability Hearing	Inmate was denied parole for four years
September 13 2000	Parole Suitability Hearing	Inmate was denied parole for four years
August 01 1998	Parole Suitability Hearing	Inmate stipulated to unsuitability for two years
December 01 1995	Parole Suitability Hearing	Inmate was denied parole for three years
December 09 1993	Parole Suitability Hearing	The inmate was denied parole for 2
August 16 1991	Parole Suitability Hearing	Inmate was denied parole for two years
September 14 1989	Parole Suitability Hearing	Inmate was denied parole for two years

When James Michael Munro petitioned the United States District Court on September 2, 2009, for the denial of his 2005 parole, it was not that he disagreed with the validity of his convictions; instead, he was challenging the board's 2005 decision, finding him unsuitable for Parole Case No..2:07-cv-01404-RSL-JLW.

The board's decision to deny Mr Munro's Parole was primarily based on his committed offence, his unstable history, unfavourable psychiatric evaluations, insufficient participation in self-help programming, insufficient parole plans, opposition by law enforcement, the victim's surviving family members, and a confidential letter opposing Munro's release. [143, 144]

The board found that the offence was carried out cruelly, and the victim had been abused during the offence. It was carried out in a manner that demonstrates an exceptionally callous disregard for human suffering. In addition, the motive for the crime was inexplicable. And once the victim died, his body was disposed of like garbage.

The second factor the board provided was that Munro was unsuitable for Parole due to his unstable social history, which is defined as a history of unstable or tumultuous relationships with other people. They based this on the fact that he dropped out of school in the tenth grade as a teenager and ran away from home on several occasions.

How do they say that is a reason for denial? he was a teenager. It is not uncommon for teenagers to run away from home and leave school in year ten. That does not make them all unstable, especially since Munro was no longer a teenager. Munro is now over 60 years of age.

Munro did have an unstable relationship with his parents; they disapproved of almost everything about him. They had also committed him to a psychiatric hospital to curb what they thought was terrible behaviour. In addition, his relationship with his sisters was also troubled, which the parole board tried to prove by asking why they had no contact with him for years at a time; it could have been that they were ashamed or did not want the media attention that comes from being related to such an offender in such a high-profile case. But in case they certainly disapproved of Munro's sexual tendencies

That is not proof that Munro is a danger to society if released.

The third and fourth factors they claimed to have used to deny Parole were his unfavourable psychiatric evaluations and his insufficient participation in self-help programmes. Munro had completed an electrical course in 1992. He was a certified Mig welder, which he obtained in 1992. In 2006, Munro completed his GED. Munro also participated in Anger and Stress management in 1988. 145

143 Suitability for Parole in California | Law pipe. https://www.lawpipe.com/California/Suitability_for_Parole_in_California.html 144 Court, United States District. "James Michael Munro, V. Martel." 2011.

As of this year, he has also been studying Paralegal and getting excellent grades. He also was working in the kitchen until recently.

The last psychiatric evaluation was on July 29, 2004. In that evaluation, the psychiatrist said that Munro posed a moderate risk of reoffending if released. The psychiatrist commented that the two remarkable things about the interview with Munro were that he lacked empathy and deviated from the truth. The psychiatrist says there seemed to be a disconnect where genuine emotion might have been expected and crying was expressed.

The board was questioned on how to rely on a five-year-old report, especially considering the potential for change in a prisoner's behaviour and mindset. Recent discussions with Munro revealed significant remorse for his actions, which was not reflected in the old report.

The fifth factor was realistic plans for release. They say Munro's plans were insufficient, and he had no marketable skills to be used when released. Munro planned to move to Michigan, where his wife lived, and she offered him a home and assistance finding work. However, he had no plans for work at the time. How can a prisoner with no idea if he will be paroled already have work lined up? It is hard enough to get a job, let alone someone with a criminal record. How can they expect every parolee to have already work lined

145 Munro, Tina. "James Munro His Life His Words." By Sharon McQuillan. 2023.

up? The fact that he had someone willing to house him and help him find work should have been enough.
It should be noted that the board commends Munro for completing all the classes necessary to graduate high school. The board also indicated that Munro had held many different jobs. The federal reports detail the various jobs he took, even if only for a short period. Munro's work product was also good. It was still not good enough for Parole. The sixth factor was the opposition to Munro's release from the victims' surviving family members and a small handwritten confidential fearful letter. Unfortunately, Munro is a Victim of the Criminal Justice System. As a person with an intellectual disability and transgender, she has never been treated appropriately. Her Socioeconomic status has further compounded her plight. Her family, her so-called Friends, and Bonin have let her down. This is a story of injustice that should not be overlooked.

Munro's last petition in August 2014 was declined partly due to David McVicker's input at the Parole hearing and the change.org petition gathering signatures to deny Munro's (James) Parole. One could argue that McVicker had no right to be at the parole hearing and use his input as he was never actually a victim of Munro's. This is a clear case of unfairness that needs to be addressed.

This was an attempt by Munro to gain attention, and hopefully, someone would come to his aid. However, Mc Vicker took it seriously; Mc Vicker also claims that on a recorded call, Munro threatened to Kill him if Munro was released. Munro, of course, denies this. No proof of the phone calls has been provided, especially when placing a call from prison; they are monitored. There was also mention of phone conversations between Munro and a Murderbillia website owner, claiming he would start killing again to continue Bonin's work. This, of course, was here say, and nothing was proven.

According to Munro, Miley kept running his mouth on the phones about how he wanted to get out and commit more crimes than Bonin did. Miley said that Munro wanted to do the same, which was a lie. Also, Miley wrote a confidential letter to the board saying he wanted to commit more crimes, which was false. Munro deserves a second chance at redemption, so she should not be denied Parole.

McVickers' petition closed with 2,605 signatures from strangers who had no idea about Munro's participation in the crime, thinking he, too, was responsible for the sexual assault on McVickers. What is most astonishing is that McVickers never vehemently opposed the release of Bonin's other accomplice, William (Billy) Pugh, who was charged and sentenced for the homicide of 15-year-old

Harry Todd Turner. William Pugh was released after only serving five years.

Neighbours of Munros paint a vastly different picture to those denying him Parole at the same time; they were never close to Munro. They acknowledged that he was always active cutting lawns and shovelling snow in the small town of St Clair; the older generation had no problems with young Munro. He was always around with a shovel on his shoulder, looking for jobs. The people around his age who claim to have known him say that he would ask too many questions and tends to exaggerate when telling stories. Not surprising, though, considering that it is pretty standard with intellectually disabled people.

Chapter 25: The Lucky Ones and how did Bonin escape Justice for so long

The following information is from files and records: Vonda Pelto was privy.

November 17, 1968, Bonin was cruising around in his mother's white Chevrolet Sation wagon when he spotted 14-year-old Billy Jones walking home; he pulled up and asked the young lad for directions to the Santa Anita racetrack, a tactic he eventually perfected. Billy tells him the racetrack is closed, But Bonin reels the boy in, stating he has a horse and is looking for somewhere to agist him. The boy gets excited about the possibility of seeing a horse. They exchange a few more words, and then Bonin introduces himself as William, but his friends call him Bill, and they share the same name; now entirely at ease, Bonin offers the boy a ride home.

No sooner than the young had got in the car, Bonin asked him if he had ever been blown; Billy, not entirely understanding, asked, "Huh, is that some sort of sex stuff?" Bonin replies, "Yeah, you know to suck dick." Billy responds oh yeah, I know, but no, I am not into that, Bonin encourages him to try it, and Billy, getting uncomfortable, asks to get out and reaches for the door handle. Still, it is locked, and realising he could not get out, his throat is suddenly dry. He began to panic; at this point, Bonin reached over with his free hand, grabbed Billy's crotch and squeezed

hard." Ouch, that hurt. Why did you do that? "Bonin replies, "Because I want to fuck you in the butt."
Bonin managed to drive to a closed shopping centre and parked around the back; he dragged young Billy out of the car and proceeded to handcuff his hands behind his back. As Billy struggled to break free, Bonin began choking him, telling him Bonin would kill him if he did not nod his head by the count of three. Billy pleaded for his life, but Bonin ignored him as he ripped his jeans to his ankles. As Billy began to scream, Bonin punched him in the face, knocking him unconscious; when Billy came to, Bonin released him and placed him at a bus stop and told him, "Do not look back, or I will kill you."
When Billy got home, his mother could see something terrible had happened, so they went to the Arcadia police station. The police now had a description of Bonin, the car he was driving and his first name.
November 26, 1968, John Treadwell hitchhiked. He accepted a ride from the monster Bonin, and John almost arrived home safe. Still, Bonin pointed a gun at his head and accelerated away. Bonin drove to a secluded spot, tied the boy's hands behind his back, and proceeded to rape John; then, he was released, not before Bonin told him, "I know where you live. Speak to no one." This was reported to the Redondo Police Department

December 4, 1968, Allen Pruitt (17) also became a victim of Bonin's lucky to escape alive; getting into Bonin's car after accepting a ride, Bonin begins the conversation by asking if Allen knew about queers. At that point, Bonin turned off the main highway and handcuffed the boy as he did the others; he pulled down Allen's jeans and forcibly inserted his penis into Allen's rectum. Allen reported this incident to his instructor at Torrance High School, who then told the Vice Principal, which delayed the incident being reported to the correct authorities.

January 2, 1969, Larence Bretman reported to Hermosa Beach Police Department that he had been sexually assaulted and robbed by a man wielding a weapon.

January 19, 1969, Jesus Monge reported to police that he had been hitchhiking and accepted a ride from A man who began talking about homosexuality and then offered Jess $20 for an oral copulation. Jesus tried to exit the vehicle but was punched in the chest and stomach; Bonin proceeded to handcuff the young man, unzip his jeans and force Jesus to copulate orally.

At this point, the police began to realise that they had a serial rapist; alerts were sent out to all law enforcement agencies in California. January 28, 1969, El Segundo police got a break. Officer Peggy Duval had spotted the white station wagon; while on patrol, she called it in to see if they could get a partial match on the plate. The lights went on, and they pulled Bonin over, "registration, please? "The officer asked. "Bonin fumbled around, then handed over his licence.

"William Bonin, aged 22. Is that you?" Bonin replied, barely audible. The officer shone the torch into the car, saw a young man in it, and told them to leave the car." What's your name, son? "Timothy Wilson," he replied. He was a 16-year-old runaway from Kansas.

"Bonin, please raise your arms". "What is the problem?" Bonin responded, "I was not speeding."

The officer proceeded to search Bonin and recovered a pair of tarnished handcuffs. "What are these for the officer asked. Would you care to explain?" This is when Bonin broke down and started to plead, "Please, you have to help me; you should incarcerate me, not let me be free because of how I am. "

"William Bonin, put your hands behind your back. You are under arrest."

That night, Bonin was charged with kidnapping, penal code S 207 and sex perversion s 288 (a). the pieces quickly fell into place, and they knew they had the man responsible for the other attacks.

Bonin was charged, and they bound him for trial in superior court; he was moved to LA County Men's Central Jail. Before the proceedings, Judge Newell Barrett had issued a court order for Bonin to undergo a psychiatric examination to determine if he was a sexual psychopath.

California law at the time stated that a "sexual psychopath is any convicted criminal, not punishable by the death penalty, who suffers from abnormal sexual desire of a kind and degree to constitute him a menace to others.

Albert Bonner, M.D. and Frederick Hacker, M.D., both psychiatrists, began interviewing Bonin. He was the first to complete his report on March 14, 1969. He described Bonin as being of average intelligence, in good contact with reality and verbalised freely, relevantly and coherently. In narrating his deviant sexual behaviour, Bonin revealed no emotional anxiety or remorse; Bonin also admitted that on each occasion that he sodomised the boys, he climaxed.

Frederick Hackers' report was more detailed and completed on March 28, 1969; along with Bonin not being completely honest with the second Doctor, it seems that the sexual assaults he experienced as a child seemed utterly abhorrent to him. He admitted he always carried handcuffs, bound his victims and that he picked up as hitchhikers and forcefully had anal sex with them. Using the handcuffs, pinning their hands behind their backs. Additionally, the defendant shows signs of depression, aside from his realistic worry about the present involvement. Hacker ends the report with a paragraph that provided the courts hope that he could be rehabilitated with Psychiatric treatment. "The defendant is undoubtedly not mentally ill by legal standards. He has sufficient capacity to know and understand what he is doing. The defendant represents a distinct danger since the mixture of uncontrolled sexual drive is explosive with a significant likelihood of recurrence. Therefore, under all circumstances, confinement of this possibly treatable individual for a prolonged period is strongly recommended.

On May 9, 1969, Bonin was formally charged with five counts of kidnapping, five counts of crimes against nature, one count of crimes against children, and two counts of sex perversion; Bonin pleaded Guilty. At trial, Bonin admitted to using all the trademark moves he later used to murder young men when he was labelled the freeway killer. Bonin was found guilty of kidnapping, two counts of crimes against nature, one count of crimes against children, and two counts of sexual perversion.

*Image SEQ Image * ARABIC93 Screenshot (Dark Reality, 2022)*

On June 4, during the sentencing hearing, the Judge decided that Bonin would be sent to Atascadero State Hospital to determine if he could benefit from treatment and to assess whether he was a Mentally Disordered Sexual Offender. Bonin arrived at Atascadero on June 17, 1969. He faced an uncertain future: he could be transferred to state prison at any time or remain in the maximum-security treatment hospital. The court had ordered a 90-day evaluation and diagnosis at Atascadero. However, if he rejected treatment, criminal proceedings would immediately resume, resulting in his transfer to prison.

In 1969, Atascadero Hospital had a relaxed environment; patients could wander the halls.
On July 24, 1969, a report noted Bonin's involvement and participation…
On July 24, 1969, the report noted that his involvement and participation had been minimal, suggesting he had little motivation to help himself. Bonin expressed that he wanted to remain at the hospital, but the staff were very aware of Bonin and still believed he was extremely dangerous; with little hope of benefiting from treatment, Doctor Hollingsworth made the decision and diagnosis that Bonin was a Mentally Disordered Sexual offender amenable to hospital treatment. He would stay for another 90 days. Despite the staff's concerns, Bonin was diagnosed with Inade-

quate Personality and sexual Deviation, and Paedophilia (Male) remained the same. Dr Edward E Edlund and Hollingsworth approved the retention decision. At this point, Bonin took on the responsibility to get better. He participated in therapy, and although his horrendous socialisation skills were on full display, he was very unpopular with the other patients. Bonin was pushy and had opinionated views. As a result, he became depressed and withdrawn. But this would not hamper Bonin; he still had friends who visited him, had full hall privileges, and had joined the industrial therapy assignment of painting the wards. Still, Bonin's report came back with poor impulse control, judgement, lack of insight, anger and lousy socialisation skills.

On September 18, Bonin was served with the commitment order, giving him ten days to request a court hearing on the decision. He was not likely to do this; he wanted to stay at Atascadero. December 1969, and things seemed to be working in Bonin's favour, but when 1970 rolled in, things had changed; Bonin was always pursuing sexual activities with other patients of his age until December 12, 1969, when another patient hit him for trying to force his sexual will on unwilling people, he was cited for sexual deviance Bonin had seduced a young mentally disabled patient aggressively and sodomised him. All his hall privileges had been revoked because of the sexual assault. Bonin then became withdrawn and only socialised with the younger patients.

On March 5, he was caught again having sodomised someone and three days later got punched again. Bonin is forcing himself on unwitting victims, Alfred Owre Jr M.D had reported. This man has not been reached in therapy. He is unresponsive to treatment. Yet, Somehow, Bonin found himself receiving another 90 days at Atascadero.

August 4, it was learned that Bonin was repeatedly sodomising and performing acts of perversion with a new friend. "Finally, a ward report puts forward an accurate account of Bonin, stating two fundamental observations, "he appears to be putting on a false front to hide his selfish intentions. He is a natural manipulator and is a past master at it. This is William Bonin, the serial killer, intelligent and clever, who can mould people to participate in perverted and horrific activities.

Early December 1970, the wheels had been set in motion to send Bonin back to court, with a report filed on December 10 determining that Bonin, while he had made improvements, proved to be manipulative, untruthful, and sexually dangerous to other males. Bonin typically victimises mentally ill or mentally disabled victims who are eager sexual converts. Since he is untreatable and all programs available to sex offenders have not produced change, the staff recommends disposition under section 6325(b) WI. In their opinion, he is sexually dangerous to males, both children and adults, signed Dr Owre and the staff.

Bonin was ordered to return to court on January 14, 1971, and was transported to the LA Men's County Jail to await trial.

After Bonin's letter requesting more treatment at Atascadero to Judge Miller, Miller called Atascadero for more information and was told directly that he was a risk and should be in prison. The doctors were ignored, and Judge Miller sent Bonin back to Atascadero. This decision left the doctors and staff furious, their professional opinions disregarded.

Bonin's manipulation was evident in his 9-page letter that convinced the Judge.

Immediately, the hospital got to work on getting rid of Bonin; he was readmitted on February 8, 1971. He was given an updated diagnosis and disposition on March 17. Anti: social personality, severe, Sexual Deviation, Aggressive Sexuality (Forcible sodomy), sexual Deviation, Sadism. Most notably, the updated disposition was transferred to the Department of Corrections.

In April 1971, Bonin's transfer to prison was approved; Bonin tried to get the decision reversed, but the doctors would not be outwitted by a man who continued to pursue homosexual encounters with unwilling participants.

On July 7, 1971, Bonin was discharged from Atascadero and sent to the California Medical facility in Vacaville. The Diagnosis Vacaville gave Bonin was Explosive personality and Homosexuality with Aggressive and sadistic tendencies, and deemed unable to be returned to Atascadero.

In May 1973, reports said that Bonin was coming to terms with his crimes and deviations that landed him in trouble. Bonin acknowledged he was homosexual and even curbed his sexual activity at Vacaville. (Bonin has learned to play their game.) his diagnosis was Explosive personality, and Homosexuality with Aggressive and sadistic tendencies was listed as improved.

On September 20, 1973, Bonin's report stated he had avoided sexual contact in the first two years at Vacaville, which seemed implausible for a man like Bonin. Bonin had not reached the maximum insight of which he might be capable, but still, he had been at Vacaville for three years, and the therapists found themselves at a loss; they no longer knew how to help Bonin. Bonin clings to his sexual orientation but states that he will no longer engage in aggressive and sadistic activity if released. His diagnosis was updated, but the therapists remained sceptical. Still unsuitable for return to Atascadero. Five months later, Doctors gave up, washed their hands of Bonin and dismissed all previous concerns about Bonin's danger to society. This decision, made with a sense of finality, marked the end of the therapists' efforts to rehabilitate Bonin.

March 24, 1974, Psychologist J.W Fleming, PhD, stated Bonin's identity as homosexual and his diagnosis was lowered to a single condition, homosexuality with some aggressive features. April 3, 1974, the council sent Bonin back to court with a recommendation for probation.

June 11, 1974, Bonin was released back into the unsuspecting public, apparently a changed man; at this point, I am appalled at the psychologists and therapists who sent this monster back into society. He was given five years' probation with the following conditions.

Do not use or possess any narcotics, dangerous or restricted drugs, or associated paraphernalia except with a valid prescription and stay away from where users congregate.

Do not associate with persons you know as narcotic or drug sellers or users.

Associate with persons disapproved of by the probation officer.

Cooperate in a plan for psychiatric or psychological treatment to be terminated only with the consent of the therapist and the probation officer.

Seek and maintain training, schooling, or employment as the probation officer approves.

Maintain residents approved by the probation officer.

Obey all laws, orders, rules and regulations of the probation department and court.

Californian sex offender registration was passed in 1947. Bonin had to register with local law enforcement wherever he lived—enacted nationally in 1994. California was the first state to pass such laws.

Bonin was discharged in June and hung around Hollywood for a while, renting an apartment at 4956 Romaine Street to socialise within the gay community and spend time at some gay bars. Bonin found the experience unpleasant and, by August 1974, was back at his parent's house. He began bartending at Pizza Burger on Brookhurst in Fountain Valley. He received $200 in monthly Social Security cheques. He became eligible for the Veterans Affairs educational benefits under the GI Bill.

Bonin found some aspects of his parole relatively easy, as he was never a drinker or a drug user in late 1974. Bonin quit bartending and started working at Dependable Drive Away in Montebello, 546 Greenwood Ave, 6 miles northeast of Downey. He is delivering trucks as needed on a per-job basis.

Around March, while driving a dark blue Opal, Bonin became anxious. He revisited past habits of constantly trolling the streets, where he found hitchhikers as easy prey as homosexual partners, even if unwilling. The encounters were of a transient and promiscuous nature because it seemed Bonin never really felt like maintaining or continuing a relationship of a homosexual nature.

Bonin booked a summer session at a nearby Cerritos junior college. He took a variety of classes, intending to continue into the fall. In another departure from the norm and trying to make progress, Bonin meets 30-year-old Sharon Nitz at a social club in Los Angeles. She has a 5-year-old mentally challenged son. Bonin and Sharon see each other often and even decide to get engaged. This was Bonin's first heterosexual encounter since Vietnam, and positive developments appear in the works. The summer of 1975 concluded uneventfully, with Bonin passing his classes and registering for the following semester. Knowing Bonin began picking up hitchhikers for sexual contact in March, it is fair to assume the activity continued during the summer, after which his life and others would change for the worse. His old Atascadero friend, Phillip Gonzalez, stayed connected with Bonin and met up in Hollywood around this time. During the evening, Bonin suggested that they pick up some boys. Gonzales asked how he would handle the situation if he got into the same trouble he had been before. Bonin told him there would never be more witnesses. Gonzales asked Bonin how he planned to eliminate them and was told, "As a matter of fact, I would kill them if I had to. Bonin managed to keep himself in check for 13 months before everything went haywire.

David McVicker was a survivor of Bonin. He was hitchhiking in a garden grove on the last day of summer, where Bonin picked him up and raped him at gunpoint David was

146 Ellingwood, Ken. "The Other Victims of William Bonin." Los Angeles Times (Online), 19/2/1996 1996. https://www.latimes.com/archives/la-xpm-1996-02-19-mn-37703-story.html.

released feeling dirty and ashamed, but he told his parents and best friend, and they went to the police. 146

In the Book Without Redemption, 14 David McVicker shares his story. On September 8, He was walking home late afternoon when Bonin pulled up alongside him. In a blue opal offering David a lift, He seemed friendly. The man was smiling and cheerful. He seemed OK. I started to get nervous when he started asking me if I had ever had sex with a man and if I liked gay people. I told him I had not and did not care what other people did and asked him to drop me off. My street was coming up anyway. I wanted to get out there fast, but that son of a bitch did not pull over. Instead, he kept driving, and when I realised He was not stopping, I freaked out. What was going on?

I was too scared to jump out of the car, but I would have if I had to. Fuck it. I sneaked the door open and got ready, but Bonin saw me and pulled out a fucking gun, pointing it at me. I couldn't believe I was 14 years old with a gun pointed at my head fuck. I couldn't believe it was happening. I did not know what to do, so I froze and said nothing. He kept on driving. I do not know how long it wasn't really long. That damn gun pointed at me with his left hand, moving with his right. You know, like you see in the movies. Well, we ended up in some place with dirt hills all around. No point in screaming cause there wasn't anyone around. It was almost dark. If I tried to run away, who knows what he would do? I didn't know how I was or how to escape. Bonin stops the car. Acting paranoid about ensuring no one was around, he removed all his clothes and ordered me to strip down. He grabbed my penis and made me touch his. It was so gross. Bonin started giving me fellatio and ordered me to suck him back.

I said no way, and he got furious, pissed off enough to put the gun right next to my neck. It was really close. It was so close I could not see it, and he told me to do it. Oh my God, that moment is burned in my memory forever. Time froze as I stared at Bonin in blank horror, wondering what the fuck was I to do. I tried to imagine my face, staring at him at that moment. A 14-year-old boy staring into unknown evil. With total fear. It scares me years later thinking about it. The moment ended when he punched me in the chest. God, he was bigger and Stronger, and I was just a kid.

I thought he would break my chest, but I did what he said. It was disgusting, and I gagged and tried to open the car door to spit on the ground, and this got Bonin really pissed off. he was so mad that he punched me in the face and screamed at me to roll down the window instead. After he calmed down, Bonin began to play with my penis and told me to do the same with his it was awful when Bonin got hard. He told me to turn around and bend over, and he tried to sodomise me; by God, what a horrible feeling fuck I hate him for doing that to me. Well, it hurt so much that I began to cry really hard. I mean, it must have made him stop. Maybe it was not exciting enough. I do not know. fuck I do not care. Anyway, the creep actually apologised for hurting me. He then put Vaseline on his fingers and on mine. He touched me, and I felt him, but nothing happened. And Bonin gave up. I thought he might punch me again because he could not do anything. Or maybe he would shoot me, dump me out of the car and leave me to die in the dirt. All these horrible things raced through my mind. I am so fucking scared. I wanted to get home so badly, really. I never wanted anything so bad in my whole life. After giving up on everything, Bonin just masturbated himself into a Rag and told me to get dressed. He asked me where I lived, and he dropped me nearby. But as I walked home, he drove up and down the street looking for where I lived. I could not get inside our house fast enough. It took me hours to calm down, telling my mother what happened. Crying and still scared to death. I knew he saw my house and would come back and get me again. I wish the memory could be wiped from my brain, but I cannot forget it. I never will.

Bonin Pulls up beside a 15-year-old boy on Beach Blvd. He tried to solicit sex from the car window, asking the boy if he knew what it meant to be gay and if the boy would sell his body for $35, but he tried picking up the wrong boy. The boy started yelling at Bonin to get the fuck out of here and kept on walking, upon which time Bonin drove up the curb and nearly ran him over. The observant boy provided police with the possible licence plate number; thus, Bonin was now on their radar screen.

October 10, 1975, Bonin was pulled over by a standard police cruiser and arrested for probation violations based on the attacks. This incident, a stark reminder of the gravity of Bonin's actions, marked a turning point in his life. Now he knows that at least one of the incidents was reported to police, and prison is a real possibility. During the arrest, Bonin utters a prophetic phrase to one of the arresting officers, further signalling Bonin's gradual decline into the monster decades in the making. Officer Patricia Johnson later testified that after getting him into the police car, Bonin chillingly told her the next time, there would not be any more witnesses. Mcvickar and the other victim positively identified Bonin. With that, he was booked by Stanton Police Department for assault and battery and soliciting sex in public. Four days later, he was sent to Fountain Valley Police Department for booking on kidnapping, sodomy and sex perversion by force charges in the brutal attack on David McVicker. All charges were incorporated together for proceedings in Orange County Superior Court. The LA Superior Court was alerted about Bonin's arrest and parole violations, thus requiring a hearing with Judge Barrett, who granted him parole a year earlier. Knowing Bonin must appear in Los Angeles for parole violations, on November 5,

Orange County Superior Court accepted a guilty plea for one count, 288, (a) perversion by force serving to lock in the LA County parole violations. Sentencing and remaining Orange County charges are to continue on December 23, labelled mentally disordered sex offender proceedings. They will occur after Bonin sees Judge Barrett in LA on December 18. Both decisions can later be consolidated for final sentencing, treating Bonin as an MDSO, given that the label by the Atascadero office gives him certain advantages in the ultimate disposition.

Before the Los Angeles hearing, Judge Barrett received a damning report from acting probation officer Clarence E Cabell, one approved by Roger Carlson, deputy Bellflower area office. This comprehensive report, dated August 6, 1974, detailed Bonin's previous violations of probation obligations, his current custody at Orange County, and other relevant facts. The report listed Bonin's earlier violations of probation obligations, notes he is in custody at Orange County, current violations, whether adjudicated or not, and other relevant facts.16

Cabell wrote that the defendant appears to be violating probation as evidenced by his plea of guilty violation of Section 288-A Penal Code. It is apparent that the defendant is not willing or capable of functioning in an open setting, and it is also evident that he is a natural and present menace to the community. Consequently, our commitment to state prison seems the only logical alternative. Therefore, the following recommendation is submitted. It is recommended that the defendant be found in violation of probation, the probation be revoked, and a sentence be imposed. Bonin's probation was withdrawn at the LA hearing, and he is scheduled for the most essential appearance in early February. Bonin was sent back to Orange County. I believe LA County District Attorney John Van De Kamp will pursue and obtain a stiff sentence on multiple charges from Bonin's 1969 arrest.

Judge Williams passed a Waterdown sentence on the one charge He pled guilty to. As a result of the 288, (a) from sex perversion by force to oral copulation despite Bonin's desire for assignment. As an MDSO to Patton State Mental Hospital located in San Bernardino County, William gives him 15 years. With a six-month minimum at the California Men's Colony. A state prison. Events will reveal this, which is yet another lucky break for Bonin. Arrived at CMC on December 31, 1975. It must be noted that Bonin's designation as a Mentally Disordered Sexual offender (MDSO) is the reason he landed at CMC East; without the MDSO tag, he would have been dealt with more severely. Meaning had time inside a dangerous state prison.

Bonin lands in a relatively safe prison and is considered an easy time when compared to other violent, high-security facilities. Child molesters are regarded as rock spiders and quite often are targets of violence. Bonin appeared back at the Los Angeles Superior Court in early February. DA Van De Kamp convinces Judge Barrett to convict on 4 counts from the 1969 unrest, a significant event in the history of criminal justice, due to parole violations, and he receives 25 years with a one-year minimum.

The documents are perplexing, but on April 21, 1976, the California Attorney General, Orange County adjusted the sentence. to a charge to a 15-year maximum. The whole sentence will be revised again in 1977. While Bonin's at CMC documents indicate a final sentence is 25 years with a one-year minimum, another part of the LA case summary suggests a term of three years minimum. The final sentence is shrouded in ambiguity, a legacy from California's indeterminate sentencing policy, which was about to change with the passing of the new 1976 California Determinate sentencing statute amendments in 1977, which meant the statute was in full effect and thus would alter Bonin's final sentence without the new law Bonin stay at California men's colony might have been much longer.

August 1977. Bonin retains a new attorney, Mark Woolpert, from San Luis Obispo, and his sentence review hearing is set for January 12, 1978. his parents continue to visit. The fiancé is no longer in contact and has stopped visiting. Over the previous year, Bonin refused to participate in Group therapy, citing [specific reasons for refusal], and is still on the waiting list for individual sessions. Prison doctors are powerless to force him into group therapy. Bonin finally started private psychiatric treatment in October 1977. Enrolled in the vocational machine shop, Bonin got an A in Algebra One and utilised the master machine shop. In the meantime, Bonin's annual 1977 Aug board report is coming up, and the psychiatric evaluation for the community release board has been renamed due to the new determinant sentence law. On July 11, the psychiatric counsel, six psychiatrists, including Doctor Owre and another old friend from Atascadero, Dr Hollingsworth, interviewed Bonin for over an hour, Preceded by a case review and a discussion. It is noted that Doctors Owre prepared the 1976 Aug Board report.

Bonin is described as inarticulate in recognising, labelling, or recognising his emotions, and he uses only one word concerning his personality. *Aggressive*, thriving in their controlled environment and kept busy. Bonin believes he overcame a negative self-image through vocational training, school friends, self-control and a positive outlook. Bonin was absolutely considered as demonstrating little psychological change during the present period of incarceration. Still, he had gained an intellectual understanding of some of the dynamic features. Doctors view him as still likely to seek sexual acts with minor boys under stressful circumstances in the community. If released, he should be in a closely supervised programme. Bonin should be encouraged to attend therapy or maintain accounts in a relationship where we can explore appropriate behaviour alternatives during stressful circumstances. On January 12, 1978, a three-member panel of the California community release board met and set about assigning a set amount of time for each convicted offence, and the total adds up to nine years and eight months. The final order in the Application of Laws section reads that special parole conditions are to be imposed, including [specific conditions]. In this case, it is the Parole Outpatient Clinic.

Seeing an opportunity to reduce the final sentence, Bonin meticulously obtains hearing transcripts, requests documents from LA and OC superior courts, and submits a written appeal that is highly lucid and well-organised, pointing out various mathematical errors and time credits. The total sentence is knocked down to 8 years and four months. Another appeal was denied on February 21, 1978, and further appeals were disallowed. Bonin's father suffered a minor stroke in December 1977. Church landed him in the Long Beach, VA hospital for two months, where his mother worked as a vocational nurse. And could assist in his care. Bonin's path forward was apparent at this point. The most he would serve had been substantially reduced, and his record at CMC was flawless. He continues to work at the vocational machine shop while planning how to get released quickly. A possible pretext arises when, in March 1978, his father suffers a second major stroke, which Lands him back in the VA hospital for at least a year and probably for good. Bonin has been in individual therapy for about seven months. According to reports, he is making good progress in acquiring a positive self-image and insight into his previous hang-ups; along with this, he acquired enough self-knowledge about himself to realise that he really wanted to become a practising adult homosexual rather than attempt to fulfil their heterosexual identity that his mother had always given him. After discussions with his parents, they apparently accepted that their son needed his identity. This is Bill Bonin at his manipulative best, playing a game honed over eight years of incarceration, many of them being psychoanalysed and picked apart by teams of psychologists, psychiatrists, and social workers. In my opinion, calculating that recent events and suitable behaviour make him eligible for early release, he writes a letter pleading his case to various prison officials. In the letter, Bonin cites four primary reasons for early release. He is helping his mother because his father is hospitalised, and two, having completed 2400 hours of vocational training with decent work reviews. He made solid progress in individual therapy, job prospects, and financial viability.

Bonin met with Dr. Owre on July 27, 1978, for what turned out to be the final August board report. It is the shortest one since Bonin arrived at CMC, and Dr. Owre breezes through his progress and recommends parole.

Diagnosis of antisocial personality and sexual deviation. Male Paedophilia was upgraded and improved with a psychiatric conclusion that his prognosis for non-recidivism is noticeably improved and better than average in the opinion of the examiner.

The Community Release Board agrees with the recommendation. Bonin returned to reside with his mother in Downey, sought employment as a machinist, received $240 a month in Social Security disability benefits, and must participate in Inpatient Outpatient Clinic therapy as part of his parole obligations. The decision has been made. The die is cast. And finally, Bonin is about to be set free, bringing a sense of closure to his long legal journey.

On August 22, a request was issued for a medical examination so he could maintain his class. One California driver's licence is in good standing and states that Bonin will be released in December 1978. Parole will be for one year, and he must participate in outpatient psychiatric treatment and will be reporting to a parole officer At the Southeast Division near his mother's home in Downey; Bonin has secured employment at Freight Movers, also in Downey, and he uses his appeal for even earlier release. It works for the last time. William George Bonim was released from state prison on October 11, 1978.

In Bonin's confessions, he reports that there were a few very, very lucky people that he could have killed, but for reasons only he knows, he did not kill them: 5 young boys and three girls.16

On 9thAugust 1979, 5 days after killing two young men, Bonin was trawling again for another victim; he found an unwitting victim, a 17-year-old boy who was hitchhiking to a friend's house in Orange County, and Bonin offered him a lift. Shortly after getting in the van, Bonin started to fondle the boy's genitals, asking, "Does this feel good? "The young man pushed Bonin's hands away, but Bonin was persistent and said that he was bisexual and the young man should try it. Bonin found somewhere to park and was still fondling the man's genitals; Bonin asked him, "Can't you get hard for me?" the young man became confused and wanted to leave. Still, Bonin insisted on talking him into moving to the back of the van. Bonin pulled down his pants, asked him if he wanted a good blow job, and tried to kiss him, but the young man turned away and told him he was not into this; Bonin still insisted that he would give the young man oral copulation and he could just jack Bonin off, Bonin had only just begun to orally copulate the young man when a patrol car arrived, Bonin was charged with Sex perversion and remained into custody the crime report is #562-395 Bonin was released on parole on August 13 1979. the officer who made that arrest likely saved that boy's life. An astonishing recommendation on the Bonin's Parole report for that offence was that jail time was not recommended as it would not serve any purpose if only they had known!!!

According to Vonda Pelto's book Without Redemption Bonin's attorney filed a writ of habeas corpus compelling his release and calling for the charges to be filed against him by September 7, 1979. The court released him and set him to appear for a disposition hearing on Friday, August 24. While the wheels were set in motion to decide this matter with possible parole violations, Bonin continued killing a parole report dated August 23, recommending that further jail time would not serve any purpose.

Chapter 26 Closing Statements to the World by Tina

Ladies and gentlemen of the world we know. I want to state to everyone who reads this book that I have spent over 43 years in prison for a crime I did not commit. Many in prison claim not guilty, but if you read this crime book. You will find out that some of us are not guilty but guilty by association, which, in this case, is incredibly sad. If you genuinely believe in the criminal justice system and feel that I, Tina Marie Munro, once James Michael Munro, am not guilty and was thrown away by the court system, then please contact the state of California Governor's office and demand my release from the prison of hell, I cannot escape. Not a day goes by that I do not think about all of this, which will haunt me for the rest of my life. I even petitioned the governor to be executed because I felt so bad. I wanted to bring Steven Wells back even if I did not do this. Still, since the courts threw me away, I can finally bring closure to the Wells family to show them how sorry I truly am.

If anyone wishes to write to me, contact the Department of Corrections under my new name,

Tina Munro C-44535, box 409089, Ione Ca 95640. I will happily correspond or text me at https://www.gettingout.com/

Go to agreements and put my CDC number in it. I will be glad to text.

Love you all.

Chapter 27 Crime Scene Photos

*Image SEQ Image * ARABIC94 Screenshot (Dark Reality, 2022)*

*Image SEQ Image * ARABIC95 Screenshot (Dark Reality,2022)*

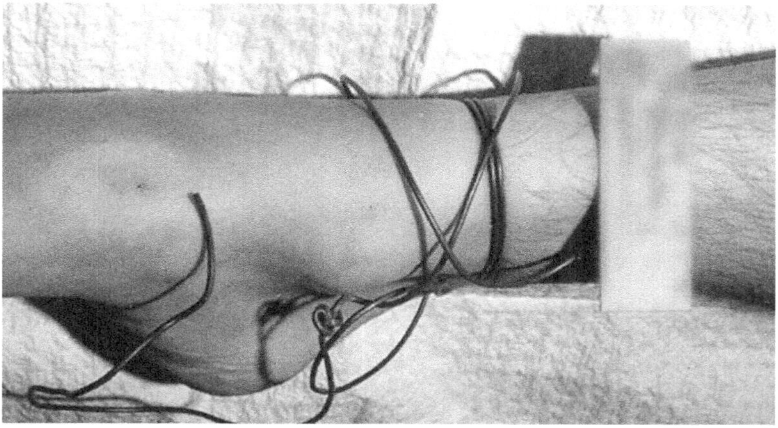

*Image SEQ Image * ARABIC96 Screenshot (Dark Reality, 2022)*

*Image SEQ Image * ARABIC98 Screenshot (Dark Reality,2022)*

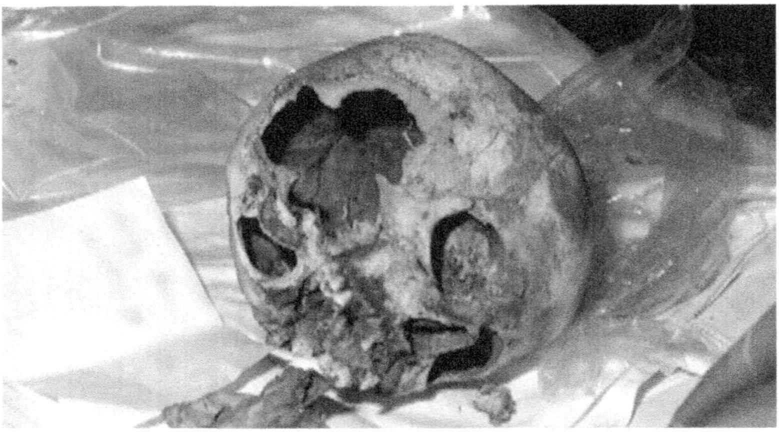

*Image SEQ Image * ARABIC97 Screenshot (Dark Reality,2022)*

*Image SEQ Image * ARABIC99 screenshot (Dark Reality,2022)*

*Image SEQ Image * ARABIC100 Inside the Death Van Screenshot (Dark Reality, 2022)*

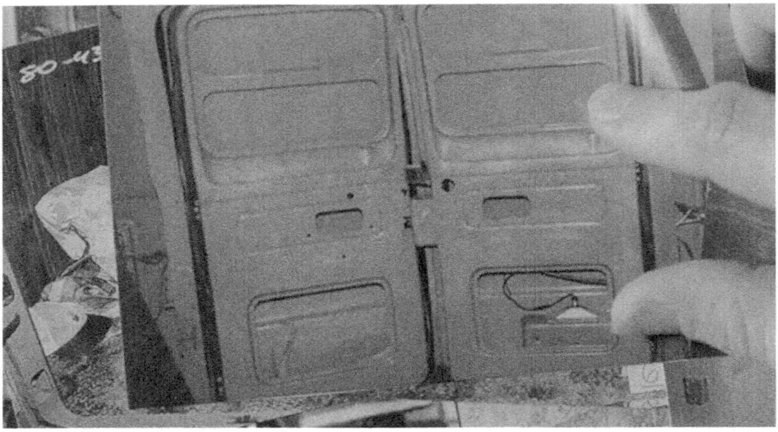

*Image SEQ Image * ARABIC101 Bonin's Death Van Doors Screenshot (Dark Reality,2022)*

*Image SEQ Image * ARABIC102 Inside the Death Van Screenshot (Dark Reality,2022)*

*Image SEQ Image * ARABIC103 Processed Death Van Screenshot (Dark Reality, 2022)*

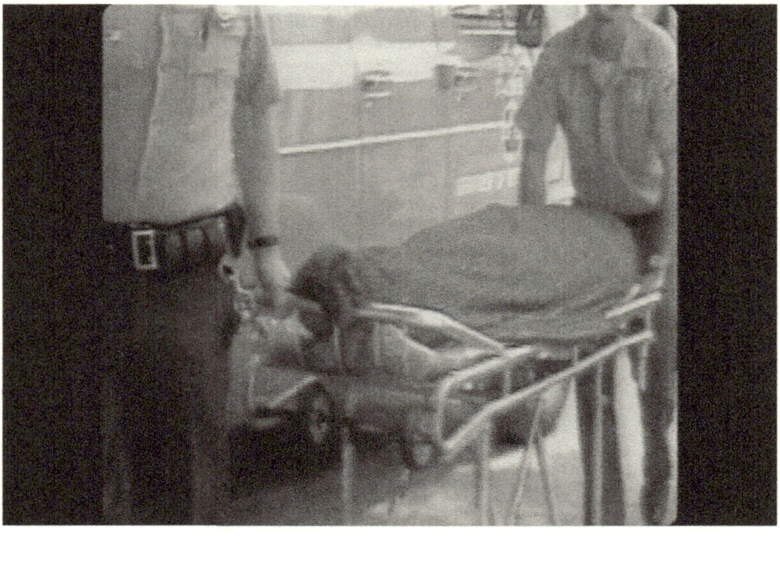

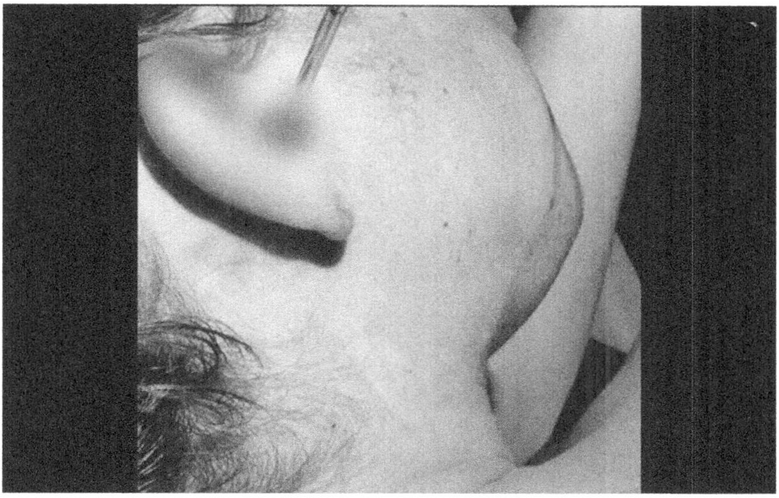

*Image SEQ Image * ARABIC104 Victim with an Ice pick in ear Screenshot (Dark Reality, 2022)*

*Image SEQ Image * ARABIC106 Detectives examine the crime scene Screenshot (Dark Reality,* ***2022)***

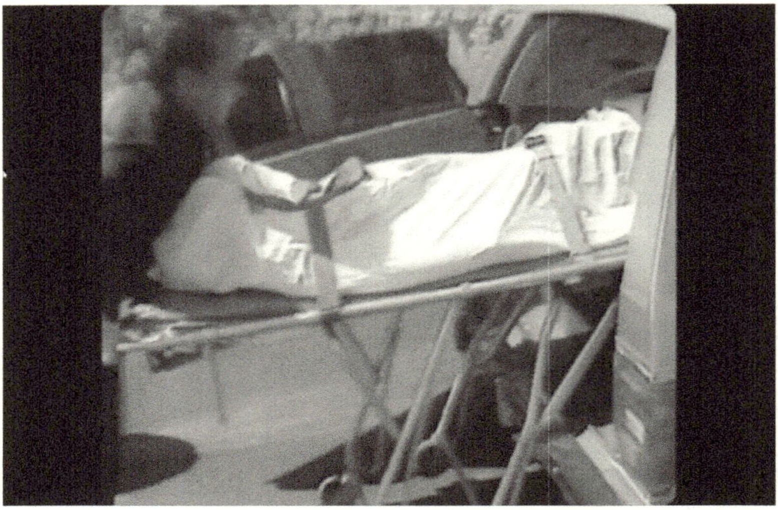

*Image SEQ Image * ARABIC107 Loading victim into coroner vehicle Screenshot (Dark Reality,2022)*

*Image SEQ Image * ARABIC108 Victim behind one of the buildings screenshot (Dark Reality 2022)*

*Image SEQ Image * ARABIC109 Victim behind one of the buildings screenshot (Dark Reality 2022)*

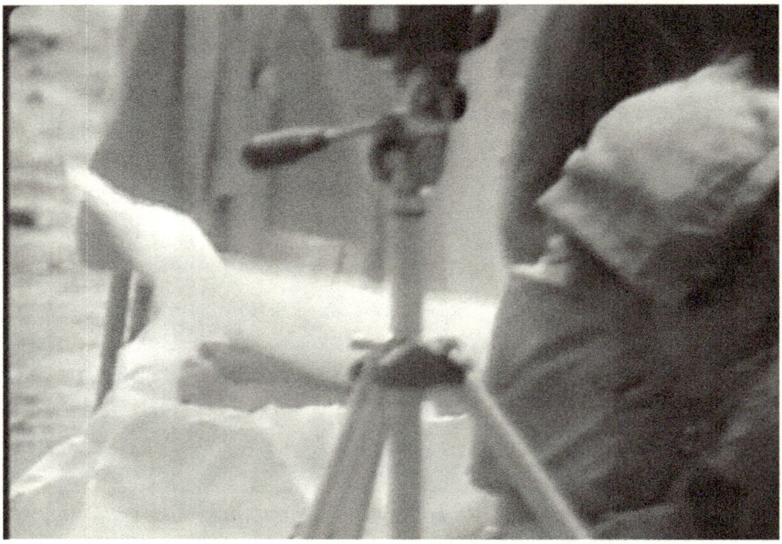

*Image SEQ Image * ARABIC110 Victim behind one of the buildings screenshot (Dark Reality 2022)*

*Image SEQ Image * ARABIC111 Outside Bonin's former home (Redfin, n.d)*

*Image SEQ Image * ARABIC112 Outside Bonin's former home, the pool is a recent addition (redfin, n.d)*

*Image SEQ Image * ARABIC113 Inside Bonin's former home (Redfin, n.d)*

*Image SEQ Image * ARABIC114 Inside Bonin's former home (Redfin, n.d)*

*Image SEQ Image * ARABIC115 Inside Bonin's former home (Redfin, n.d)*

*Image SEQ Image * ARABIC116 Inside Bonin Former Home (Redfin, n.d)*

*Image SEQ Image * ARABIC117 Inside Bonin Former Home (Redfin, n.d)*

*Image SEQ Image * ARABIC118 Inside Bonin Former Home (Redfin, n.d)*

*Image SEQ Image * ARABIC119 Inside Bonin's former home (Redfin, n.d.)*

Families Find Bonin Trial an Ordeal

2 Embittered Mothers Take Stand in County Phase of Murder Case

By JERRY HICKS,
Times Staff Writer

Jerri Fox was at the William Bonin murder trial in Orange County Superior Court on Tuesday only because she had to be. Sandra Miller was there because she wanted to be.

Both women profess bitter hatred toward the man accused of killing their sons.

Bonin, already convicted of 10 Los Angeles murders, is accused of slaying four other young men in Orange County.

One of them, Dennis Frank Fox, 18, was Jerri Fox's son. Another of the four, Russell Rugh, 15, was the son of Sandra Miller.

Both women testified last year at the penalty phase of Bonin's Los Angeles trial, where he was eventually sentenced to the gas chamber. Both took the witness stand when testimony began Tuesday in Bonin's Orange County trial, three years after he was arrested.

But only Mrs. Miller will be back in court today. Mrs. Fox said during a recess Tuesday that the trial would simply be too much for her.

Please see BONIN, Page 5

CLIFF OTTO / Los Angeles Times

Waiting out a recess in William Bonin's murder trial are, from left, Steven, Sandra and Bernie Miller, the half brother, mother and stepfather of Russell Rugh, allegedly a victim of Bonin.

CLIFF OTTO / Los Angeles Times

William Bonin, right, seated with his attorney, William Charvet, during Bonin's murder trial in Orange County Superior Court.

*Image SEQ Image * ARABIC120 Outside Bonin's former home pool is a recent addition* ***(Redfin, n.d)***

*Image SEQ Image * ARABIC121 Outside Bonin's former home pool is a recent addition (Redfin, n.d)*

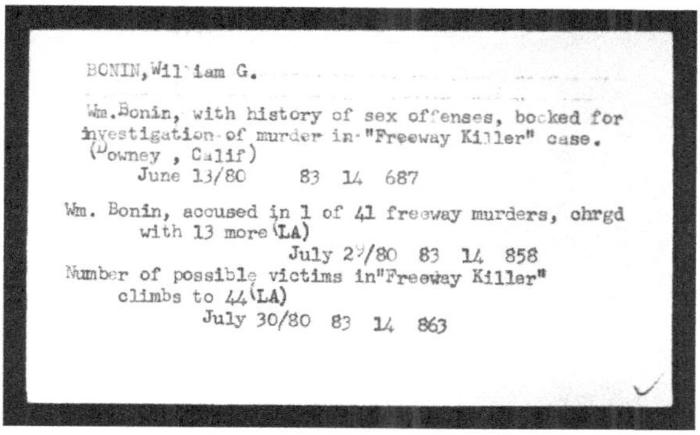

BONIN, William G.

Wm. Bonin, with history of sex offenses, booked for investigation of murder in "Freeway Killer" case. (Downey, Calif)
June 13/80 83 14 687

Wm. Bonin, accused in 1 of 41 freeway murders, chrgd with 13 more (LA)
July 29/80 83 14 858

Number of possible victims in "Freeway Killer" climbs to 44 (LA)
July 30/80 83 14 863

*Image SEQ Image * ARABIC122 Ancestry.com. Associated Press, Name Card Index to AP Stories,1905-1990C*

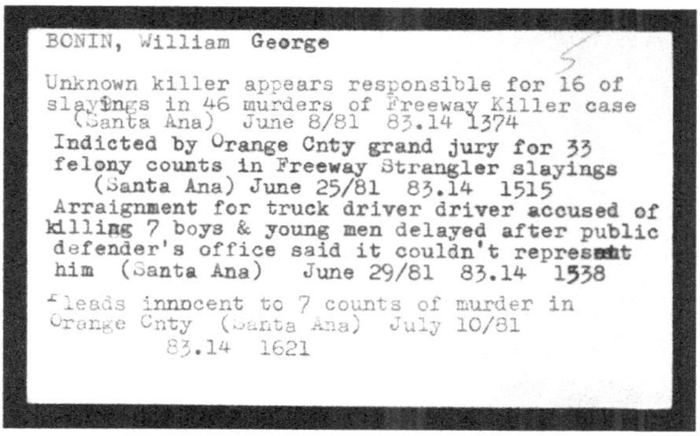

BONIN, William George

Unknown killer appears responsible for 16 of slayings in 46 murders of Freeway Killer case (Santa Ana) June 8/81 83.14 1374

Indicted by Orange Cnty grand jury for 33 felony counts in Freeway Strangler slayings (Santa Ana) June 25/81 83.14 1515

Arraignment for truck driver driver accused of killing 7 boys & young men delayed after public defender's office said it couldn't represent him (Santa Ana) June 29/81 83.14 1538

Pleads innocent to 7 counts of murder in Orange Cnty (Santa Ana) July 10/81 83.14 1621

*Image SEQ Image * ARABIC123 Ancestry.com. Associated Press, Name Card Index to AP Stories, 1905-1990*

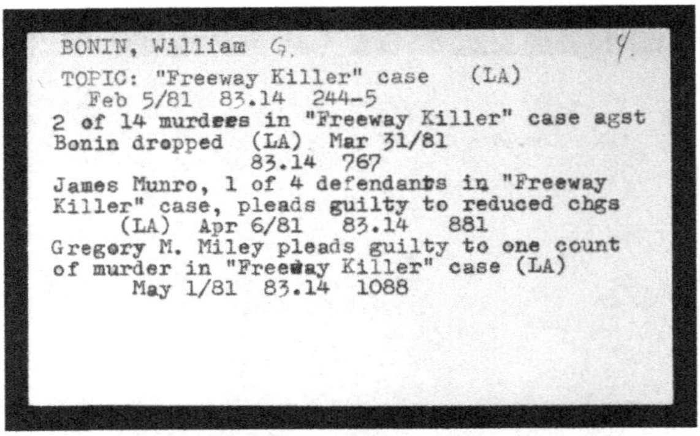
BONIN, William G. 4.
TOPIC: "Freeway Killer" case (LA)
Feb 5/81 83.14 244-5
2 of 14 murdees in "Freeway Killer" case agst Bonin dropped (LA) Mar 31/81
83.14 767
James Munro, 1 of 4 defendants in "Freeway Killer" case, pleads guilty to reduced chgs (LA) Apr 6/81 83.14 881
Gregory M. Miley pleads guilty to one count of murder in "Freeway Killer" case (LA)
May 1/81 83.14 1088

*Image SEQ Image * ARABIC124 Ancestry.com. Associated Press, Name Card Index to AP Stories, 1905-1990*

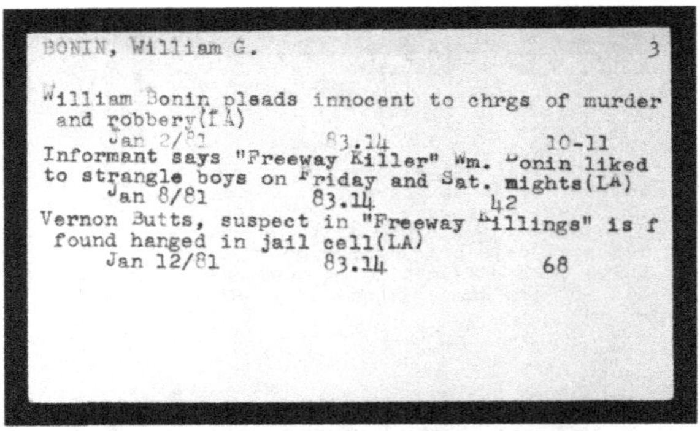
BONIN, William G. 3
William Bonin pleads innocent to chrgs of murder and robbery(LA)
Jan 2/81 83.14 10-11
Informant says "Freeway Killer" Wm. Bonin liked to strangle boys on Friday and Sat. nights(LA)
Jan 8/81 83.14 42
Vernon Butts, suspect in "Freeway Killings" is f found hanged in jail cell(LA)
Jan 12/81 83.14 68

*Image SEQ Image * ARABIC125 Ancestry.com. Associated Press, Name Card Index to AP Stories, 1905-1990*

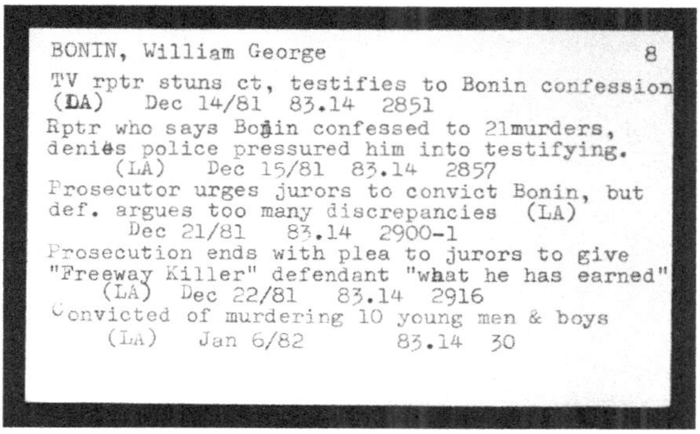

BONIN, William George 8

TV rptr stuns ct, testifies to Bonin confession
(DA) Dec 14/81 83.14 2851
Rptr who says Bonin confessed to 21murders,
denies police pressured him into testifying.
(LA) Dec 15/81 83.14 2857
Prosecutor urges jurors to convict Bonin, but
def. argues too many discrepancies (LA)
Dec 21/81 83.14 2900-1
Prosecution ends with plea to jurors to give
"Freeway Killer" defendant "what he has earned"
(LA) Dec 22/81 83.14 2916
Convicted of murdering 10 young men & boys
(LA) Jan 6/82 83.14 30

*Image SEQ Image * ARABIC126 Ancestry.com. Associated Press, Name Card Index to AP Stories, 1905-1990*

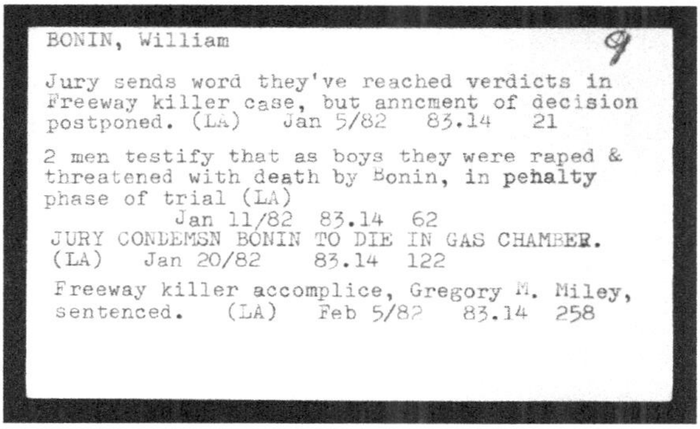

BONIN, William 9

Jury sends word they've reached verdicts in
Freeway killer case, but anncment of decision
postponed. (LA) Jan 5/82 83.14 21

2 men testify that as boys they were raped &
threatened with death by Bonin, in penalty
phase of trial (LA)
Jan 11/82 83.14 62
JURY CONDEMSN BONIN TO DIE IN GAS CHAMBER.
(LA) Jan 20/82 83.14 122

Freeway killer accomplice, Gregory M. Miley,
sentenced. (LA) Feb 5/82 83.14 258

*Image SEQ Image * ARABIC127 Ancestry.com. Associated Press, Name Card Index to AP Stories, 1905-1990*

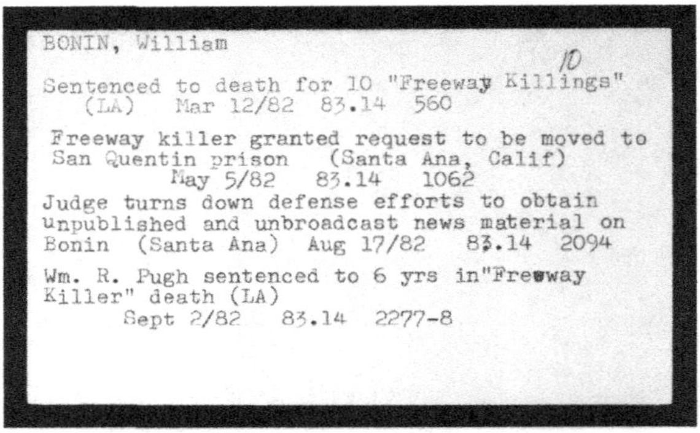

BONIN, William

10

Sentenced to death for 10 "Freeway Killings"
(LA) Mar 12/82 83.14 560

Freeway killer granted request to be moved to San Quentin prison (Santa Ana, Calif)
May 5/82 83.14 1062

Judge turns down defense efforts to obtain unpublished and unbroadcast news material on Bonin (Santa Ana) Aug 17/82 83.14 2094

Wm. R. Pugh sentenced to 6 yrs in "Freeway Killer" death (LA)
Sept 2/82 83.14 2277-8

*Image SEQ Image * ARABIC128 Ancestry.com. Associated Press, Name Card Index to AP Stories, 1905-1990*

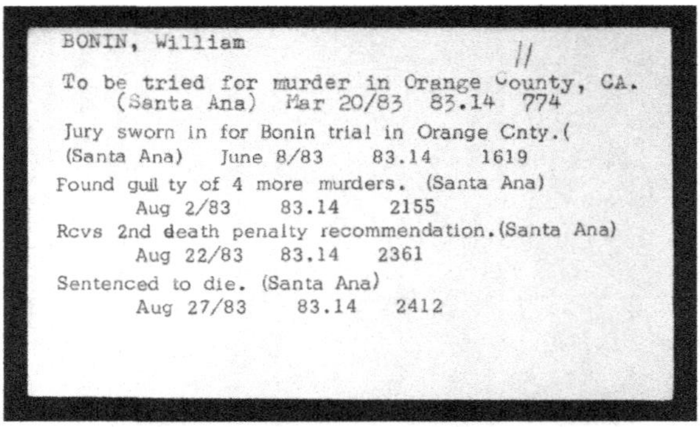

BONIN, William

11

To be tried for murder in Orange County, CA.
(Santa Ana) Mar 20/83 83.14 774

Jury sworn in for Bonin trial in Orange Cnty.(
(Santa Ana) June 8/83 83.14 1619

Found guil ty of 4 more murders. (Santa Ana)
Aug 2/83 83.14 2155

Rcvs 2nd death penalty recommendation.(Santa Ana)
Aug 22/83 83.14 2361

Sentenced to die. (Santa Ana)
Aug 27/83 83.14 2412

*Image SEQ Image * ARABIC129 Ancestry.com. Associated Press, Name Card Index to AP Stories, 1905-1990*

Murderbillia

Murderbillia is a controversial topic, which I am not going to get into a moral debate about. However, I am including it in the back of my book, as many people collect various items from convicted felons. If you are interested in collecting or are a collector, I recommend visiting the website at

https://www.murderauction.com/.

It is run and owned by William Harder, and you'll find all sorts of memorabilia, not just those related to crime.

Happy
Birthday

DOING TIME
Stories from the mind
of a Death Row Prisoner
Book One
William Bonin

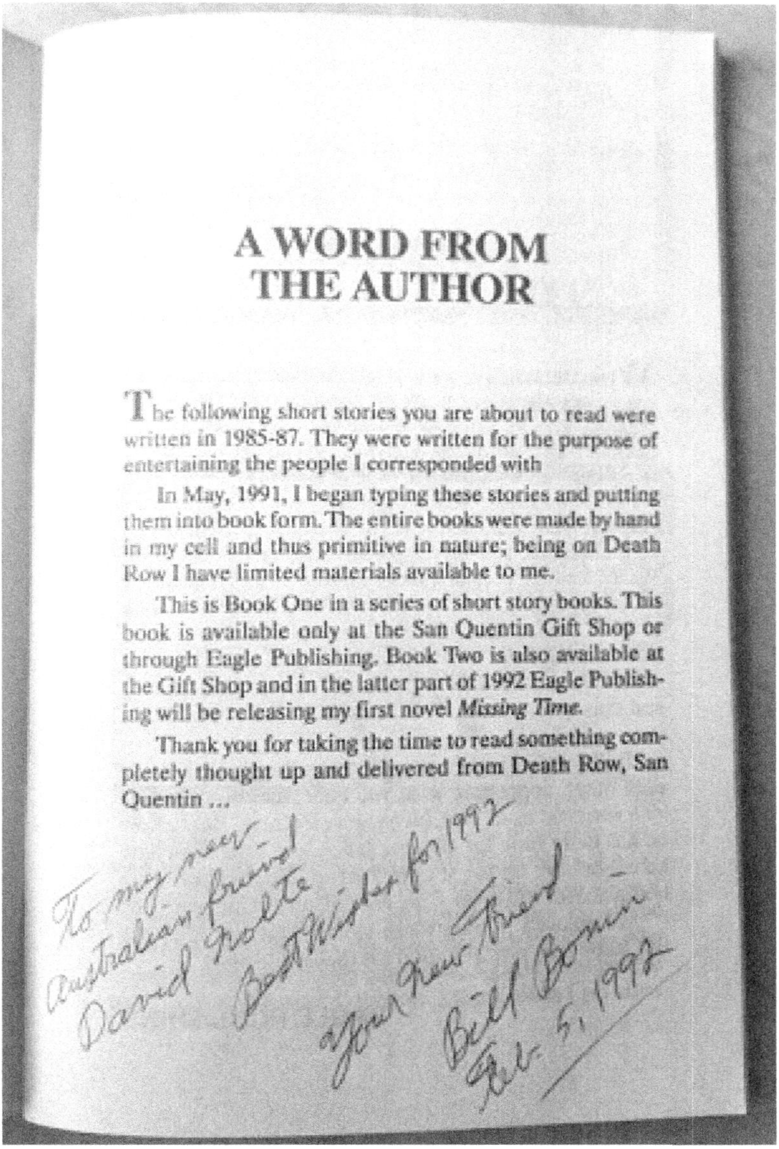

A WORD FROM THE AUTHOR

The following short stories you are about to read were written in 1985-87. They were written for the purpose of entertaining the people I corresponded with

In May, 1991, I began typing these stories and putting them into book form. The entire books were made by hand in my cell and thus primitive in nature; being on Death Row I have limited materials available to me.

This is Book One in a series of short story books. This book is available only at the San Quentin Gift Shop or through Eagle Publishing. Book Two is also available at the Gift Shop and in the latter part of 1992 Eagle Publishing will be releasing my first novel *Missing Time*.

Thank you for taking the time to read something completely thought up and delivered from Death Row, San Quentin ...

To my new Australian friend David Nolte
Best Wishes for 1992
Your New Friend
Bill Bonin
Feb. 5, 1992

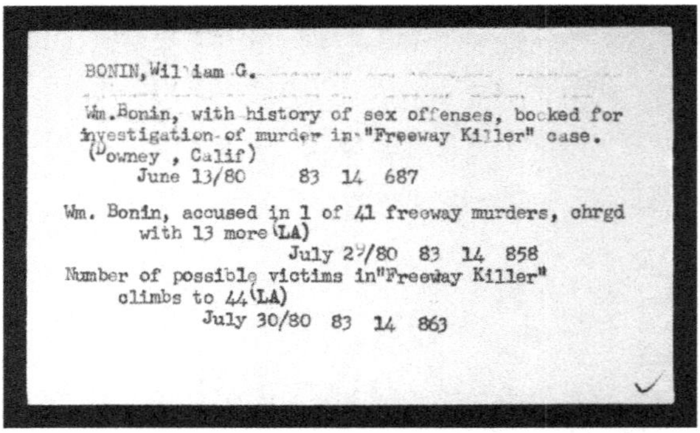

BONIN, William G.

Wm. Bonin, with history of sex offenses, booked for investigation of murder in "Freeway Killer" case. (Downey, Calif)
June 13/80 83 14 687

Wm. Bonin, accused in 1 of 41 freeway murders, chrgd with 13 more (LA)
July 29/80 83 14 858

Number of possible victims in "Freeway Killer" climbs to 44 (LA)
July 30/80 83 14 863

*Image SEQ Image * ARABIC130 Ancestry.com. Associated Press, Name Card Index to AP Stories, 1905-1990*

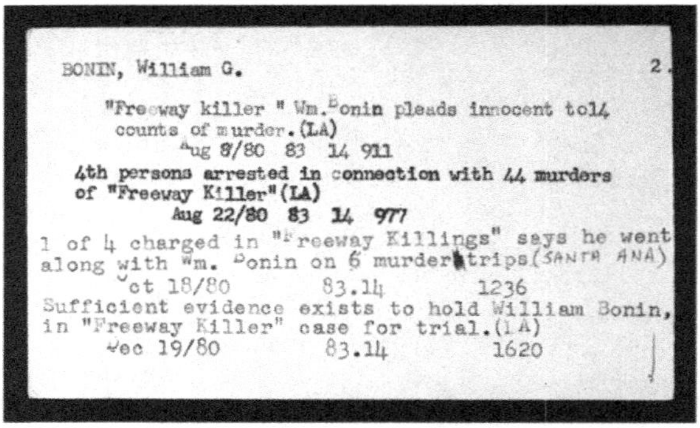

BONIN, William G. 2

"Freeway killer" Wm. Bonin pleads innocent to 14 counts of murder. (LA)
Aug 8/80 83 14 911

4th persons arrested in connection with 44 murders of "Freeway Killer" (LA)
Aug 22/80 83 14 977

1 of 4 charged in "Freeway Killings" says he went along with Wm. Bonin on 6 murder trips (SANTA ANA)
Oct 18/80 83.14 1236

Sufficient evidence exists to hold William Bonin, in "Freeway Killer" case for trial. (LA)
Dec 19/80 83.14 1620

*Image SEQ Image * ARABIC131 Ancestry.com. Associated Press, Name Card Index to AP Stories, 1905-1990*

Photos and Illustrations

Image Reference List

IMDb. (n.d.). James Munro. IMDb. https://www.imdb.com/name/nm9551254/

Wikipedia contributors. (2024, July 22). Sonny Barger. Wikipedia. https://en.wikipedia.org/wiki/Sonny_Barger

Blanco, J. I. (n.d.). William George Bonin | Photos | Murderpedia, the encyclopedia of murderers. http://www.murderpedia.org/male.B/b1/bonin-william-photos.htm

"U.S., School Yearbooks, 1880-2012"; School Name: North High School; Year: 1963

Dark Reality. (2022, October 25). The Freeway Killer (William Bonin) - Lost Murder Tapes [2022] [Video]. YouTube. https://www.youtube.com/watch?v=9h4nYtrvxhA

Orphelinat Franco-American. (n.d.). CardCow.com. https://www.cardcow.com/865283/lowell-massachusetts-orphelinat-franco-american/

Hermit, W. (n.d.). Jethro Tull - Long Beach 1979. https://thewitchwoodrecords.blogspot.com/2013/12/jethro-tull-long-beach-1979.html

Kuroski, J. (2024, February 24). William Bonin, the "Freeway killer" who terrorised Southern California. All That is Interesting. https://allthatsinteresting.com/william-bonin

File: Gregory Mathews Miley Mug shot 1980.jpg - Wikimedia Commons. (1980, August 23). https://commons.wikimedia.org/wiki/File:Gregory_Mathews_Miley_Mug_Shot_1980.jpg

IMDb. (n.d.-a). Billy Pugh. IMDb. https://www.imdb.com/name/nm12843752/

"U.S., School Yearbooks, 1880-2012"; School Name: Bolsa Grande High School; Year: 1976

Thomas Glen Lundgren (1966-1979). - Find a Grave. . . (1966, March 24). https://www.findagrave.com/memorial/54053478/thomas_glen-lundgren

Mark Duane Shelton (1961-1979). - Find a Grave. . . (1961, December 19). https://www.findagrave.com/memorial/115644189/mark_duane-shelton

File: William Bonin's Ford Econoline murder van.jpg - Wikimedia Commons. (1980). https://commons.wikimedia.org/wiki/File:William_Bonin's_Ford_Econoline_murder_van.jpg

IMDb. (n.d.-b). Donald Hyden. IMDb. https://m.imdb.com/name/nm12843382/

IMDb. (n.d.-b). Donald Hyden. IMDb. https://m.imdb.com/name/nm12843382/

Dave Louis Murillo (1962-1979). - Find a grave. . . (1962, May 22). https://www.findagrave.com/memorial/99304631/dave_louis-murillo
Robert Christopher "Bob" Wirostek (1960-1979) -. . . (1960, October 30). https://www.findagrave.com/memorial/216968371/robert_christopher-wirostek#view-photo=21508139
9
"U.S., School Yearbooks, 1880-2012"; School Name: Orange High School; Year: 1980
Ronald Craig Gatlin (1961-1980). - Find a Grave. . . (1961, August 3). https://www.findagrave.com/memorial/85406438/ronald-craig-gatlin
John Fredrick Kilpatrick (1964-1979). - Find a... (1964, February 24). https://www.findagrave.com/memorial/199908077/john_fredrick-kilpatrick
"U.S., School Yearbooks, 1880-2012"; School Name: Montclair High School; Year: 1978
James Michael Macabe (1967-1980). - Find a Grave. . . (1967, March 31) https://www.findagrave.com/memorial/191138304/james_michael-macabe
IMDb. (n.d.-c). Glenn Barker. IMDb. https://m.imdb.com/name/nm12843754/
Russell Duane "Rusty" Rugh II (1965-1980) - Find a... (1965, March 18). https://www.findagrave.com/memorial/203273903/russell_duane-rugh
Wiki, C. T. S. K. D. (n.d.). TURNER Harry Todd. Serial Killer Database Wiki. https://skdb.fandom.com/wiki/TURNER_Harry_Todd
Wiki, C. T. S. K. D. (n.d.-b). WOOD Steven John/Gallery. Serial Killer Database Wiki. https://skdb.fandom.com/wiki/WOOD_Steven_John/Gallery
"U.S., School Yearbooks, 1880-2012"; School Name: Columbus High School; Year: 1980
Lawrence Eugene Sharp (1962-1980). - Find a Grave. . . (1962, November 3). https://www.findagrave.com/memorial/194418367/lawrence-eugene-sharp\
Darin Lee Kendrick (1961-1980). - Find a Grave. . . (1961, January 31). https://www.findagrave.com/memorial/213194869/darin_lee-kendrick
File: Sean Paige King Freeway Killer William Bonin 1980.jpg - Wikimedia Commons. (1980, July 30). https://commons.wikimedia.org/wiki/File:Sean-_Paige_King_Freeway_Killer_William_Bonin_1980.jpg
King_Freeway_Killer_William_Bonin_1980.jpg
Wikipedia contributors. (2024b, July 28). Chevrolet Chevette. Wikipedia. https://en.wikipedia.org/wiki/Chevrolet_Chevette

James Wilfred "Jamie" Trotter (1965-1979) - Find. . . (1965, June 12). https://www.findagrave.com/memorial/50898187/james_wilfred-trotter

Gannon, F., & Gannon, F. (2021, September 18). Victims Spotlight: The suspected victims of the scorecard killer. Wicked Horror. https://wickedhorror.com/features/victims-spotlight-the-suspected-victims-of-the-scorecard-killer/

Freeway Killers arrested in 1980. . . - RareNewspapers.com. (n.d.). https://www.rarenewspapers.com/view/688434?imagelist=1

Blanco, J. I. (n.d.-b). William George Bonin | Photos | Murderpedia, the encyclopedia of murderers. https://murderpedia.org/male.B/b1/bonin-william-photos.htm

Redfin. (n.d.). 10282 Angell St, Downey, CA 90242 - 4 beds/2 baths. Redfin. https://www.redfin.com/CA/Downey/10282-Angell-St-90242/home/7412861

Dr Theodore Kaczynski. (2021). The infamous Downey house where Freeway Killer Bill Bonin grew up. Reddit. Retrieved August 10, 2024, from https://www.reddit.com/r/serialkillers/comments/nugxrn/the_infamous_downey_house_where_freeway_killer/

Ancestry.com. Associated Press, Name Card Index to AP Stories, 1905-1990 [database online]. Provo, UT, USA: Ancestry.com Operations, Inc., 2013. Original data: Associated Press File Drawers of National, International, News Feature Name/Subject Cards, 1937–1985. Microfilm. Associated Press Corporate Archives, New York, NY.

Wiki, C. T. C. M. (n.d.). William Bonin. Criminal Minds Wiki. https://criminal-minds.fandom.com/wiki/William_Bonin

FilmRise True Crime. (2021, August 19). World's Most Evil Killers - Season 5, Episode 4 - William Bonin - full episode [Video]. YouTube. https://www.youtube.com/watch?v=xjWJBEHaipo

Bibliography

'The Vietnam War is to blame for the 14 '. *United Press International,* 17 August 1983.

'William George Bonin'. Clark County Prosecuting Attorney. http://www.clarkprosecutor.org/html/death/US/bonin322.htm.

. 1980. *San Bernardino Sun,* 19 October pp. 11.

'Accused Freeway Killer William Bonin vowed while he was '. 1981. *United Press International,* 26 November.

'Bizarre trial twists through the courts'. 1981. *The Southeastern Missourian,* 12 February

'Californians Shocked Anew by Grisly Murder Case'. 1981. *The Argus- Press,* pp. 2.

'Delay Granted man accused in homosexual murders of boys, young men'. 1981. *Eugene Register-Guard* 22 September, pp. 33.

'Freeway killer allegedly tortured victims'. 1981. *Record-Journal,* 5 November, pp. 14.

'Freeway Killer case now twisting through courts '. 1981. *The Dispatch,* 5 Feb, pp. 2.

'Freeway Killer case shocks folks'. 1981. *The Tuscaloosa News,* 5 February, pp. 2.

'Freeway killer Cases Shock Many residents '. 1981. *The Press Courier,* 5 February, pp. 3.

'"Freeway Killer' Murders May Involve 44 Victims'. 1981. *Ocala Star Banner,* 7 February, pp. 4.

'Freeway killer suspect faces Court'. 1981. *Record- Journal,* 21 Sept, pp. 21.

'"Freeway Killer" trial reveals tales of homosexual torture'. 1981. *The Day,* 3 February pp. 41.

'Freeway killers' story ghastly tale of horror'. 1981. *Gadsen Times,* February 5 pp. 9.

'Freeway Killers story ghastly tale of horror '. 1981. *Gadsen Times,* 3 February pp. 40.

'Freeway Killings Suspect Lies, Guessing '. 1981. *The Press- Courier,* 23 April 1981, pp. 4.

'Freeway slayings suspect indicted'. 1981. *Record-Journal,* 25 June, pp. 12.

'He calls killings a "good nightmare". 1981. *Boca Raton News,* 5 February 1981, pp. 5.
'Innocent Plea Entered In " Freeway Killer"'. 1981. *The Press Courier,* 9 May 1981, pp. 3.
'More than one Freeway Killer suspected'. 1981. *Lakeland ledger,* 9 June, pp. 14.
'Plea Entered'. 1981. *The Press Courier,* 29 January, pp. 2.
'Pugh Claims Innocence'. 1981. *The Evening News,* 10 May pp. 4.
'Suspect denies guilt in slayings'. 1981. *The Bulletin,* 9 May, pp. 23.
'Suspect Pleads Innocent '. 1981. *The Tuscaloosa News,* 10 May, pp. 2.
'Trail of Death now twists through courts'. 1981. *Daily Union*, pp. 4.
Vernon Butts, who confessed to taking part in the grisly Freeway Killer murders of young men and boys. He was found strangled with a towel in his Jail cell Sunday'. 1981. *United Press International,* 11 January.
'10 L.A. Freeway Killings '. 1982. *Toledo Blade,* 6 January pp. 7.
'Around the Nation; California Murderer Gets Death Sentence'. 1982. *The New York Times,* March 13, 1982, section 1, pp. 8.
'Bonin Witness sentenced'. 1982. *The Telegraph,* 9 September pp. 3.
'Death sentence imposed on "monster' murderer'. 1982. *The Vancouver Sun,* 12 March pp. 69.
'Freeway Killer Accomplice Gets 25 Years to Life Sentence'. 1982. *Lodi News-Sentinel* 4 February, pp. 29.
'Freeway Killer Bonin convicted for 10 Killings; awaits sentencing'. 1982. *Ellensburg Daily Record.*
'Freeway Killer sentenced to Die'. 1982. *The Pittsburgh Press,* 12 March, pp. 9.
'Freeway killers' fate is Pondered'. 1982. *Reading Eagle*, pp. 3.
"Freeway" figure gets six years '. 1982. *Reading Eagle,* 7 September pp. 70.
'Gas chamber mulled for homosexual killer'. 1982. *The Telegraph,* 7 Jan, pp. 19.
'Jury Deliberates'. 1982. *The Press- Courier,* 12 May, pp. 2.
'Jury still out in Murder case'. 1982. *Lodi News -Sentinel* 11 May, pp. 20.
'The Mother and two brothers of convicted Freeway Killer'. 1982. *United Press International,* 18 January.
'Pugh sentenced in Strangling'. 1982. *Sarasota Herald-Tribune,* 3 September, pp. 9.

'Retarded Youth Meted 15 Year Sentence '. 1982. *Eugene Register-Guard,* 16 March, pp. 5.
'Sex Offender guilty in torture killings of 10 boys'. 1982. *Pittsburgh Post Gazette,* 7 January, pp. 2.
'Teenager convicted of manslaughter'. 1982. *Times Daily,* 2 September, pp. 34.
'Teenager convicted of manslaughter in death '. 1982. *Lodi News- Sentinel,* 18 May 1982, pp. 4.
'Trial Delayed'. 1982. *The Press Courier,* 14 April pp. 2.
'Young Armenian Faces Assassination Charges '. 1982. *Lodi News -Sentinel* 7 May 1982, pp. 2.
"People v. Bonin 1989." In. 2009. Supreme Court of California, In Bank.
"Freeway Killer." In. 2010. Image Entertainment.
"William Bonin." In. 2022. *World Most Evil Killers Series 5, Episode 2*
'Find a Grave'. 2023. https://www.findagrave.com/virtual-cemetery/1485060.
AP. 1980. 'Freeway Killer Feared', *The Evening News*, pp. 13.
———. 1981. '"Freeway Killer " Murders May Involve 44 Victims ', *Ocala Star-Banner,* 7 Feb, pp. 4.
———. 2000. 'As home to infamous vehicles junkyard is a field of nightmares ', *Toledo Blade,* 3 September, pp. 10.
Barabak, M. (1982). 'Death by execution is the only just penalty for Freeway killer William Nonin', *United Press International,* 19 January.
Birke, D. (2010). "" The Freeway Killer"." In.
Bovsun, M. (2008). 'Murder Down the Freeway', *Daily News,* 25/3/2008.
Butler, Vonda L Pelto Ph.D. and Michael B. 2022. *Without Redemption Creation & Deeds of Freeway Killer Bill Bonin His Five Accomplices and How One Who Escaped Justice* (Flotsam Publishing).
Carangelo, L. (2018). *James Munro and the FREEWAY KILLERS* (Access Press).
Circuit, U.S Court of Appeals for the Ninth. 1995. "William George Bonin, Petitioner appellant, v Authur Calderon, As Warden of San Quentin State Prison; James Rowland, Director of the Californian Department of Corrections, l Respondents-Apelles " In *59 F.3d 815*
Collins, J. (1996). 'Lawrence Eugene Sharp: He loved an old dog named Fred and fishing with his dad', *The Orange County Register.*
Court, United States District. 2011. "James Michael Munro, v. M. Martel." In.

Deutch, L. (1981). 'Southern Californians Shocked Anew by Case', *Waycross Journal-Herald,* 9 Feb, pp. 20.

———. 1981. 'Trail of Death now twisting through courts ', *The Lewiston Journal,* 5 Feb 1981, pp. 10.

Deutsch, L. (1981). '"Freeway Killer " California is shocked by gruesome murders involving black magic, homosexuality, torture', *Kingman Daily Miner,* 15 February 1981, pp. 16.

Donnelley, P. (2009). *501 Most Notorious crimes* (Bounty et al.).

Ellingwood, K. (1996). 'The Other Victims of William Bonin', *Los Angeles Times,* 19/2/1996.

Filkins, D. (1996). 'Clues from Condemned Mans Past', *Los Angeles Times*

Government, United States. 2013. "Change in Terminology: "Mental Retardation" to "Intellectual Disability." In.

Gribben, M. (2008). 'No more Witnesses', Accessed 28/09. https://web.archive.org/web/20080605043559/http://www.trutv.com/library/crime/serial_killers/predators/bonin/witnesses_3.html.

Harold, S. (2003). *The Serial Killer Files* (Random et al. Group).

Harriet, C. (1996). 'Page One -- Boys ' Killer Led a Twisted, Tortured Life ', *San Fransisco Chronicle* February 19, 1996.

Hyman, J. (1982). 'Bonin sentence applauded by victim's father', *The Day,* 11 March, pp. 49.

Keel, A. (2022). "The Freeway Killer Lost Murder Tapes " In, 1.24min. IMDb Pro.

L Romney, K Ellingwood. (1996). 'There is Still No Closure for Dead O.C Boys Family', *Los Angeles Times.*

Locke, M. (1996). 'California executes 14 boys " murderer', *The Hour,* 23 Feb, pp. 2.

———. 1996. 'Défense still fighting as 'Freeway Killer' awaits death', *The Tuscaloosa News* Feb 19, 1996.

MacWilliams, B. (1996). 'Glen Norman Barker: Sandy-haired boy grew up without a father ', *The Orange County Register.*

———. 1996. 'Russell Rugh: Teen-ager opposed death penalty in school essay ', *The Orange County Register.*

Maloney, J J. (2009). "William Bonin." In *Crime Magazine.* Online

Munro, J. Michael. (1999). 'In the Eyes of a Killer ', Accessed 25/09. http://www.mansonfamilypicnic.com/munro2.htm.
———. N/A. 'In the Eyes of a Killer: The Californian Freeway Killings'. http://www.clarkprosecutor.org/html/death/US/bonin322.htm.
Munro, T. (2023). "James Munro His life His words." In, edited by Sharon Mc-Quillan.
N/A. 1981. 'An 18-Year-old suspect in the string of Freeway Killer....', *United Press International,* May 9
———. 1981. 'Testimony Points to Bonin', *The Bulletin,* 15 November, pp. 5.
———. 1982. 'Freeway Killer Sentenced to Death in Gas Chamber', *Record-Journal,* 13 March, pp. 12.
———. 1982. 'Teenager to Stand Trial for Diplomats murder ', *Times Daily,* 6 May 1992, pp. 31.
———. 1987. 'Details Told on Capture of Gay Killer', *The Press Courier* 2 November, pp. 2.
Newton, M. (2006). *The Encyclopedia of Serial Killers* (New York).
Pelto, Vonda L. 2007. *"Without Remorse: The Story of the Woman Who Kept Los Angeles Serial Killers Alive"'* (Seven Locks Press).
Philbin, Tom Philbin & Michael. 2009. *The Killer Book of Serial Killers* (Sourcebooks: USA).
Press, Associated. 1996. 'Execution is set fort Freeway Killer', *Reading Eagle* 19 Feb, pp. 6.
R, C, Jorss. (1998). "Freeway Killer Accomplice Ask Governor Wilson for Execution or Parole " In, 2.
Rasmussen, A. (2022). "Freeway Killer ' Terrorized Southern California During Year Long Murder Spree'. https://www.investigationdiscovery.com/crimefeed/serial-killer/freeway-killer-terrorized-southern-california-during-yearlong-murder-spree.
Rehabilitation, Californian Department of Corrections and. 1982. "Executed Inmate Summary: Willliam George Bonin." In.
UPI. 1980. '2 charged in 14 murders ', *The Press Democrat,* 30 July
———. 1981. 'Freeway killer allegedly tortured victims', *Record-Journal,* 5 Nov, pp. 14.

FREEWAY FEAR

THE DRIFTER, VICTIMS AND BONIN

WRITTEN BY
SHARON MCQUILLAN

Index

B

C

D

E

F

P

R

S

T

V

W

About the Author

Armed with her recent triumph of a bachelor's degree in criminology and criminal justice from Griffith University, Sharon has equipped herself with knowledge and strives to understand the intricacies of crime and justice. Her heart beats for fairness and truth, advocating for all souls' rights and dignified treatment. Sharon's unwavering commitment to justice is a source of inspiration for all. Sharon's journey is anchored by her role as a devoted mother to five adult children. Her family's unwavering love and shared encouragement have been the wind beneath her wings, enabling her to chase her dreams confidently.

Her insights into the criminal mind have found a platform in Serial Killer Magazine, where her contributions have shed light on the darkest corners of human behaviour.

You can contact Sharon at

s.mcquillan.criminologist@gmail.com

Freeway Fear by Sharon Mc Quillan

Mental Health Resources

Resources:

If you or someone you know is struggling with mental health issues, here are some resources that may be helpful:

Australia:
- Lifeline Australia: 13 11 14 (24/7 crisis support and suicide prevention services)

- Beyond Blue: 1300 22 4636 (support for anxiety, depression, and suicide prevention)

- Headspace: headspace.org.au (mental health support for young people aged 12-25)

- SANE Australia: 1800 18 7263 (support for people affected by complex mental health issues)

- Black Dog Institute: blackdoginstitute.org.au (research and support for mental health)

USA:

- Mental Health America: mhanational.org (resources and support for mental health)

- National Institute of Mental Health (NIMH): nimh.nih.gov (information and resources for mental health)

- 988 Suicide & Crisis Lifeline: Call or text 988 (24/7 confidential support for people in suicidal crisis or emotional distress)

- Substance Abuse and Mental Health Services Administration (SAMHSA): 1-800-662-HELP (4357) (helpline for substance abuse and mental health services)

- National Alliance on Mental Illness (NAMI): 1-800-950-NAMI (6264) or text NAMI to 741741 (support for mental health issues)

UK:

NHS: nhs. UK/mental health (information and support for mental health)

Mind: mind.org.uk (support and services for mental health)

Mental Health UK: mental health-uk.org (resources and support for mental health)

Samaritans: 116 123 (24/7 confidential support for people in distress)

Mental Health Foundation: mentalhealth.org.uk (information and resources for mental health) mental health-uk.org (resources and support for mental health)

Samaritans: 116 123 (24/7 confidential support for people in distress)

Mental Health Foundation: mentalhealth.org.uk (information and resources for mental health)

Made in the USA
Middletown, DE
15 January 2025

69222944R00305